SAVAGISM AND C̶ ̶ ̶

SAVAGISM AND CIVILITY

INDIANS AND ENGLISHMEN IN
COLONIAL VIRGINIA

BERNARD W. SHEEHAN

Indiana University

CAMBRIDGE UNIVERSITY PRESS

Cambridge
London   New York   New Rochelle
Melbourne   Sydney

Published by the Press Syndicate of the University of Cambridge
The Pitt Building, Trumpington Street, Cambridge CB2 1RP
32 East 57th Street, New York, NY 10022, USA
296 Beaconsfield Parade, Middle Park, Melbourne 3206, Australia

First published 1980
Reprinted 1980

Printed in the United States of America

Typeset and printed by Heritage Printers, Inc.,
Charlotte, North Carolina

Library of Congress Cataloging in Publication Data
Sheehan, Bernard W

Savagism and civility.
Includes index.
1. Indians, Treatment of–Virginia.
2. Indians of North America–Virginia–First contact with
Occidental civilization.
3. Virginia–History–Colonial period, ca., 1600–1775.
4. Indians–Public opinion.
5. Public opinion–Great Britain.
I. Title. E78.V7S53   975.5'02   79–18189
ISBN 0 521 22927 8 hard covers
ISBN 0 521 29723 0 paperback

To my mother and father

CONTENTS

PREFACE

———

This book inquires into the failure of white men to understand the nature of native societies in America. In a sense it is the history of a misperception, of the distance in the early years of colonization between what Europeans had been taught to expect in the New World and what greeted them when they arrived. I have avoided the temptation to draw a direct causal connection between the content of the white man's intellect, or even his emotions, and the collapse of native society. Europeans lacked the power to wish the Indians dead or, in the first stages of settlement, to effect their demise. The relations between the two societies were more complex, and the process of disintegration more prolonged and tentative, than can be explained by the European vision of native society. Besides, colonization introduced into the new continent forces far more destructive than ideas. Yet ideas were important. The story of cultural conflict in America cannot be told without attention to the conception of the Indian held by white men, if only because so many Europeans seemed determined to treat him as an abstraction. Hence this book concentrates on the tension between idea and reality in Anglo-Indian relations in Virginia.

I have been struck most forcefully not by the power of ideas to stimulate certain kinds of activity, as for example ignoble savagism to generate violence or noble savagism to tempt Europeans to abandon familiar ways, but by the profound inability of the reigning European ideas to offer even a glimmer of truth about the meeting of white and Indian in America. Englishmen certainly behaved toward Indians in certain ways because they believed them to be savages, but more important was the irony that they continued to believe them savage even when circum-

stances inspired an utterly different sort of relationship. Because
the English were trapped by the disjunction between savagism
and civility, they could never grasp the reality of their dealings
with the native inhabitants of America. They could never perceive that they had found a people as deeply loyal to their own
ways as the English were to theirs; or that they had come upon a
capable people who had much to offer concerning the secrets of
survival in America. Of course we have no reason to believe that
the results would have been any different in the long run even
if the English had suddenly stumbled on a bonanza of anthropological wisdom. As it turned out, the English proved incapable, despite the evidence, of transcending the limitations of
their conventional way of interpreting alien people.

The meaning of the story can be found in the tendency of
societies to reconcile the curious with the familiar. Sixteenth-
and seventeenth-century Englishmen, after all, were as dependent as other human beings on conventional definitions of
reality. Discomforted by the intrusion into their world of a new
continent and an unknown people, they reached for the formula
that had long satisfied their needs. They assimilated this new
intelligence through a process of abstraction that condensed
complexities and conformed enigmatic and obscure information to a time-honored prescription. Many abstractions prove
useful in adjusting the tensions and easing the trials of life.
But some, savagism for one, raise a barrier against understanding, set men at odds with reality, and in the end nurture tragedy.

I have incurred the usual debts in writing this book. My
colleagues in the profession have been free with their time and
generous in giving advice. Only the author can know how the
book would have turned out without their help. The entire
manuscript benefited from readings by Robert F. Berkhofer,
Jr., Herbert H. Kaplan, Walter T. K. Nugent, Martin Ridge,
and Alden T. Vaughan. The chapter entitled "Bestiality" endured the criticism of a departmental seminar whose membership included Maurice G. Baxter, Richard M. Dorson, Robert
H. Ferrell, William H. Harris, Richard S. Kirkendall, David M.
Pletcher, Gerald Strauss, and John E. Wiltz. At a critical moment in the making of the manuscript Thad Tate rendered
valuable counsel.

A major portion of the research was completed at the Huntington Library, where I enjoyed generous support, one of the world's great collections of rare books, stimulating conversation, sybaritic surroundings, and unflagging cooperation from the staff. I am indebted to Charles S. Hyneman, R. Emmett Tyrrell, Jr., and John Von Kannon for their help, and to the Earhart Foundation for two summer fellowships. From Indiana University I received a sabbatical leave, aid from the Office of Research and Graduate Development, prompt service from the library, and efficient typing in the history department. I owe Anne Richards thanks for a lesson in the art of copyediting.

This book is dedicated to my mother and father in gratitude for years of trust and patient encouragement.

Bloomington, Indiana   B. W. S.
September 1979

INTRODUCTION

The discovery and colonization of the New World afforded Europeans an extraordinary opportunity to expand their knowledge of the human condition. Explorers, traders, and colonists encountered new peoples with distinctive physiognomies and curious ways of organizing their lives, who provided a vast new field for ethnological investigation. Of course few Europeans reached America bent on a dispassionate examination of its population and resources. They sought practical ends—trade, settlement, proselytization—and their vision of the new continent tended to be subordinated to those ends. Moreover, virtually every observer in some sense aped medieval travelers by noticing the curious and exotic aspects of native life. Despite the imperatives of practicality and a taste for the bizarre, the age of discovery accumulated a substantial body of accurate information about the continent and its inhabitants. But this rich display of knowledge added very little to the European conception of man's place in the universe,[1] mainly because throughout the early years of exploration and settlement European thinking and feeling about the native people of America occurred within the limits of the customary division between civility and savagism. Until the nineteenth century few serious European thinkers transcended this limitation.

The idea of the savage derived from the primal myth in European culture. It defined a condition antecedent to the formation of society and the inception of history in which men lived free of the complexities and limitations that have since become part of human existence. Genesis gave the conception vital support by describing the passage of man's ancestors from the bliss of the Garden to the tribulations of life on earth. Psychologi-

1

cally, savagism rested on the atavistic longings of human beings to abandon the world of adversity and drift into the comforting realm of nothingness; or, conversely, it drew on the fear that human life hovered on the edge of the abyss and might at any time slip into a state of unrelieved violence and insecurity. Thus savagism elucidated human origins and explained contemporary peoples who, by remaining attached to the simple existence of the primal age, failed to replicate the European mode of life, but it left open the nature of that presocial condition. Savages might be either noble or ignoble, either the guardians of pristine virtue or the agents of violent disorder.[2]

Savagism assumed meaning only in the sense that it inverted the civil condition. Civil men labored for their bread, pacified their sexual urges in marriage, and formed a complex pattern of social arrangements. They lived in a world of order and discipline that was defined by political authority, a system of law, and the requirements of religious morality. Depending on one's point of view, a savage either lacked these advantages or enjoyed a state of enviable innocence by being free of them. In either case, as an ignoble or noble savage, his mode of life was clearly demarcated from the civility that Europeans believed characterized their own manner of living. Although the barrier between the civil and savage conditions seemed impenetrable, most commentators allowed for movement between the two. In one mood Europeans sought a return to original innocence. In another they were convinced that they had once been mired in savagism and had managed by dint of hard work and the blessings of Providence to reach the civil stage of life. Ignoble savagism conveyed the impression of childishness and immaturity, of stunted growth; civility assured European society that it had achieved adulthood. This assurance, however, did not obviate the possibility of a slide back into the savage state. The ignoble savage always loomed as an external threat to Europeans and as an internal danger because he represented primal urges that, although subdued, remained part of the human condition. In the eighteenth century this relationship between savagism and civility would be transformed into a formal theory of staged development. In the sixteenth and seventeenth centuries, it served as a way of categorizing disparate cultures and explaining to Europeans how their own world had come to be and why it was different from the world inhabited by American Indians.[3]

The myth, of course, preceded the experience. Europeans knew what they would find in the New World long before experience had an opportunity to intrude on their convictions. They encountered savages in America because their minds and their senses had been molded by a powerful mythic formula that equated societies less elaborately organized than their own with the primal condition. This myth enabled Europeans to make sense out of America, to reach an accommodation between the new continent and a venerable abstraction basic to European beliefs. Unfortunately, the American native as savage bore little resemblance to the real Indian. As a consequence Europeans went to the New World ill-equipped to understand or deal with the societies they met there. Tension arose immediately between what Europeans thought they saw and what actually existed, but no means were available to reconcile anthropology with myth. Once classified as a savage, the Indian could be expected to play out his role in relation to the civil order. Either he would make the transition to civility or he would resist the influence of European society and face destruction.

For Englishmen of the sixteenth and early seventeenth centuries the doctrine of savagism served deeply felt social needs. They lived with an intense fear that the coherence of life might disintegrate. Shakespeare encapsulated the danger brilliantly in the discourse on order in *Troilus and Cressida*: "Untune that string," and "discord follows." And no wonder: It was a tumultuous age. The breakup of the old religion and the international conflict that ensued threw Englishmen on guard against internal and external enemies. As English religious opinion edged closer to Continental Protestantism, millennial stirrings sparked expectations of profound social change. Neoplatonism took hold in the universities and stimulated a new interest in mystical thinking. In the intellectual underground, Hermetic philosophy, the Judaic Cabala, and alchemy gained numerous adherents who sought a simple insight into the mystery of life. Although the new cosmography did not dethrone man from the center of the universe, it seriously under-

mined traditional certainties and initiated a drastic transformation in the postmedieval conception of the physical world.
In politics the influence of Machiavelli shattered the moral
underpinnings that had supported the Christian state. Simul-
taneously the Elizabethan age experienced economic changes
that impaired the integrity of village life, caused substantial
shifts in population, and convinced the aristocracy that it had
entered a period of crisis. Hence the turn of the sixteenth
century was a time of deep melancholy. Even the expansive
optimism and dreams of chivalric romance that haunted the
generations of Sidney and Essex ended in death and betrayal.
Transported to the New World, the threat of disorder became more acute when the English confronted a native people
who represented for them the antithesis of humane social
arrangements.[4]

The earliest impressions transmitted from America were
paradisaic. The new continent stimulated prelapsarian yearnings for a haven from the insecurities and distractions of European life. Although the English entered the field of colonization late, long after the European experience should have
yielded more realistic evidence, they were no less inclined than
the Spaniards and French to see the New World and its inhabitants through the rose tints of paradisaic innocence. Even
the wealth expected from the new continent, largely gold and
precious metals, was translated into a mythic remedy for Europe's ills. Treatment of the Indians through the paradisaic
formula turned them into an ideal to which Europeans appealed in their chagrin at the shortcomings of their own way
of life. The paradisaic formula left the Indians in a curiously
insubstantial state. Not only was their way of life seen from the
perspective of the white man's world, but it lacked the particularities of a real social order. And yet native Americans
were real enough to make a distinctive mark on the history of
English colonization in the New World. When they resisted the
invasion of their territory or asserted the strength and integrity
of their society, Englishmen tended to stress the ignoble side of
the doctrine of savagism.

The English vision of the natives had been split from the
outset and remained divided throughout the history of the

relationship between the two peoples. But with the establishment of the Virginia colony English opinion made a discernible shift toward ignoble savagism. The images were ready-made, available for use in appropriate circumstances. Once the English began the hapless ordeal of building a civil order in America and became entangled in a delicate relationship of dependence and antipathy with the Powhatans, they were much quicker to seize on the negative portrayal of native life.[5]

In the ignoble savage Englishmen perceived a creature devoid of social discipline, violent by nature, inclined to devour even his own, and repulsive in his personal habits. He was a servant of the devil, a threat not only to English interests in the New World but also to the welfare of mankind. This extreme depiction of the ignoble savage came close to depriving the Indian of his humanity. Although never stated explicitly, the language of savagism disclosed that doubts about the Indian's right to membership in the human family lurked in the imagination of many Englishmen. Images of the Indian as beast drew on legends of monsters, wild men, and quasi-human creatures that had long been part of the European tradition. Thus ignoble savagism incorporated the American native within the bounds of European sensibility and offered Englishmen a plausible explanation for the resistance that Indians presented to colonization.

In fact savagism merely fed the white man's internal needs. It provided no realistic interpretation of the relationship Indians and Englishmen constructed in the New World. It did not, for example, explain the dependence of the English colonists on the native society. As savages, Indians were expected to draw sustenance from the bounty of nature or to survive meagerly on the fruits of hunting and gathering. The native people of Virginia derived a major portion of their food from farming, a practice quickly noted and exploited by the English. John Smith brought the Jamestown settlement through its first two years by confiscating and wheedling corn from the Indians, and the colony continued to depend on the native farmers until the early 1620s. Although they occasionally acknowledged and regretted their dependence, the English failed utterly to see the incompatibility between reality and their conception of Indians as savage people. Even while subsisting on Indian corn, they stressed the scarcity that they believed inevitably afflicted those unable to transcend the savage condition.

Savagism placed no permanent impediment in the way of progress. Even when the Indian was portrayed in bestial terms, there was still hope for his salvation. He participated to some degree in the common human inheritance which, in Christian terms, meant that he would benefit from the preaching of the Gospel. Englishmen lacked the missionary zeal of Spaniards and Frenchmen. Moreover their relations with the Indians were never quite conducive to successful proselytization. Still, they accepted the obligation to teach the Indians Christianity and to raise them from the primitive habits of the savage state. As civil men they could do no less. They made only a feeble effort, but the main reason for their failure was the refusal of the Indians to respond. The native people found many of the white man's artifacts attractive, but they would not abandon their children to English teachers or give up the gods that had served them well. Few Indians went over to the colonists, though more colonists than the English wished to remember threw in with the Indians. In the sense that the doctrine of savagism harbored the beginnings of a theory of development, it predicted the conversion of the native people. When the conversion failed to occur, it served as well to explain the incorrigibility of the Indians. In neither case did it offer an intelligible solution to the problem of Anglo-Indian relations.

Above all, ignoble savagism argued persuasively for the inevitability of violence between Englishmen and Indians. The English clearly expected conflict to erupt. Spaniards' accounts of their experiences in the New World described orgies of violence between conquistadores and native warriors. Although the English generally dissociated themselves from Spanish brutality, they obtained their first insights into the native societies from Spanish sources. In addition, explorers, fishermen, traders, and would-be colonists who plied the Atlantic coast during the sixteenth century counseled caution in dealing with the Indians. The English took the advice and arrived in the New World armed and prepared for a hostile reception. In fact the reception was as often friendly as it was hostile. Indians sought ends similar to those that motivated European policy. They wished to trade, and they hoped for allies against local enemies. Each side attempted to manipulate the other, and both were prepared for violence. It came because both societies ranked war as an important human activity, because their interests diverged, and because the English envisioned the Indians as a savage menace to civil order.

The uprising of 1622, the culminating event in Anglo-Powhatan relations, occurred when the Indians became convinced that the integrity of their society demanded an all-out assault on the English. Peace of a sort had reigned for some eight years. Actually the peace was more a period of armed tension in which the English drifted into the interior, established a firm economic base, and imposed political order on their new colony, while the Indians were required to serve English purposes and gradually declined in strength. Under Powhatan and Opechancanough the native people had resisted conversion by the English, but through the process of acculturation their society, by 1622, had reached a point of crisis. Opechancanough and the war leader Nemattanew apparently sought to inflict vengeance on the English and assuage the tensions of native life by annihilating the colony in one blow. For the English the attack cleared the air. It settled whatever doubts may have remained concerning the implications of savagism, and they proceeded to the systematic conquest and dispersal of the Powhatan people.

The English decision to subjugate the Indians rested on the experience of over a century. They had known about the native people at least since the early years of the sixteenth century, and beginning with the publications of Richard Eden in the 1550s a substantial literature had developed dealing with the New World and its native inhabitants. What Waldseemüller, Ramusio, and de Bry did for the Continent, anthologizers such as Eden, Richard Hakluyt, and Samuel Purchas did for England. The major writings dealing with Spanish, Portuguese, and French exploration and colonization were collected, translated, and widely circulated. There can be little doubt that great numbers of literate Englishmen found the subject fascinating, though perhaps not quite fascinating enough to please

a promoter like Hakluyt. Strange peoples were inherently interesting and the travel literature contained great amounts of
reasonably accurate and usable information. In addition, the
literature confirmed the English predisposition to conceive of
the native people as savages. Thus the material almost never
came through for its own sake. Eden, Hakluyt, and Purchas,
among others, pursued a variety of ends other than the precise
portrayal of the people of America. They were concerned with
empire, economic improvement, the defense of Protestantism,
and proselytization, and only marginally with the indigenous
cultures of America. The Indian figured in their accounts because he could not be avoided in the New World and might
serve the white man's purposes. He might people an empire,
form a market for European goods, aid the English in their
contest with Catholic Spain, or abandon devil worship for the
truth of Christianity. Inevitably Englishmen reconciled the
presence and character of the native people with their own
interests. This requirement was the major function of savagism.
It allowed the English colonizer to incorporate the Indians into
the primal myth of Western Christendom, and to subject the
Indians to the fundamental needs of English thinking and feeling. No amount of contrary evidence concerning the savage
concept could release the native people from subjection to a
universal idea. For the Powhatans it offered no consolation,
though to Englishmen it explained the natives' demise.

1

PARADISE

The search for the terrestrial paradise assumed a special urgency in the Elizabethan period. International turmoil and internal tension made the anticipation of some chiliastic fulfillment unusually comforting. Yet the Elizabethan explorers and colonists invented nothing new. Western European travelers and writers about distant lands had sought paradise for a millennium. That the New World should eventually have served their purposes was inevitable. When the English began exploration and colonization in the late sixteenth century, they showed the same proclivity for engaging in paradisaic fantasy as other European peoples. Indeed, the tendency was so pervasive as to lead one to suppose some deep-seated psychic or mythic origins that urged Europeans to see virtually any strange land as the repository of prelapsarian virtue.[1]

Although few doubted the existence of the terrestrial paradise, its actual location and the route to it remained obscure. Besides Scripture, one of the principal sources of information on the earthly paradise was the adventures of Sir John Mandeville, a popular writer who traveled largely in his own imagination. His *Travels* had already swept the Continent by the time that the first English version appeared in 1496. A number of later editions came out in the sixteenth century, and Hakluyt included a Latin selection in his *Principall Navigations* in 1589. Mandeville admitted that he had never seen paradise but gave the traditional medieval description of its location.[2] "Men say that Paradise terrestre is the highest lande in all the worlde, and it is so high that it toucheth nere to the cycle of the Mone, for it is so high y^t Noes floude might not come thereto which covered all the earth about." Paradise lay beyond the land of

9

Prester John, separated from the world by a wilderness of "hils great rocks and other myrke land, where no man may see a day or night . . ." A wall of moss surrounded it, and from it flowed the four great rivers of the world. One of these rivers fed what "some call the well of youth, for they that drinke thereof seme to be yong alway, and live without great sicknesse, and they say this well, cometh from Paradise terrestre, for it is so vertuous . . ."[3] Great obstacles stood in the way, but Mandeville left little doubt of the rewards awaiting those who attained paradise.

Scarcely a spot touched by European explorers did not yield evidence of paradise. Sebastian Munster found it in Calicut. There the harmony of the birds' singing was so ravishing that "the inhabitantes lyue in greate pleasure, as though they were an earthly paradise . . ." They "lyue as it were in continual springe tyme." Stephen Batman thought the Fortunate Isles possessed the right attributes, though he knew well enough that the earthly paradise was in the East. Henry Hawkes favored the Philippines. He reported in 1572 "that sitting vnder a tree, you shall have such sweete smels, with such great content and pleasure, that you shall remember nothing, neither wife, nor children, nor haue any kinde of appetite to eate or drinke, the oderferous smels will be so sweete." One of Richard Eden's travelers found it in Ethiopia, on a high mountain, closer to its traditional location.[4]

But no region could compete with America as the location of the earthly paradise, or at least as the segment of the world most endowed with the virtues of paradise. Although the continent seemed to devour explorers and settlers with startling regularity, reports from the New World remained strongly paradisaic until the English became entangled in the business of building colonies. Then the land resisted exploitation and the native people made life uncomfortable for expectant colonizers. The Puritans who came on the New World scene in the second and third decades of the seventeenth century preferred the image of the perilous wilderness to the conception of the earthly paradise.[5] Even after colonizing commenced, propaganda sustained the tendency to magnify the richness of the land. In order to protect investments, agents of the Virginia Company persisted in exaggerating its potentiality. Colonies always required more capital and new settlers. At its most intense the rhetoric of paradise did more than stretch a point or two. It raised America above the normal expectations of human existence. In a profoundly radical way it threw open the new continent to demands that no ordinary portion of the globe could satisfy. Though distorted, the formula remained pervasive in the Elizabethan and early Jacobean periods. Few Englishmen showed the good sense to agree with Samuel Purchas's characterization of the Jesuits' effort in Paraguay as a "Lunaticke Paradise," or to complain that, although never seen, paradise had become a "commonplace in mens braines, to macerate and vex them in the curious search hereof."[6] Most found it easier to adopt the comfortable paradisaic mode in describing the strange sights they beheld in America.

Columbus placed the earthly paradise in Paria, at the highest point of land on the globe.[7] In the succeeding years paradise and the New World became inseparable. Before touching the new land navigators were enveloped in the paradisaic odors that wafted from the shore. These unearthly impressions struck Arthur Barlowe off the coast of Georgia in 1585. For Marc Lescarbot a "warm wind" carried from the Canadian coast "odours incomparable for sweetness." "We did stretch out our hands as it were to take them, so palpable were they . . ." The experience was familiar enough for Michael Drayton to enshrine it in poetry. In approaching Virginia, "Earth's onely Paradise," sailors could expect their "Hearts to swell" "When as the Lushious smell/Of that delicious Land,/Above the Seas that flowes,/ The clear Wind throwes, . . ."[8] With tedious regularity viewers of the new continent referred to it as the "yet unformed Occident," the "garden of Eden," "this earthly paradise," and "this paradise of the worlde."[9]

Often enough the first experience after landing in America confirmed the olfactory premonitions. The land looked rich with potential. Just before an Indian attack injected reality into his dream, George Percy could find nothing on the shores of Chesapeake Bay "but faire meddowes and goodly tall Trees, with Fresh-waters running through the woods." He "was almost rauished by the first sight thereof." Richard Hakluyt, a man fully as practical as Percy, employed similar language in his "Discourse on Western Planting." He quoted Jean Ribaut's description of Florida:

> Wee entred (saieth he) and viewed the Countrie, wch is the fairest, frutefullest, and pleasantest of all the worlde, aboundinge in honye, waxe, vension, wilde fowle, fforrests, woodds of all sortes, palmetrees, cipresses, cedars, bayes, the highest and greatest wth also the fairest vines in the worlde wth grapes accordinge wch naturally wth oute arte or mans helpe or trymmynge will growe to toppes of oaks and other trees that be of wonderfull greatnes and heighte. And the sighte of the faire meadowes is a pleasure not able to be expressed with tongue, full of herons, curlues, bitters, mallardes, egriphts, woodcockes, and all other kinde of small birdes, with hartes, hindes, bucks, wilde swyne and all other kynde of wilde beastes . . .

In keeping with his task of instructing the queen in the advantages of empire, Hakluyt compiled an inventory of the New World's resources. But the effulgence of the rhetoric and the prediction that wealth would be obtained "wth oute arte or mans helpe" contained profound paradisaic implications. John Smith, according to Purchas, left no ambiguity about Virginia's possibilities. He had traveled on three continents, but he held Virginia "by the naturall endowments, the fittest place for an earthly Paradise."[10]

Sir Walter Ralegh made paradise his obsession. He discovered it, he thought, in Guiana in 1595, and it haunted him for the rest of his days. Finally it destroyed him. Though in some ways he knew better, Ralegh apparently found himself powerless to resist the dream of perfection contained in the paradisaic memory. Even gold and imperial dominion, embodiments of worldly ambition, were symbols of his impassioned search for the boundless dreamworld of paradise and El Dorado.[11]

In the sobering confines of his prison, where he spent some thirteen years waiting for James I to see the folly of détente with Spain, Ralegh contemplated the problem of paradise. He entertained no doubts that such a place existed and that it was not a utopia, which by his definition did not exist, but an actual geographic region. It was a place, he wrote, "in respect to the fertility of the soil, of the many beautiful rivers and goodly woods that the trees (as in the Indies) do always keep their leaves, [and] was called Eden, which signifieth in the Hebrew, *pleasantness*, or *delicacy* . . ." His deepest wish was to find paradise in the southern continent of the New World, in Guiana, and for it to fulfill his craving for perfection.[12] Yet doubts arose. The East and West Indies may have been blessed with perpetual spring and summer, but they were also afflicted with thunder and lightning, earthquakes, diseases, "venomous beasts and worms," and other inconveniences. Moreover, such places may be called "vicious countries" because "nature being liberal to all without labour, necessity imposing no industry or travel, idleness bringeth forth no other fruits than vain thoughts and licentious pleasures." Ralegh concluded his discussion of the earthly paradise with the reluctant concession that it was probably where the ancient sources said it was—in Mesopotamia.[13] But that was the temperate Ralegh, eager to prove his orthodoxy, fearful that his hopes for release would be dashed.

Ralegh's hatred of the Spaniards did not extend to a refusal to follow in their path. Since the 1530s they had been combing the Orinoco basin and the mountains beyond for wealth equal to the treasures found in Mexico and Peru. The location of this sought-after bonanza was the legendary city of Manoa, where reigned the gilded king who covered himself with rosin and rolled in gold dust. Ralegh already knew the stories, but he heard them firsthand from Antonio de Berrio, whom he captured in Trinidad in 1595.[14] Ralegh thought Berrio had actually seen Manoa, and the idea fired his imagination: "If any else shalbe enabled thereunto, and conquere the same, I assure him thus much, he shall performe more than euer was done in *Mexico* by *Cortez*, or in *Peru* by Pacaro, whereof the one conquered the Empire of Mutezuma, the other of Guascar, and Atabalipa, and whatsoever Prince shall possesse it, that Prince shalbe Lorde of more gold, and of a more beautifull Empire, and of more Cities and people, then eyther the king of Spayne, or the great Turke." Guiana "hath yet her Maydenhead," in Ralegh's vivid phrase; it awaited the arrival of the English to set "their glad feet on smooth Guianas brest . . ."[15]

"There are in many places of the world," wrote Ralegh, "especially in America, many high and impassable mountains,

which are rich and full of gold . . ." This was his immediate
quest. He believed that a fabulously rich gold mine waited in
Guiana to support the creation of a British empire. As his
friend Chapman wrote of Elizabeth's reign: "Then most admired Soueraigne, let your breath/Goe foorth vpon the waters,
and create/A golden worlde in this our yron age." Gold preyed
on his mind for twenty years. Finally, in 1617, James I turned
him loose, and he made one last desperate effort to locate the
mine. It eluded him. His men fell into a fight with the Spaniards, contrary to the explicit orders of the crown, and James
executed the death sentence that had hung over Ralegh's head
since 1603. He had sought in Guiana "a very Paradise, and so
excellent in all perfections and beauties, that nature seems only
here to have her Temple . . ." Surely he had found "a landskip
of that excellent perfection, which no Art could better, hardly
imitate . . . a very earthly Paradise, and therefore doubtlesse is
full of strong promises . . ."[16] That the promises remained unfulfilled only served to emphasize that his quest transcended the
ordinary desires of men.

Spanish success in extracting gold from paradise was widely
publicized in England. Holinshed recorded that the Spaniards
yearly took four or five hundred ducats of gold from the "earthlie paradise." They found "gold euerie where; for their is in
maner no river, nor mountaine, and but few plaines that are
vtterlie without it."[17] The Spanish histories translated and
published in England in the sixteenth and early seventeenth
centuries set the English an enticing example. Gómara had recorded Cortez's brazen message to Montezuma: "I and fellowes
have a certayne disease of the harte, and golde healpeth us."
The English knew how readily the disease had been cured.
But Mexico paled before the wealth of Peru. Acosta claimed
that the Potosí silver mines yielded thirty thousand pieces each
day.[18] The Inca Atahualpa filled a room with gold and plate
for Pizarro. The descriptions of the Temple of the Sun in Cuzco
must have awakened otherworldly fantasies. One of the Spanish chronicles printed by Purchas valued a throne and a foun-
tain taken from the temple at 1,320,000 pesos.[19] And this was
only a small portion of the precious metals sent home by the
Spaniards.

Lest the appalling greed of this quest for riches appear too patent, Acosta submitted an ingenious justification. Had the gold not been placed in the New World by God, Europeans would not have been attracted to the new lands and would not have spread Christianity. God used human desires for his own ends.[20] Indeed the Spanish accounts revealed a certain ambivalence on the question of gold. The consequences of the discovery of such wealth were not totally beneficial. Time spent searching for it might have been devoted to establishing a stable European society in the New World. It caused the destruction of native life and disrupted the economy of Europe. Moreover, the attitudes of the Indians toward precious metals raised serious questions. It seemed that the denizens of paradise used gold and silver for a variety of decorations but at the same time valued it very little. They were contemptuous of Spanish greed. The natives of Chile, so the story went, slaked the avarice of one Spaniard by pouring molten gold down his throat.[21]

The English found testimony that "the same golden mettal dothe also lie incorporate in the bowlles of the Norwest parties . . ." Coronado had been told of Indians who wore "on their bodies golde, Emeralds, and other precious stones, and are served commonly in golde and silver, wherewith they cover their houses: and the chiefe men weare great chaines of golde well wrought . . ." North of Florida, if one could believe the Spanish and Huguenot accounts, lay a great city, heavily populated and rich in gold and precious stones. The same information came in concerning the people of the Far North.[22] Martin Frobisher made three voyages to the northern regions between 1577 and 1579, returning with tons of valueless ore, which the assayers labored over for five years. Someone could always be counted on to find gold in Frobisher's rocks, though in fact none existed. Frobisher's reputation suffered somewhat for his failure, but the expectation that the new land would yield golden riches persisted.[23] At Roanoke the colonists searched diligently for a mine. The Jamestown adventurers had been instructed to "digg myne and searche for all manner of Mynes of Goulde Silver and Copper . . ." Captain Newport returned in the summer of 1607 with a barrell of ore, which at first sight seemed promising. One observer wrote that "we an falne vpon a lande, that promises more, then the lande of promise: In steed of mylke we fynde pearle. & golde In steede of honye . . ." Hope faded the next day when the ore was found to be worthless. Virginia was "more Lyke to prove the Lande of Canaan then the Lande of ophir." "In the ende all turned to vapore . . ." But Newport made another voyage to Virginia determined to return with the gold "he confidentlie beleeued he had broughte before."[24]

The association of gold with a paradisaic New World became a fixation with many writers. Christopher Marlowe made gold a major theme of his play *Tamburlaine*. In that play, the Tartar conqueror represents England, and the gold of the New World is a major motivation for his activities.[25] The governor in the *Jew of Malta* is even more explicit: "Desire of gold, great Sir?/That's to be gotten in the Westerne Inde." In response to the importunities of Scapthrift in Jonson's *Eastward Ho*, Seagull launches into a golden fantasy: "I tell thee, gold is more plentiful there than copper is with us; and for as much red copper as I can bring, I'll have thrice the weight in gold. Why, man, all their dripping-pans and their chamber-pots are pure gold; and all the chains with which they chain up their streets are massy gold; all the prisoners they take are fethered in gold . . ." Lest his listeners miss the point, Seagull transforms the image into the more familiar picture of a garden, where men can live freely, "without sergeants, or courtiers, or lawyers, or intelligencers . . ." In the paradise of Cuba, wrote Robert Greene, was "enrapt,/As in the massy storehouse of the world,/Millions of gold . . ." Who could doubt, then, that "among the Sun-burnt *Indians*,/That know no other wealth but Peace and pleasure,/She shall find Plutus, god of riches . . ."? The metal "burned with a quenchles fire" that "Inflames our thirsting hartes unstaunched in desire."[26]

The tendency to identify the New World with paradise and gold seemed to stimulate the English appetite for illusion. At Whitehall in February 1613, a masque written by George Chapman and staged by Inigo Jones was performed to celebrate the marriage of Princess Elizabeth to Frederick, the Elector Palatine. A great artificial rock the height of the hall contained a mine of gold. The theme was the wealth of Virginia. Baboons scampered about representing an antimasque, a threat to civilization. In the directions for staging, the theme took second place to the display of the setting and the costumes that adorned the masquers. A viewer could scarcely doubt that Virginia would yield fantastic wealth or that it represented an enchanted dream-world. Witness the costumes:

> Then rode the chiefe Maskers, in Indian habits, all of a resemblance: the ground cloath of silver, richly embroidered, with golden Sunns, and about every Sunne, ran a traile of gold, imitating Indian worke: . . . betwixt euery pane of embroidery, went a rowe of white Estridge feathers, mingled with sprigs of golde plate; vnder their breasts they woare bawdricks of golde, embroidered high with purle, and about their neckes, Ruffes of feathers, spangled with pearle and silver. On their heads high sprig'd-feathers, compast in Coronets, like the Virginia Princes they presented. Betwixt euery set of feathers, and about their browes, in the vnder-part of Coronets, shin'd Sunnes of golde plate, sprinkled with pearle: from whence sprung rayes of the like plate . . . Their legges were adorn'd, with close long white silke-stockings: curiously embroidered with golde to the Middle-legge.

> And ouer these (being on horse backe) they drew greaves or buskins embrodered [sic] with gould, and enterloc't with rewes of fethers; altogether estrangfull, and *Indian* like.

> In their Hands . . . they brandisht cone darts of the finest gould.

A glimpse of reality intervened. These bogus Indians sported olive skin and wore shoulder-length black hair. But their horses were hung with "sunnes of Gould and Ornamentall Iewells. To euery one of which was tackt a scarffing of Siluer; that ran sinnuousely in workes ouer the whole caparison, euen to the daseling of the admiring spectators."[27] If the courtly company found the spectacle dazzling, it was doubtless because the New World had long been seen as a golden illusion.

Gold possessed magical properties that transcended its monetary value. Sixteenth-century Englishmen lived in an age in which magic retained its grip upon the human imagination.[28]

The intense yearning for the golden age, the search for the earthly paradise, and the easy tendency to attribute paradisaic qualities to the New World all revealed how deeply attached Englishmen remained to ancient modes of thinking and feeling. The roots may have been primordial, but surely the pagan and Christian traditions supplied ample justification for the paradisaic search. The Renaissance had revived interest in Hesiod, Pindar, Virgil, and Ovid and awakened memories of a golden age in which men lived unvexed by the anxieties of the world. Throughout the Middle Ages and into the modern era astrology held out hope that men would find a way to enlist the power of the stars in their own interests. The revitalization of Neoplatonism in the sixteenth century fogged the distinction between matter and spirit and infused the material world with spiritual power beyond the ordinary expectations of men. It was one thing to become rich by following the path of the Spaniards, but it was another to find in the New World the answer to all the conundrums that for millennia had plagued humankind.[29]

In its extreme form the paradisaic theme took on gnostic dimensions. John Dee, a friend of explorers and colonizers, dabbled in the most arcane mystic arts and attributed extraordinary powers to man. Through the ancient tradition of Hermeticism, he sought to release men from the limitations of the body and identify them once again with the divine intellect. Man would be raised to a position of equality with God. Dee was a magus, a member of the paradisaic priesthood, who devoted his life to the search for the special knowledge that would reveal the mysteries of human existence.[30] Promoters of exploration and colonization and those who did the actual work were more practical, but they were clearly touched by the same fondness for paradise. What Dee sought to reveal in the magical proceedings of his study, Englishmen from Eden to Purchas hoped to find in the New World.

The search seemed always to return to gold. Through the Hermetic formulas, alchemists attempted to reduce all minerals to the most basic substance, gold, not because it commanded wealth and power but because it contained the secret of life. The alchemical process engaged the practitioner in the profoundest of human rituals, a symbolic repetition of the mystical drama of passion, death, and resurrection. In the Hermetic philosophy minerals possessed heavenly qualities. The moon generated silver, Mercury quicksilver, Venus cooper, Mars iron, Jupiter tin, Saturn lead, and the sun gold. The sun symbolized God; hence knowledge of gold implied knowledge of God. When alchemists attempted to change other metals into gold, they were, in effect, attempting to perfect nature; by transforming the mineral substance, the alchemist repeated the divine process. Few claimed the secret knowledge of the alchemists, but everyone knew the wondrous properties of gold.[31]

The relationship between the sun and gold led to the popular belief that gold would be found in the warmer regions, where the sun poured its golden rays onto the earth. Frobisher's search for gold in the North raised some eyebrows and his failure confirmed the ancient legend. After all, Solomon had obtained his gold from Ophir, a rich country to the south. Ralegh's quest in Guiana, with its clear paradisaic overtones, conformed to the expectations of the age. "This ought to be consydered for a general rule," wrote Eden some fifty years before, "that the nearest vnto the south partes of the world betweene the two Tropikes vnder ye *Equinoctial* or burning lyne, where the sunne is of greatest sorse, is the chiefest place where gold is engendued . . ." Vespucci had given it as his opinion that "yf there bee any earthly Paradjes in the worlde it can not be farre from these regions of the south . . ."[32]

Belief in the existence of a golden, paradisaic world simplified what should have been an extraordinarily difficult anthropological problem. Europe had come upon strange people before, in Asia and Africa, and had usually found it easier to rely on the ancient formulas to explain their existence, even after acquiring extensive knowledge of them and establishing actual relations. All the more reason to expect, therefore, that when the New World appeared with a sizable native population Europeans, and the English among them, should fall back on their primary myth (or its negation) in incorporating these new facts into their view of the world. Indeed the newness of America probably made it imperative that some form of the paradisaic myth be employed in describing and explaining it.

Asia and Africa had long come within the purview of Europe. An extensive literature and a rich deposit of legend offered Europeans a certain comfort in dealing with these continents and the people who inhabited them. When the New World burst upon the scene without warning (through perhaps not without some vague expectations on the part of its discoverers), Europe at first could scarcely believe in it, and then began the inevitable process of reconciliation. Travelers returned with the news that this new land exhibited all the lineaments of that mythic place to which European man yearned to return. And the people who lived there possessed qualities fitting for the inhabitants of a paradisaic land.[33]

This explanation solved the anthropological problem, but only by denying its existence. Conceived as paradise, the continent evinced a striking insubstantiality. The intangibility of the odors that transmitted the first evidence of the New World's existence was indicative of the incapacity of the paradisaic formula to create a description of an existing portion of the earth that bore any more than a faint resemblance to reality. Even Hakluyt, in attempting to list the potential resources of the continent, fell into the conventional quietistic formulation. The particulars were no doubt accurate enough, but the context bore no connection to the world in which those resources might have been discerned and used. Certainly gold was a substantial commodity. The Spaniards had proved the point. But in the paradisaic mode it could not be simply a resource. It became a symbol of mythic possibilities. Inevitably, the inhabitants of paradise–the native peoples of America–assumed the properties attributed by Europeans to the new continent. The same lack of substance that characterized paradisaic treatments of the continent affected European conceptions of the native Americans.

Henri Baudet has pointed out that the original expression of the paradisaic myth celebrated "the glorification of all things primitive, the cultureless as a characteristic of the true, the complete, the only and original bliss . . ."[34] In the sense that paradise was a condition to be hoped for, it predicted boundless possibility. As a source of anthropological definition, it described human beings largely by negation, even though the negation formed the summation of human happiness. The reasons for this paradox were not difficult to find. Deriving in large measure from the early chapters of Genesis, the myth described a mode of life enjoyed by humankind before the loss of paradise. Men had experienced only the later condition, and had found it wanting. What they yearned for, the paradisaic way of life, was inevitably conceived of as the opposite of what they knew. Thus perfection took on the form of a societal void. Men would live in paradise when they ceased to be identified with the complex of attachments and historical accretions that made up society. Alien peoples, about whom very little was known, appeared to have already reached that state—or perhaps never to have left it. They deserved the name savage because they lived a rudimentary existence similar to the life enjoyed by the ancestors of Christian Europeans before they were driven from paradise and required to fashion a culture and endure the inconvenience of history. But, of course, this definition of savage existence offered the savage nothing of his own. Instead, it deprived him of the elements of culture and bound him irretrievably within the skein of European thought processes.

The negative traits generally assigned to the savage condition virtually drained the conception of anthropological meaning. The character of the savage was defined by the absence of the modes of life familiar to Europeans. Lacking letters, the noble savage enjoyed no intellectual life. He was more likely to be antiintellectual on the grounds that thinking inevitably led to unhappiness. The savage state required no system of law because no basis for abrasiveness existed among men. Life went on without the benefit of political order and without the need for kings, magistrates, or rulers of any kind. Apparently the inhabitants of paradise engaged in little or no activity. The environment yielded plenty without the need for cultivation. Art was a useless affectation, though gold served as adornment if not as money. No exchange of goods took place; therefore, no one became rich. Violence was foreign to the experience of noble savages. Either the absence of war made weapons useless or, conversely, the absence of weapons made war useless; neither existed. People went naked. Sexuality implied perfect innocence and marriage proved unnecessary. Hence noble savages enjoyed a life without bound and apparently without substance.[35]

Few employed the totality of the paradisaic vision, but virtually every observer in the Elizabethan era saw one or more of the characteristics of paradisaic man in the people of the New World. "The unripe side of the earth," wrote John Donne, setting the principal motif, "produces men like Adam before he ate the apple." Indeed, other strange places called forth similar descriptions. According to Mandeville the people of Sumatra

> go al naked and they scorne all them that are clade for they say that God made Adam & Eve all naked . . . and there is no woman we-ded, but women are all common there, and they forsake no man. And they say God commaunded to Adam & Eve . . . Encrease & multiply and fyll the earth, and no man may say there, This is my wife, & no woman may say, this is my husbande. And when they have any children they give them to whom they will of men that haue medled with them. Also the lande is all common, for every man taketh what he will, for that one man hath in one yere now, an other man hath another yeare. Also all the goods, as corne, beastes and all maner thing of that country are all in common. For there is nothing under locke, as riche is one man as an other . . .

In the state of nature clothing represented familial attachments or private property; it set bounds to human existence. Life's "superfluities they vtterly contemne, as hynderances of theyr sweete libertie, forasmuch as they are gyuen only to play and Idelnes." Savages denied the basic principle of society: the division of goods. "For it is certeyne," wrote Peter Martyr, "that amonge them the lande is as common as the sonne and water: And that Myne and Thyne (the seedes of all myscheefe) have no place with them." The American natives lived in a "goulden worlde, without toyle. lyuinge in open gardens, not intrenched with dykes with hedges, or defended with waules. They deale trewely one with another, without lawes, without bookes, and without Iudges." Just as the landscape lay open, without obstruction, human relationships were direct, without the interference of societal machinery. French geographer, Pierre d'Avity pushed the principle perilously close to a denial of the natives' human attributes. He believed that the Chichimecas of New Spain and certain natives in Brazil were the most "barbarous" people in the New World. They led a "sauage and brutush life, without commanders, without laws, without any forme of civilitie, or pollicie . . ." But, more seriously, they "shew not in their actions any discourse of reason, but what they need for their entertainment; Since in them doth darken the vnderstanding, and passions blind the judgment: they doe not eleuat their thoughts aboue the earth, and they doe not thinke but of things that are present." Innocence, modesty, honesty, and openness characterized paradisaic life, but this portrayal did not credit the native with intellectual discrimination or thought of the future.[36]

Of course the paradisaic formula could not work in its fullness. The real world was bound to intrude. Travelers and colonists observed native life and recorded what they saw, which could never quite conform to the paradisaic vision. Marc Lescarbot, for example, described the Indians of Canada in conventional paradisaic terms, but he obviously found it difficult to sustain the conceptualization. Native justice, he reported, rested on the principle of nature: "that one must not offend another." They lived by neither divine nor human law. Yet the Indians often quarreled, and the "Sagamos" administered justice. Wrongdoers were beaten or required to compensate the injured party, "which is some form of dominion." A prisoner who offended his captors risked being thrust into the "pot." After his death no one would revenge him, for "there is no account made of a man's life that hath no support." Only a real society could grant support; the noble savage required none. In the spring of 1607, Gabriel Archer observed real Indians on his voyage up the James River and his description was similarly ambiguous. After discussing the resources available in Virginia and the prospects for exploiting them, he noted in contrast the absence of initiative on the part of the native inhabitants. They have "no commerce with any nation, no respect of profitt, neither is there scarce that we call meum et tuum among them . . ." Yet the "kinges know their owne territoryes, & the people their severall gardens . . ." For Archer the paradisaic interpretation of native life justified the English assertion of ownership over the lands and resources of Virginia, even though he recognized the actual possession by the Indians. The tension between the rhetoric and the reality became striking when an accurate perception of native life supported the savage theory. Archer had recorded realistically that the Indians "dwell as I guesse by families of kindred & allyance so 40^tie or 50^tie in a . . . small village . . ." In commenting on the massacre of 1622, John Smith noted the same arrangement of native life, but he clearly associated it with the way "wilde naked natives live . . ."[37]

The language of paradise frequently shaded off into ambiguity in other ways. The image of the garden, for example, held paradisaic implications, but it evoked a more complex set of images of the native peoples. Laudonnière found Florida peopled by an extraordinary race of natives. The chief Satourioua greeted the Frenchmen draped "with a great Harts skinne dressed like Chamois, and painted with devices of strange and divers colours, but so lively a portrature, and representing antiquity, with rules so justly compassed, that there is no Painter so exquisite that could finde fault therewithin: the naturall disposition of this strange people is so perfect and well guided that without any ayd and favour of artes, they are able by the helpe of nature onely to content the eye of artizans, yea even those which by their industry are able to aspire unto things most absolute."[38] Nature remained the operative concept, but the native society had clearly managed achievements to rival the best of Europe. In the early seventeenth century, Englishmen discovered extensive cultivation in Guiana which they depicted in images of the garden. After landing in Canada, Poutrincourt heard Indians playing fifes and compared the beauty of the sound to the harmony produced by shepherds in France. A century before, Peter Martyr described a meeting between Bartholomew Columbus and an Indian king on Hispaniola. Thirty of the king's wives and concubines, naked "sauynge . . . theyr pryuie partes," preceded him, holding date branches and singing and dancing. The virgins of the company were utterly naked. The women's "faces, brestes, pappes, handes, and other partes of theyr bodyes, were excedynge smoothe and well proportioned . . ." The Spaniards thought they had met the "beautyfull Dryades, or the natyue nymphes or fayes of the fontaynes wherof the antiquites speake so muche." The nymphs delivered the date branches to Columbus "with loue curtesy and smylynge countenaunce," fed the hungry Spaniards, and then put them to bed. John Smith's account of his first encounter with Powhatan contained similar pastoral elements.[39]

The pastoral image of the Indians and their world gained a measure of reality from the observations of travelers and colonists. True enough, the garden motif drew on a long tradition and came to the New World in the baggage of the Europeans. The original genre, initiated by Virgil, had been rediscovered in the Renaissance, and sixteenth-century English writers such as Spenser, Sidney, and Drayton had breathed new life into it.[40] Although closely enmeshed in the paradisaic conception, it added substance to the landscape, frequently through a catalog of potential resources. Barlowe's experience off the Georgia coast in July 1585 prompted him to anticipate "some delicate garden, abounding with all kind of adoriferous flowers." Doubtless he knew what he would find. Once on land he offered an extensive description of resources that could only have come from careful examination.[41] The middling landscape tended to be rich in expectation or actually cultivated. And the Indians who lived in such circumstances took on a certain substance. In the garden Indians danced and sang and carried on the simple activities of their rudimentary life. Or they engaged in the elaborate ceremonials that courtly poets associated with pastoral existence. Nevertheless, the garden image granted only minimal integrity to native culture.

Noble savages tended to be passive. Their world, after all, required few of the exertions that Europeans associated with civilized life. Some were virtuous, prudent, and grave, possessing the self-assurance of pristine nature.[42] These attributes constituted a decisive native character, one that the white man might respect or at least recognize as deserving of serious attention. But for the most part the paradisaic image defined the native personality in such quiescent and submissive terms as virtually to deprive the Indian of any personality of his own. Although he did not use the paradisaic image explicitly, Bartolomé de Las Casas limned natives of almost infinite passivity

in his compulsion to indict the Spaniards for inhumanity. He depicted natives as

> very simple, without sutteltie, or craft, without malice, very obedient, and very faithfull . . . , very humble, very patient, very desirous of peace making, and peacefull, without brawles and struglings, without quarrelles, without strife, without rancour or hatred, by no means desirous of reuengement.
>
> They are also people very gentle, and very tender, and of an easie complexion, and which can sustayne no trauell, and doe die very soone of any disease whatsoeuer, in such sorte as the very children of Princes and Noble men brought up amongst us, in all commodities, ease, and delicateness, are not more soft then those of that countrey: yea, although they bee the children of labourers. They are also very poore folke which possesse little, neither yet do so much as desire to have much worldly goodes, & therefore neither are they proud, ambitious, nor couetous.[43]

Driven by a piety of overwhelming self-abnegation, Las Casas sought a native personality equally supine. Moreover, he portrayed a native people fully compatible with the paradisaic image. His Indian society lacked the elemental signs of a real culture. As with the noble savage, the inhabitants of America served someone else's purpose. For Las Casas their gentleness contrasted with Spanish brutality, and they were ideal pupils for his teachings. But they seemed to possess none of the complex substance out of which culture takes form.

Although Las Casas exhibited profound hatred of his own people, he did not call into question the legitimacy of European culture. He believed that American natives should be transformed into good Christians. Nor did he express himself technically in the language of paradism. These tasks were left to Montaigne, whose *Essays* were translated into English by John Florio in 1603,[44] though they had been widely known in England for a generation. Montaigne formulated the major radical critique of European culture offered in the Renaissance.

Ostensibly, Montaigne intended to check the universalizing tendency of Europeans that compelled them to condemn all other ways of life as inferior. He believed that Europeans, by adopting the relativistic view of culture, would perceive the good in other societies because they would see them as merely different. Yet the consequences of this process were markedly paradoxical and led ultimately to the employment of categories even more inclusive than those Montaigne condemned.[45] Native society might have benefited from a moderate infusion of relativism into the anthropological thinking of Europeans, if Montaigne had not been after bigger game. He mounted a full assault on European culture, and he could sustain it only by opposing European life to the pristine design of nature represented by the societies of the New World. For the Indians the consequences were predictable. They became instruments that served the white man's purposes, but they did not emerge with a character of their own.

Montaigne rested his account of native life on solid sources. He knew the travel writers, but he also relied heavily on a servant who had spent twelve years in Brazil and on a conversation of sorts with three natives of that country. As a result he acquired a fair amount of accurate information about native life, and he managed to communicate some of it dispassionately. Even when he condemned the Spaniards' destructiveness, he took the time to describe the life they destroyed.[46]

Because his writings were heavily tendentious, Montaigne made free use of the concepts of pristine nature and the noble savage. The information offered by his servant could be trusted precisely because the fellow was "rough-hewen" and lacked the subtlety that cast suspicion on the utterances of Europeans. Indeed Europeans might profit from the virtues of innocence and candor that held sway in America. For Europeans to censure American natives as "savages" revealed how confined they were by the limited horizon of their own world and how incapable of appreciating the values of another. It might be more appropriate, asserted Montaigne playfully, to attach the term "savage" to the "bastardyed" life Europeans had created with the aid of "artificial devices." More directly, he argued that "there is no reason art should gaine the point of honour of our great and puissant mother Nature." European inventions have "surcharged the beauties and riches of her workes. . . ," so that "where ever her puritie shineth, she makes our vaine and frivolous enterprise wonderfully ashamed." In the opposition of nature and art Montaigne placed himself squarely on the side of nature. Virtue resided not in the "corrupted taste" of Europe but in these "countries that were never tilled. . ."[47] Cultural relativity made way for a mythic taxonomy of life in America.

Montaigne believed that in the New World he had found evidences of the "golden age" that Lycurgus and Plato could only surmise. In keeping with this vision, he formulated in negative terms the classic characterization of savage life. Native society "hath no kinde of traffike, no knowledge of Letters, no intelligence of numbers, no name of magistrate, nor of povertie; no contracts, no successions, no partitions, no occupations but idle; no respect of kindred, but common, no apparell but naturall, no manuring of lands, no use of wine, corne, or mettle. The very words that import lying, falshood, treason, dissimulations, covetousnes, envie, detraction, and pardon, were never heard of amongst them." The ancients could not have improved in poetry and philosophy on the simplicity of Indian life; nor would they have believed that their own "societie might be maintained with so little art and humane combination." Montaigne's design for an ideal society left little room for the modalities of real life. Perhaps between riches and poverty lay some median relationship to the world's goods. A common respect for kindred seemed to imply a familial basis for social organization. The absence of vices no doubt assumed the existence of virtues. But otherwise life among the inhabitants of America was devoid of substance–"all naked, simply-pure in Natures lappe."[48]

Montaigne wrestled with the problem of cannibalism. He seemed more fascinated than appalled by it. Though he could not defend the practice, he was reduced to the assertion that the Indians did not eat human flesh for nourishment, but for the nobler motive of revenge. Still, Europeans could not claim superior virtue. Their own practices were far more "barbarous." Moreover, Indian wars were "noble and generous." They fought not to gain new lands, for they were already furnished with every necessity, but out of "meere jelousie of vertue." Montaigne saw no danger to Europeans in associating with American natives. Because his comparisons always worked to the disadvantage of the white man, he feared the consequences of the relationship for the Indians.[49]

Montaigne's intentions were polemical, and hence what he wrote about the New World and its inhabitants must be seen in that light. He wished to censure his own society and the Indians became an instrument for that end. And yet intentions aside, the burden of his language and the categories of human existence that came so easily to mind revealed more than alienation from European culture. He attacked society itself, and, if one can credit his theriophilistic tendencies, the very integrity of the human condition.[50] The Indians benefited little from this mode of argument. Although in the course of discussion Montaigne made reference to many particular traits of native life, the theoretical structure of his thought excluded any serious consideration of Indian societies. The negative language of paradism made the Indians the inhabitants of an institutional void or at best a reflection of Europe's unfulfilled ideals. Montaigne revealed his proclivity to make Indians into white men in recording the observations of his native informants in response to questions concerning their experience in France. As Montaigne remembered the episode, the Indians wondered why the large, bearded, armed men who attended the king allowed themselves to be ordered about by a beardless child. Nor could they understand why "there were men amongst us full gorged with all sortes of commodities, and others which hunger-starved, and bare with need and povertie, begged at their gates."[51] Indians may indeed have made such observations, but so also would noble savages, primed with the white man's ideals and yearning to return to their equalitarian paradise.

Sir Thomas Chaloner broached the same theme of nature against civilization in his translation of the *Praise of Folie* by Erasmus. The happiest of men, according to the great humanist, were those "who altogethers maie abstaine from medlyng with any sciences, and follow Nature onely for theyr guide and maistres. . . for Nature abhorreth counterfeityng. . ." The least counterfeited among the human species were *"fooles, doltes, ideotes, and paches,"* and, as it turned out, men whose lives imitated the "bluntnesse of brute beastes." These simple people were free from the primal human anxiety, the fear of death.

"They are not tawed, nor plukt a sunder with a thousande thousand cares, wherwith other men are oppressed. Thei blushe at nothyng, they doubt nothyng, they coveite no dignitee, they envie no mans fortune, they love not peramours; and lastly if they be veraie brute Naturalles, now they sinnne not, as doctours doe affirme." Montaigne and Chaloner drew on an enduring mode of social criticism that held obvious implications for the travelers and colonists who encountered native people in the New World.[52]

In 1606 Marc Lescarbot, a lawyer from Vervins, accompanied Poutrincourt to Acadia. He stayed for a year, found the country attractive (the winter was mild), and observed the manners of the Indians. On returning he wrote his *Histoire de la Nouvelle France*, which was published in Paris. The same year Richard Hakluyt arranged for the appearance of an English translation of the portions of Lescarbot's book that dealt with the most recent French efforts in the northern continent and with the Indians. Lescarbot was enthusiastic about the potential of the New World, and Hakluyt hoped his work would quicken support for English colonization.[53]

Lescarbot accepted the paradisaic conceptualization. His Indians were of a "noble heart" and lived by the law of "Nature." In addition, like Las Casas and Montaigne, he had an eye for the constituent parts of native culture and even a commitment to cultural relativism. "It is a small matter," he wrote, "to know that people differ from us in customs and manners, unless we know the particularities thereof. . .; but the fair science is to know the manner of all nations of the world. . ." The Indians feared nothing in war except shame and reproach. He found them vengeful but trusted that Christianity would cure this defect. Indians were temperate in "venereal action," though not in the eating of meat. Lescarbot recognized the importance of gift giving in native culture and noted the liberality and generosity of native character. Indians were frank and hospitable people. They showed piety in providing for their parents in old age and mercy toward wives, children, and enemies. Yet when he came to explain native traits, he relied on the contrast between nature and civility and ultimately judged the Indians by the white man's standards. "Our savages," he wrote, "although they be naked, are not void of those virtues that are found in men of civility." They practiced the justice that only nature could teach.[54]

Lescarbot's genuine sympathy for the Indians contrasted sharply with his disrelish of Frenchmen. He seemed inordinately determined to record his opinions of his countrymen. An injustice had been done him in the French law courts ("the plague of our lives"), and hence he had fled to America "to avoid a corrupted world." Of course he found in Acadia a society that fulfilled much of the youthful promise that Europe had disappointed.[55]

The Indians lived in common, "the most perfect and most worthy life of man," which had characterized the "ancient golden age." The great shortcoming of Christianity was its failure to restore the common life. It was the American natives who retained "this mutual charity, which hath been taken away from us since that *mine* and *thine* have come into the world." The French confirmed their fall from grace by digging up the Indian dead and stripping the bodies of beaver skins. "A thing that maketh the French name to be odious and worthy of disdain among them, which have no such sordid quality at all, but rather having a heart truly noble and generous, having nothing in private to themselves, but rather all things common. . ." Native longevity stemmed from the harmony of their lives and from the small store they put in worldly goods. "They have not that ambition which in these parts gnaweth and fretteth the minds and spirits, and filleth them with cares, making blinded men to go to the grave in the flower of their age. . ." Moreover the Indians were free of corruption, the "fostering mother of physicians and of magistrates," and of the law suits that "consume both our years and our means." "From such afflictions," wrote Lescarbot, "do proceed the tears, fretfulnesses, and desolations which bring us to the grave before our time." In contrast, the Indians maintained the two principles of marriage that were derived from nature: the authority of the father and the industry of the husband, both of which were in decline in France. Because the native women nourished their own children, they loved them more deeply than did European women: "Likewise their breasts are no baits of love, as in these our parts, but, rather, love in those lands is made by the flame that nature kindleth in everyone, without annexing any arts to it, either by painting, amorous poisons, or otherwise." Tacitus, Lescarbot noted, praised the Germans for the same reasons.[56]

Lescarbot, it seemed, got on badly with his fellow colonists. Danger in the New World, he wrote, came "not from the people that we call savages, but from them that term themselves Christians and yet love but the name of it—cursed and abominable people, worse than wolves, enemies to God and human nature." The Indians were more open, generous, and humane precisely because they were "less civilized." He recognized faults in the Indians, though the one that seemed to strike him most forcefully was their table manners. They ate vast amounts of food. Still, Hercules, an ancestor of the Europeans, consumed more—a whole ox at a time—and greater gluttons, Lescarbot contended, could be found now in France than among the savages.[57]

Edmund Spenser made his contribution to the disgruntlement of the age by contrasting the "antique world," in which man was in his "freshest prime," with his own time, in which "the world is runne quite out of square." A situation "once amisse growes daily wourse and wourse." The golden age had become a "stonie one." Men once "form'd of flesh and bone,/ are now transformed into hardest stone. . ." Life could scarcely be more bleak or the future less promising. In his hymn to Guiana, Chapman proved more hopeful for the future, but only because the scene of English activities would soon shift to the New World. Tame savages, gold, and fertile fields were the least of the advantages that could be expected from colonization.

> There *Learning* eates no more his thriftlesse bookes,
> Nor *Valure* Estridge-like his yron armes.
> There *Beaute* is no strumpet for her wantes,
> Nor Gallique humours putrifie her bloud:
> But all our Youth take *Hymens* lightes in hand,
> And fill each roofe with honor'd progenie.
> There makes *Societie* Adamantine chaines,
> And ioins their harts with wealth, whom wealth disioyn'd.
> There healthfull Recreations strowe their meades,
> And make their mansions daunce with neighborhood,
> That here were drown'd in Churlish *Auarice*.

The strength of his claims for Guiana rested on the deep pessimism of his vision of European life as it was lived in his own time. A colonist as knowledgeable and realistic as John Smith fell into a similar argument in recommending New England to his countrymen. In the New World, he claimed, Englishmen would be free of rents and fines. Nor would lives be consumed in "tedious pleas in law." "Multitudes to occasion such impediments to good orders, as in popular States," would not be found in New England. There, "every man may be master and owner of his owne labour and land; or the greatest part in a small time. If hee have nothing but his hands, he may set vp this trade; and by industrie quickly grow rich; spending but half that time wel, which in England we abuse in idlenes, worse or as ill." The New World opened magnificent vistas to Englishmen largely because they felt so confined on their little island. "Heer nature and liberty affords vs that freely," wrote Smith, "which in *England* we want, or it costeth vs dearely."[58]

Ralegh put the radical critique of European life into broad historical terms. All nations, he wrote, had evolved from the same primitive conditions. In the earliest ages men fed on acorns and roots, lived in rude cottages, and covered their bodies with skins of animals. Gradually life changed. Weapons became more proficient and so did hunting and warfare. At first, bodies of water had been crossed on rafts made of trees, but then methods improved, culminating in the age of sail. Although all men once had the same "want of instruction," in time they developed farming, laws, and philosophy. But the results had not been entirely salutary. Men now had greater opportunities for vice and injustice. They once lived in houses of clay and timber; now they inhabited palaces of stone that were painted, carved, and adorned with gold. As a result men were now known by their houses rather than their houses by them. "We are fallen from two dishes to two hundred; from water to wine and drunkenness; from the covering of our bodies with skins of beasts, not only to silk and gold, but to the very skins of men." Time, he concluded, would exact its revenge for the excesses of mankind.[59]

Profound fears and misgivings, it seemed, plagued the Elizabethan age.[60] Dreamy pictures of paradise provided release from

insecurity and self-doubt and supplied the basis for an indictment of European life. The noble Indian represented a shining
example of how life had been in a better age and would be
again once men managed to transcend the limitations of the
present. But, of course, the paradisaic vision was narcissistic at
best. Insofar as Englishmen employed it as a lens through which
to see native peoples, they saw mainly themselves. Even when
a trace of objectivity appeared in the tendency toward cultural
relativism, it arose from European discontent and led quickly
to an idealization of the American natives. At the deepest level
the paradisaic conception derived from a primal existential
doubt. Although it supported a richly optimistic vision of the
future, it did so only by activating an acute pessimism about
the present and a woefully distorted vision of life in America.

The paradisaic conception furnished no theoretical basis
from which Englishmen might grasp realistically the character
of native society. It did not necessarily inhibit various observers' attempts to perceive certain aspects of native culture ac-
curately, but it did prevent them from discerning the full lineaments of native social order. Moreover, the paradisaic doctrine
supported the European tendency to drain native life of its
content. Description seemed invariably to fall into the negative
mood. Paradise, after all, was a state Europeans had lost. By
associating native society with that sense of loss, observers not
only misperceived the native world, but they also came close
to denying it the very substance of human existence.

On a practical level paradism exaggerated the resources of
the New World and the ease with which they could be exploited. In this process the Indians played an ambiguous part.
For all their virtues, they had failed to use what nature provided. James Rosier described the Maine coast as "a land, whose
pleasant fertility bewraieth it selfe to be a garden of nature,
wherein she only intended to delight hir selfe, hauing hitherto
obscured it to any, except to a purblind generation, whose
vnderstanding it hath pleased God so to darken, as they can
neither discerne, vse, or rightly esteeme the vnualuable riches
in middest whereof they live sensually content with the bark
and outward rinds, as neither knowing the sweetnes of the inward marrow, nor acknowledging the Deity of the Almighty

giuer. . ." The New World awaited the exploitative touch of English yeomen, miners, and merchants. "VIRGINIA," announced Michael Drayton, "Earth's onely Paradise./Where Nature hath in store/Fowle, Venison, and Fish,/And the fruitfull'st Soyle." Smith found New England as God had made it, and he concluded that the land need only be "cultured, planted and manured by men of industrie, judgment, and experience" to fulfill the hopes of Englishmen. Even allowing for the hyperbole of promotional literature, expectations for America's future were high. These expectations derived from the perception of the New World as paradise.[61]

Stephen Parmenius, a Hungarian Protestant and a friend of Hakluyt who perished with Gilbert on a voyage to Newfoundland in 1583, wrote a poem in Latin inaugurating the voyage that brilliantly summarized the positive vision of the New World. He began with a certain ambivalence toward his adopted country that persisted throughout the poem. On the one hand England had achieved worldwide recognition as a prosperous and active nation, but on the other these accomplishments had imposed heavy burdens that could be relieved by the establishment of colonies in America. Parmenius told his countrymen that, fortunately, "A land unruled by kings has been preserved/For you through many centuries. . ." The New World had been spared the burden of history. It had "not felt the weight/Of Babylon, the Persians' might, nor known/Victorious Macedon, and never was Subdued by Rome. Nor has the Moslem wail/Disturbed those regions: there no scheming hand/Of Spain rejects the early church of God. . ." The origins of the people of America struck Parmenius as mysterious. Were they perhaps of "ancient ancestry," "inheriting from times/Gone by a land of woods and fertile fields/And cities needing not the rule of law?" "The Golden Age began. . ./In such communities, and thus men lived/In blessedness. . ." The world (though apparently not the Indians) had since been "cheapened" by passing through the ages of silver, bronze, and "dull Hard Iron." But now it had come full circle and stood at the brink of another age of gold. "Well could it be that that great time has come,/That round the globe we see peace-loving men/Promote an Age of Gold? . . ." Only the English seemed deserving of this new age. The rest of the world remained sunk in corruption. Should the English prove unable to "justify the claim/That in our land there dwells a Golden Race. . . ," there would come "A time in which the pagan tribes may move/Together, under Gilbert's leadership/Into new cities. . . ," a time when families would be brought together and laws decreed.

> Then people, innocent
> Of crime and falsity, will rather wear
> The crown of lasting purity than sink
> Their minds and bodies into sinful lust
> And base indulgence: nor will they seek wealth,
> Nor yet for glory ride the fickle whim
> Of senseless masses. Freedom and the use
> Of talents will not be repressed by wealth,
> Nor will the poor divert their strength in feuds
> Against the rich, based on the claim that all
> Are citizens. Each man will take the part
> That duly falls to him. Then Mother Earth
> Will yield to all, from little effort, rich
> Provisions from her ample store of goods:
> No cares will then oppress the youth with age,
> And labouring will not deprive a man
> Of time to make a living through his own
> Abilities.[62]

Parmenius voiced the yearnings of an age. The world seemed so intolerable, so out of joint, so lacking in justice and tranquility that only a return to paradise could assuage human unhappiness. Paradise waited in the New World for Englishmen to begin the process of realizing its potential. The native people who lived there were expected to take part in the proceedings and to share in the results of English efforts. They would do so, of course, only at the expense of their way of life. When they resisted, Englishmen turned to another version of the doctrine of savagism, to the ignoble side of the conception.

2

IGNOBLE SAVAGISM

Once the English became colonists and began in Virginia to recreate the civil order of England, they seemed less inclined to envision the native people as noble savages. Yet they did not abandon the savage motif. Indians were still people whose manner of life could be defined by the absence of European civility. It required only a modest twist in logic to construe savages who merited admiration because they had been preserved from the burdens of history as savages devoid of nobility precisely because they lacked the usual signs of civil virtue. When Europeans identified the good life with the lost paradise, the Indian was considered a virtuous exemplar. When they worried about the disintegration of established values, the Indians tended to fall into the opposite category and to pose a threat to civil order. Both the noble and ignoble images rested on the broader concept of the savage. Both assumed the existence of human beings who lived without the usual restraints of social discipline. Of course the two forms of savagism had long been part of the arsenal of ideas Europeans drew on to explain the characters of alien peoples. The concept shifted from one side to the other as need arose. While engaged in the arduous task of establishing their own version of order in the New World, the English found it easier to perceive native society as an ignoble threat than as a noble ideal.

Defined as ignoble savages, the native people of the New World occupied a special place in the European imagination. Possessing none of the components of an ordered society, their only grip upon the world seemed to be the undifferentiated rage that they released upon anyone foolish enough to come within reach. Ignoble savages violated all the limitations imposed on ordinary men by social usage. Violence, treachery, brutality, and destruction were the foundations of savage existence. Still, these unpleasant attributes paled before the deeper meaning of the ignoble savage motif. American Indians were expected to be vicious because they represented, in the European imagination, the antiprinciple to humane existence. Europeans believed that life could be properly ordered only if the summation of disorder could be perceived. Virtue could not exist without a corresponding vice. Christian theology accepted the role of Satan in a world created and governed by God. The recognition of civility implied knowledge of incivility. Furthermore, the process was more than academic. It involved a real struggle in the European soul to resist the temptations of incivility, the dangers of violence, brutality, and disorder that men found within themselves. The Indians saved European society from itself. If the Indians were really beastlike creatures who devoured their own, they were dangerous and should be resisted. But they also released Europeans from the inner knowledge that they were themselves bestial—or could become so if ever the safeguards of civility weakened. For this reason the Elizabethan age identified ignoble savagism with the devil and all his works. Satan knew his friends. He knew that ignoble savages would follow his command in seeking to devour the innocent and the virtuous. Thus Indians became more than dangerous savages in the European imagination; they became the agents of demoniacal ruin.

Where paganism continued to exist or where heathens and savages threatened Christian civilization, the designs of the devil would be found. To the Hebrews the Egyptians had been barbarous because they worshiped idols; to medieval Christians the Mongols were the "detestable race of Satan, whose teeth are bloody and their jaws ever ready to eat the flesh of men, and to drink human blood." Christianity and civilization, in the European view, arose precisely at the expense of Satan's power. American Puritans seemed particularly inclined to link the wilderness and savagism with the nefarious activities of Satan, but the idea was deeply embedded in European life and played an important role in the formulation of the ignoble savage theme long before the Puritans began their struggle to create God's kingdom in the New World.[1]

James I acknowledged the close kinship between savagism and Satan in his treatise *Daemonologie*. The "wild partes of the worlde" afforded greater opportunity for mischief, "because where the Devill findes greatest ignorance and barbaritie, there assayles he grossliest . . ." The ignorance of God that prevailed among savages was as likely to attract the devil as was a conscious commitment to his cause. "The working of the divell in mens soules (being an inuisible spirit)," counseled a major religious handbook of the day, "is with such vnconceiueable sleight & crafty conueiance that men in the state of nature cannot possibly feele it, or perceive it: for how can a blind man see, or a dead man feele." Natural men were necessarily unregenerate. They would become civil when they received God's grace and abandoned their alliance with the devil.[2]

People who adored idols or who appeared to be in easy concourse with the devil were surely uncivil in their mode of life. "Such are at this day," wrote Thomas Palmer, "the barbarous people of the East and West *Indies*, that worship the vgly shapes of Divels, of the Sunne, Moone, Starres, of the Elements & of other Creatures." Idolatry violated the divine order and placed men in league with Satan. It also set them at war with the human condition itself. Witchcraft, for example, had long been identified with cannibalism. "Where the Anthropophagi doo inhabite, are many spirites, whiche doo the people there very much harme." Explorers and settlers were quick to identify the man-eaters in the New World, and they were easily convinced that these fearful enemies of humankind did the work of the devil. During the first voyage to Virginia in 1607, George Percy met them on Dominica and recognized them immediately as ignoble savages. "They are continually in warres, and will eate their enemies when they kill them, or any stranger if they take them. They will lap vp mans spittle, whilst one spits in their mouthes in a barbarous fashion like Dogges. These people and the rest of the Ilands in the West Indies, and Brasill, are called by the names of Canibals, that will eate mans flesh . . .: they worship the Deuill for their God, and have no other beliefe."

A society with such loathsome habits, akin to the behavior of animals, was inevitably allied with Satan.[3]

The presence of the devil in the savage world opened that sensitive question of the natives' humanity. George Abbot, later Archbishop of Canterbury, conceded that the natives of the Caribbean must have been under the influence of Satan, "it were otherwise incredible, that any who have in them reason, and the shape of men, should be so bruitishly ignorant of all kinde of true religion, and vnderstanding devotion." By themselves Indians could boast a human shape and reason; in concert with the devil they fell into brutishness and irreligion.[4] A revealing exchange on the religion of the Canadian Indians took place between Marc Lescarbot and Samuel de Champlain. The latter contended that the native people lived without law, but that they believed there was one God who created all things. Lescarbot doubted this and demanded to know what ceremony the Indians employed in worshiping God. Champlain replied that "everyone did pray in his heart as he would," which seemed to be just the opening Lescarbot sought. It was precisely this absence of ceremony, he argued, that led him to "believe, there is no law among them, neither do they know what it is to worship or pray to God and live the most part as brute beasts . . ." Moreover, the Indians lived in subjection to their shamans, who were agents of Satan. Later, when discussing the West Indian natives, he agreed that their gods may have been devils. Lescarbot presented a generally friendly portrayal of native society, but he accepted the familiar connections among irreligion, devil worship, and brutishness.[5]

In the literature, iconography, and imagination of the Middle Ages, the devil frequently appeared in the guise of an animal. Martin Luther entertained visions of Satan as an ape; James I called him "God's Ape." Wild men, who dwelled in the forest and whose humanity was ambiguous, often revealed themselves as incubi. Hence Shakespeare drew on a long tradition when he created Caliban, whose monstrousness stems from his origins. The misalliance of an incubus and the witch Sycorax engendered this monster who is more than a monster: "a devil, a born devil," a "demi devil," a "thing of darkness." Although Sycorax came from "Argier" (presumably Algeria) and thus is

African, she worships Setebos, the Patagonian god. Antonio Pigafetta, the loquacious chronicler of Magellan's circumnavigation, described a meeting with a Patagonian giant who cried the name of Setebos when the Spaniards made the sign of the cross. He feared that the god would enter his body and make it burst if any more Christian signs were made in his presence. For the Spaniards, Setebos was a devil to be exorcised in converting the natives to Christianity and curing their monstrousness. Bestiality called into question the humanity of the native people and associated them with the dark forces of the universe.[6]

The close relationship Europeans established between civility and Christianity and their preoccupation with Satan led to an intense interest in the religions of the American natives. Most often, Indian religion came out badly, though a few observers found at least something to admire. Thomas Palmer explained that the "secret and wonderfull despensation of the good pleasure of God" had implanted natural law in varying strengths in the hearts of men, "whence there ariseth such strange worshipping of God amongst the Heathen."[7] Still, it was the variety that proved unsatisfactory to the Christian conscience. When explorers and settlers praised native religion, it was usually because they recognized traces of their own beliefs. Peter Martyr told of Columbus's exchange with an elderly Cuban chieftain, who addressed the Spaniards after observing them at Mass. Columbus, he said, had recently subdued many lands and instilled fear in the people, but he should remember that two rewards awaited men after death: "the one fowle and darke" for those who were "iniurious and cruell to mankynde," and the other "pleasaunt and delectable" for those who "loued peace and quietnes." Hence he cautioned the Spaniard to hurt no man wrongfully. Surprised at the percipience of this native moralist, Columbus could only respond that he had been sent to protect the innocent and instruct the people in the true religion. Louis Le Roy reported a similar belief among the Americans: "The soules of the dead go into other places according to such workes as they have done in this life." In both cases these traces of Christian belief were coupled with a paradisaic description of native life. Native religion proved worthy of praise because, like paradise, it reflected European ideals, not because it could claim legitimacy as the Indians' peculiar possession.[8]

Thomas Hariot made a conscious effort to investigate religion among the Carolina Indians. They worshiped a number of gods but ranked one above the others, "which hath bene from all eternitie." This god, they believed made the waters first, out of which he formed all creatures. Mankind was held to be the progeny of one of the gods and the first woman. The Indians gave their gods human shape and built temples to worship their images. They believed in the immortality of the soul and reward or punishment in the afterlife. According to their works, men either went "to heaven the habitacle of gods, there to enjoy perpetuall bliss and happinesse, or els to a great pitte or hole . . . , there to burne continually." Hariot attended carefully enough to the content of the natives' religious opinions, but only because he saw some potential for change, not because he respected the integrity of native life. "Some religion they have alreadie," he noted, "which although it be farre from the truth, yet beyng as it is, there is hope it may bee the easier and sooner reformed." He began the process immediately and, if his own account can be believed, met with some success. The Indians, apparently, "were not so sure grounded" or confident in their manner of belief and thus "were brought into great doubts of their owne, and no small admiration of ours . . ."[9]

Other commentators found it difficult to discover any religious opinions among the native peoples. Francis Bacon thought it extraordinary that the Indians had names for particular gods but no name for God, which proved to him that they possessed some general notion of divinity "though they have not the latitude and extent of it." Verrazzano reported that he could find no signs of religion at all among the Indians. He admitted that his impressions may have derived from the language difficulty. Yet, so far as he could tell, the natives lived without either religion or law, acknowledged no first cause, and recognized no god, not even the sun, moon, or planets. Apparently they neither built temples nor carried on any ceremonies of adoration or sacrifice. "We suppose that they have no religion at all . . . ," he wrote. This gap in native culture proceeded from ignorance, and Verrazzano believed that it would be easily filled by the Europeans.[10]

Most white men met a more formidable obstacle in the New World than ignorance or theological error. Even when native religion was discussed with relative objectivity, it was seldom that the devil did not have a place in it. Abbot thought ignorance was itself the work of Satan. He praised the Indians for their friendliness and their "open and plaine behaviour" and noted that in some parts of the West Indies they believed in the immortality of the soul, but that they also adored the devil. "The Mexicans, and other people of America," wrote Ralegh, "were brought by the Devil under his fearful servitude, in which he also holdeth the Floridians and Virginians at this day." John Smith began his experience in the New World with a deep suspicion of the native people of Virginia. Experience validated his distrust, though the Indians, in Smith's view, were not so savage as to be without religion.

All things that were able to do them hurt beyond their prevention, they adore with their kinde of diuine worship; as the fire, water, lightening, thunder, our ordinance, peeces, horses, & c. But their cheife God they worship is the Diuell. Him they call Oke & serue him more of feare then loue. They say they haue conference with him, and fashion themselues neare to his shape as they can imagine. In their Temples they haue his image euill favouredly carued, and then painted and adorned with chaines copper, and beades, and couered with a skin, in such manner as the deformity may wel suit with such a God.

Smith saw a good deal more of the New World than did most Englishmen, which only confirmed in his mind the common opinion of the time. Indians were pagans and paganism enjoyed a special place in the realm of Satan.[11]

The most impressive treatment of native religion came from the pen of José de Acosta, the Spanish Jesuit. He concentrated on Mexico and Peru and was obviously fascinated by what he found. Few English observers in the Elizabethan period had seen the great civilizations of middle America, and none had written about them in detail. Acosta described for his English readers a culture rooted in religious experience and rich in symbol and ceremony. It was clear that the religion of the Aztecs profoundly touched him. He wondered whether the devotion that Mexicans brought to a religion of such rigor and austerity–a religion that served Satan–might be applied to Christianity. Although he detected similarities between the two faiths, he recoiled with a verbal shudder from the satanic character of Mexican religion. He wrote of the ceremonial life of the Aztecs:

> It is common and generall to have vsually one of these three things, either cruelty, filthines, or slouth; for all their ceremonies were cruell and hurtefull, as to kill men and to spill blood, are filthy and beastly, as to eate and drinke to the name of their Idolls, and also to pisse in the honour of them, carrying them vpon their shoulders, to annoint and besmeere themselves filthily, and to do a thousand sortes of villanies, which were at the least, vaine, ridiculous, and idle, and more like the actions of children then of men. The cause thereof is the very condition of this wicked spirit, whose intention is alwaies to do ill, provoking men still to murthers and filthines, or at the least to vanities and fruitelesse actions, the which every man may well know, if he duly consider the behaviour and actions of the Divell, towardes those he sets to deceive.

Acosta granted the Aztecs the minor consolation of being the victims of Satan's power, though he cautioned them to look carefully at the devil's deceptions.[12] If the most impressive religioculture of the New World were held in thralldom to the devil, what more could be expected of the less sophisticated peoples confronted by the English?

The sacrifice of human beings seemed the most spectacular evidence of satanic influence. The Spanish portrayals of Mexico and Peru left nothing to the imagination. Thomas Nicholas translated Gómara's description of a melancholy episode that took place during the conquest of Mexico. "The *Mexican* Priests . . . stripped fiftie Spaniards captives as naked as they were borne, and with their fine rasors opened them in the breastes and pluckt out their hartes for an offering to the Idolls, and sprinckled their bloud in the ayre."[13] Just one of Montezuma's vassals sacrificed 20,000 victims a year, and sometimes 50,000. Pierre d'Avity described a similar scene and added some detail, but he was more interested in the bloody proceedings

of the Incas. The Mexicans, he contended, sacrificed only prisoners they took in war; the Incas destroyed their own.

> In Peru they did sacrifice children from the age of foure
> yeres vnto ten, and especially for the prosperitie of the
> Ingua in his enterprises of warre: and vpon the day of his
> coronation they did sacrifice two hundred young children.
> They did also sacrifice a good number of those virgins
> which they drew out of monasteries, for the Inguas seruice.
> When he was grieuously sicke, some man of qualitie, or
> some sorcerer (where there were many) telling him that
> he was past hope of recouerie, they did sacrifise his sonne
> to Viracoca or to the Sun, beseeching him that he would
> rest satisfied therewith.

Another account pictured a Peruvian temple, the pillars hung
with the carcasses of men and children, their skins tanned to
reduce the odor. Nailed to the walls and pillars were heads
treated and shrunken to the size of a man's fist. Samuel Purchas
did not exaggerate when he referred to the Peruvian sacrifice
of children as "most vnkind and vnnaturall."[14]

The Spanish sources prepared the English for the worst. They
expected to find widespread sacrifice of children and innocent
victims on the northern continent. In fact they found little.
Laudonnière claimed that the Florida natives sacrificed the
firstborn male. The priests placed the child's head on a block
and clubbed him to death. On one occasion, the French saw
such a ceremony. William Strachey believed that the Virginia
Indians were addicted to a similar practice: "Yt maiewell be
by the subtile Spirritt the malitious enemy to mankind whome
therefore to pacefie and worke to doe them good (at least no
harme) the priests tell them doe these and these Sacrifices vnto,
of these and these things, and thus and thus often, by which
meanes not only their owne children but Straungers are some-
tymes sacryficed vnto him."[15] The principal evidence concerned
the apparent murder of the "Black Boys" by Powhatan's people
in their huskanaw ceremony. The story originated with William
White, a Jamestown laborer who had spent some time with the
Indians. John Smith printed the first account of it; Strachey included the story in his work and attributed it to George Percy.
As Smith described the ceremony, it involved both murder and

cannibalism. Each year the natives selected fifteen young boys, painted them white, and "spent the forenoone in dancing and singing about them with rattles." They were then gathered at the base of a tree. The men of the village armed themselves with reeds and formed two lines leading to the boys. Five young men made their way through the lines and each led one boy out, while protecting him from the men's blows. The native women wept and cried out and prepared for the funerals of their children. At this point Smith faltered in his account: "What else was done with the children, was not seene, but they were all cast on a heape, in a valley as dead, where they made a great feast for all the company." When questioned about this custom, the Indians replied that the children were not all dead, "that the Oke or Divell did sucke the bloud from their left breast, who chanced to be his by lot," but that the others were kept for nine months in the forest before returning to become "Priests and Coniurers." Purchas learned from John Rolfe that the children were not sacrificed, and made this clear in his later version of the story.[16]

Europeans placed the major blame for the triumph of Satan among the Indians on the shamans. These priests were "the ministers of Sathan," whose influence in Indian society made the people the "naked slaves of the divell." The natives served Satan out of fear and were driven by the priests to the horrid crime of sacrificing their children. Writers compared the priestly class to "popish Hermits" and "English Witches." The English perceived implicitly that the shamans played a critical role in the maintenance of stability in Indian society. They acted as physicians, rainmakers, prophets, and intermediaries with an assortment of native divinities. No public and few private activities could take place without the ministrations of a shaman. It appeared to European observers that the priests held the reins of power among the native people. As a consequence the very substance of native life was contaminated by the presence of the devil, who worked his will through the influence of his agents. Moreover, the priestly class constituted the major obstacle to the success of European ways in the New World. In 1609, as part of a general plan to subject the Powhatan Indians to English authority, the Council of Virginia ordered Sir Thomas Gates to eliminate the priests, to "proceede even to dache with these murtherers of Soules and sacrificers of gods images to the Divill . . ." By resisting the Europeans, the shamans defended their own positions, but they also guarded the integrity of the native social order. To the white man, they did the work of Satan.[17]

The presence of Satan in the New World was an intensely serious matter. Cortez smashed the Aztec idols in order to convert the Indians to Christianity, but also because he feared the power of the devil. When Indians invoked the influence of their gods, Europeans usually reacted with a mixture of contempt and ill-concealed apprehension. Hakluyt reported that as Drake sailed along the eastern coast of South America the native people burned fires and performed other ceremonies as "a sacrifice . . . to the devils." The Indians prayed that shoals would be formed and storms arise to wreck the English ships, "whereof (as it is reported) there have been divers experiments." At about the same time, far to the north, sailors from Frobisher's second voyage captured an elderly Eskimo woman whom they suspected of being either a devil or a witch. They "plucked off" her "buskins" "to see if she were cloven footed." The Pamunkey Indians submitted John Smith to three days of conjurations in order, apparently, to discover the intention of the English in coming to their country. Smith reckoned that his end had come, though he endured the ordeal with remarkable equanimity. He wrote later that the episode made him feel "As if neare lead to hell,/Amongst the Devils to dwell." The Virginia colonists themselves seemed to have been attracted by the demonic power of the Indians. Thomas Dale and John Rolfe remembered that the early colonists had begun the practice of wearing a lock of hair on the left side. They took the style from the Indians, who had adopted it because the devil appeared to them with a similar coiffure. "A faire vnlouely generation of the *Loue-locke* Christians," commented Purchas, "imitating Saluages, and they the Diuell."[18]

George Percy recounted an incident that revealed the extraordinary sway exercised by Satan in America. When, in a skirmish with the English, it became clear to the Indians that their arrows would not dent armor, they fell "into their exorcismes coniuracyons and charms throweinge fyer vpp into the skyes Runneinge up and downe wth Rattles and makeinge many dyabolicall gestures wth many erigramantcke Spells and incantacious Imageinge . . ." "Butt nether the dievall whome they adore nor all their Sorcerres did anytheinge Avayle them for our men Cutt downe their Corne Burned their houses and besydes those wch they had slayne brought some of them prisoners to our foarte." Percy gloated too soon over the superiority of English arms. An event soon took place "ocasyoned by the Salvages Sorceries and Charmes" that gave him reason for pause. While Sir Thomas Dale "wth Some fo the better sorte" visited an Indian house "A fantasy possessed them thatt they imagined the Salvages were sett upon them eache man Takeinge one another for an Indyan And so did fall pell mell one upon An other beatinge one another downe and breakeinge one of Anothers heades, that Mutche mischiefe might have bene donn . . ." Fortunately the English God proved as potent as English arms. The fantasy dissipated and each man understood his error.[19] But the Indians and Satan had made their point.

In his discussion of education for the benighted natives of Virginia, John Brinsley issued a warning concerning the dangers of consorting with the savage minions of Satan. "Wofull is the case," he wrote, "of all those amongst whom Sathan reignes." Life, Brinsley believed, was fraught with menace among people ignorant of Christ, but was particularly dangerous among the Indians, who adored Satan and sacrificed to him as a god. It should not be surprising, he concluded, that "honest and understanding Christians" should be reluctant to move to Virginia. "Manifold perils" awaited them in the New World, "especially of falling away from God to Sathan, and that themselves, or their posterity should become utterly savage, as they are."[20] Proximity to savagism brought Englishmen in reach of the devil and placed them in danger of losing their souls and their civility.

Creatures of the devil and ignoble savages the Indians may have been, but the English found them remarkable attractive physically. The native skin color was free of the negative connotations that the English attached to blackness. Travelers who touched the African shore invariably commented on "those fryed Regions of blacke Brutish Negars." The curse of Ham did not have the same meaning for the Indian that it did for the African. Along the Guinea coast Robert Baker encountered "a number of blacke soules,/Whose likelinesse seem'd men to be,/ but all as blacke as coles."[21] Similarly, few observers failed to note the Indians' color. Usually, the Europeans saw them as "olive," "tawney," "brown," or "brasse." Less often, Indians were depicted as black or even white. Seldom was any value linked to color, though it may be that Europeans would have preferred Indians of a lighter hue. At least they often seemed relieved when they became convinced that the Indians' darker skin tone was artificially induced by the sun and various protective ointments.[22] Physically, the Indians cut impressive figures. White men were virtually unanimous in their praise. "They are wel featured in their limbs," wrote Verrazzano, "of meane stature, and commonly somewhat bigger then we, brode breasted, strong armes, their legges and other partes of their bodies well fashioned, and they are disfigured in nothing . . ." Of a chief's wife in Guiana, Ralegh said he had "seldome seene a better fauored woman"–high praise from an expert.[23]

Although they marked the difference in color, Europeans were as apt to view the Indian's physical structure through conventional images as they were his manner of life. Savagism impinged upon pictorial images as well as verbal images of the native people, resulting in representations of them as wild men or monsters. They no doubt derived from the more generalized ignoble savage formula, as the information from the New World concerning the native physiognomy was overwhelmingly favorable. Still, for virtually all visual portrayals of the Indians in the Elizabethan period, experience seemed to count for little. An artist as talented as John White, who saw real Indians and was extraordinarily sensitive to the particularities of their culture, employed conventional forms in painting the native body. Though his Eskimos were of the correct stature and bore the right complexion, a heavy layer of clothing concealed their bodies. Indians from Carolina sported modish Renaissance figures and could not be distinguished physically from ancient Picts. Of course, both were savages. Jacques Le Moyne was similarly conventional in depicting the Florida natives. The engravings of the work of White and Le Moyne by de Bry were even more rigidly stylized. Portraits of the American natives free of the conventional structure did not become common until the middle of the seventeenth century. Except for the more stereotyped representations of wild men and monsters, and the European fixation with scenes of cannibalism, Indians were generally spared depiction as ignoble savages.[24]

Pictures of Indians revealed the common native customs of decorating the body, a practice particularly abhorrent to Elizabethan moralists. It was common for preachers of the period to censure women for painting their faces and indulging in excessive adornment. Thomas Tuke summed up the current clerical opinion in 1616 in his *Treatise against Painting and Tinctvring of Men and Women.* He associated the cosmetic art with an assortment of vices—murder, poisoning, pride, ambition, adultery, and witchcraft—but he condemned it principally because if offended nature and was inspired by the devil. Mainly, "painting and tinctvring" seemed to be the vice of corrupt civilization. Yet Tuke could not resist bringing in the savages. He recalled Holinshed's description of the painted Picts and claimed that the custom had been originated by Medea, a sorceress. The "Heathen and Infidels," it seemed, had been the first to adopt the practice. The moral was plain enough: "Seeing therefore we have cast off their Barbarisme & Infidelity, let vs also lay aside their other vanities and adulterous devises," for the use of cosmetics "doe ill become the *bodies of Saints,* which are *Temples* of the holy Ghost . . ."[25] The travel literature contained numerous descriptions of the use of bodily adornment. To many observers, the various physical markings conveyed the impression of a people insufficiently respectful of the human body. The Brazilian practice of opening a hole in the lower lip to hold a bone or fish defied human decency. Only a savage people who lacked a sense of the proper limits of behavior would so defile the body. Such words as "deform," "disfigure," and "mishapen" were used to describe this native practice. When referring to a similar custom among the Virginia Indians, John Smith said that the most "gallant" among the natives was "the most monstrous to behould." Observers readily linked the Indians' apparent lack of respect for their bodies with ignoble savagism.[26]

The distinctive manners of the Indians also supplied impressive evidence of ignoble savagism. "These wilde men of *America* have no more civilitie in their eating, than in other things," wrote Andrew Thevet, "for they have no lawes to take the good, & to eschue the euil, even so they eat of al kinds of meats at al times and houres, without any other descretion." They drank warm blood, ate raw flesh, "Ants eggs, Worms, Serpents, Frogges, Earth, Wod, Dung of wilde beasts, and keepe the Bones of Fishes and Serpents, to grinde and eate afterwards." "They neither use table, stoole, or table cloth for comlinesse: but when they are imbrued with bloud, knuckle deepe, and their knives in like sort, they vse their tongues as apt instruments to licke them cleane . . ." Native table manners conformed to the stereotype of a savage people. Observers were reminded of barbarous Turks, Germans, Gauls, and contemporary Irishmen. More important, they noted the brutishness of native habits.[27]

Without the benefit of social discipline, savages could be relied upon to manifest the vices that civility condemned. "They are inconstant in everie thing, but what feare contraineth them to keepe," maintained Smith, adding that the natives were "craftie, timerous, quicke of apprehension & very ingenuous. Some are of a disposition fearefull, some bold, most cautelous, all Savage. Generally covetous of copper, beads, & such like trash. They are soone moved to anger. and so malitious, that they seldom forget an iniury . . ." He noted that the Indians did not steal from their own because they feared the revelations of their conjurers, which he saw as an added argument for their treacherousness. (It might have been better interpreted as a demonstration of the integrity of native culture.) They were an idle, improvident, ignorant, and scattered people who left the land as God had made it. Or, as Edward Waterhouse paraphrased Oviedo after the massacre of 1622: The Indians were "by nature sloathfull and idle, vitious, melancholy, slouenly, of bad conditions, lyers, of small memory, of no constancy or trust." Ralegh believed that he had discovered the ultimate in native greed and social disorder in Guiana. There he found a tribe of cannibals who would sell children of the tribe for three or four hatchets, and for a few more would part with even their own daughters. Savagism provided no solid base from which to erect a secure and virtuous society. As ignoble savages Indians were undependable—or, perhaps, dependable only in their inconstancy. The larger iniquities would also be noted, but because Europeans stressed the social incoherence of the savage state they often saw an Indian of paltry, contemptible vices. He was cowardly, naive, cautious, crafty, greedy, malicious, treacherous, and most of all unstable. Europeans never felt secure in his presence, though they might disdain rather than fear him.[28]

Savage people established no firm roots in the soil. Without centers of population or extensive cultivation of the land, they remained few in number. They moved from place to place and seemed incapable of attaching themselves securely to the world in which they lived. Constant warfare took a heavy toll on their small population, as did the spread of disease through their "ymoderate vse" of women. The savage Indians of the central plains "goe together in companies, and move from one place to another, as wilde Moores of Barbarie called Alarbes doe, following the season and the pasture of the Oxen." Acosta found the Chichimecas a striking example of ignoble savagism. They lived by hunting and gathering and did not farm. Apparently they did not even live together except when small bands attacked the Spanish settlements to murder and rob. Efforts to conquer them failed because they possessed no towns to destroy, no fields to burn. Marauding parties retreated into the remotest regions where the Spaniards could not pursue them. Few could ever be found. The Chichimecas seemed to have no leaders; hence, their attacks were diffuse and unpredictable. In Elizabethan terms, savage people—ignoble and noble—took on a curious insubstantiality.[29]

Europeans detected all manner of political arrangements in the New World. Indian leaders became kings, queens, and princes; familial forms of society became classical republics. Alexander Whitaker found "a rude kinde of Common-wealth" in Virginia. Yet most observers seemed more fascinated with what they perceived as a political void. Ignoble savages lived without the enjoyment of a commonweal. As Acosta put it: "In some places, they are yet more barbarous, scarcely acknowledging any head, but all command and governe in common, having no other thing, but evil, violence, unreason, and disorder, so as he that most may, most commaunds." In a society in which the people could not pronounce the letters "L, F, R" because they had neither "Law, Faith, nor Rulers," the men were cruel without measure and the women infinitely lascivious. The consequence of the collapse of internal order was the imposition of despotism. Ignoble savagism generated its own order in the classic scenario for the rise of tyranny. The savages themselves could neither perceive nor prevent this process. Their incivility denied them any knowledge of history. Because they remembered nothing, they were ripe for despotism. Thus, Smith explained the rule of Powhatan. He imposed order in his savage domain by means of his arbitrary will. "The more that men approach to reason," argued Acosta, "the more milde is their government and lesse insolent; the Kings and Lords are more tractable, agreeing better with their subiects, acknowledging them equall in nature, though inferiour in duetie and care of the commonwealth. But amongst the Barbarians all is contrary, for that their government is tyrannous, vsing their subiects like beasts, and seeking to be reverenced like gods." [30]

Europeans had described other people of strange manners in the language of ignoble savagism. Writing of the Tartars, Hakluyt referred to "their unmercifull lawes, their fond superstitions, their bestiall lives, their vicious manners, their slavish subjection to their own supereours, and their disdainfull and brutish inhumanitie unto strangers . . ." "They are rather Monsters then men, thirsting and drinking bloud, tearing and devouring the flesh of Dogges and Man." Tartars were a "savage" and "barbarous" people. So filthy were their manners that they always attacked upwind so that their odor would not reveal their presence.[31] Lapps were similarly slandered. They wandered from place to place in search of animals to hunt, and "they know no arte nor facultie." It was reported that in Estotiland the people lived by hunting, but despite the cold they went naked and had not the wit to cover themselves with the skins of beasts. "They are a very fierce people, they make cruell warres one with another, and eate one an other."[32] The Africans fared no better. They were "a people of beastly living, without a God, law, religion, or common wealth, and so scorched and bared with the heat of the sunne, that in many places they curse it when it riseth." In the Moluccas the people possessed only spices—a curious form of poverty—"in fyne, all thinges with them are despicable and vile . . ." Many of these negative judgments could be attributed to European ethnocentrism, as could the common view of the American Indians, but the pattern revealed a deeper antipathy. Perhaps the perfection of the dystopic form could be found in the *Polyhistor* of Solinus, published in English translation in 1587. The people of Atlantis, he wrote, "are altogether void of manners meete for men. None hath anie proper calling, none hath any speciall name. They curse the Sunn at its rising, and curse him likewise at his going downe: and because they are scorched wyth the heate of his burning beames, they hate the God of light. It is affirmed that they dreame not, and that they vtterlie abstaine from all things bearing lyfe."[33] Europeans saw the peoples in foreign lands as savages, not simply as strange beings with abhorrent manners.

The English had long held the Irish in low regard. Since the late twelfth century, when the Norman lords made their first penetration into Ireland, fighting had been intermittent between the two societies. The Anglo-Irish of the Pale constituted a distant outpost of English culture, sometimes mediating between English and Irish, more often required to defend themselves against the assaults of the Gaelic lords. In the last third of the sixteenth century, the English renewed their determination to expand the Pale and to spread English ways throughout the island. At the same time that they awakened to the potential of the New World, they began the last stage of the conquest of Ireland. The two enterprises became reciprocal training grounds for English imperial expansion. Personnel moved from one arena to the other; and the ideology that explained English conquest in Ireland supported the establishment of civility in America.[34]

Englishmen knew the meaning of ignoble savagism before they began the final subjugation of Ireland, although the Irish experience lent a certain technical clarity to the definition and doubtless added to the intensity and bitterness of English belief. Apparently the English never saw the Irish as noble savages. It may be that the alacrity with which they applied the negative doctrine to Ireland derived from the accounts of the Spanish conquests in America. The English justified their activities in Ireland by casting them as part of the suppression of a provincial revolt, but they resorted to the propaganda of savagism far too readily for it not to reveal the basis of their thinking about the Irish.[35] Yet the problem of origins was less significant than the evidence afforded by the Irish venture, which indicated that savagism engaged the English mind in universal definitions. Who might be termed a savage at any given moment mattered less than the tendency to invoke the savage concept in roughly similar situations. The idea of savagism revealed no more about the Irish than it did about the American Indians. It did say a great deal about the failure of the English to perceive the discrete integrity of an alien society and the English habit of seeing relations with the rest of the world through all-encompassing formulas.

Ireland and America involved, for the English, similar experiences. Both places were inhabited by people at a comparable level of technological development. Both afforded an opportunity for the English to replace a savage mode of existence with their own version of civility. The Irish reminded Edmund Spenser of the Sythians and Persians he had read about in Herodotus and Diodorus Siculus. Sir Henry Sidney compared Shane O'Neill, the Irish chieftain in Ulster, to the Huns, Vandals, Goths, and Turks. Moreover, the English saw themselves in the Irish. The ancient Britons resembled the Irish of the sixteenth century—John White, at least, had drawn them that way. The English performed a proper Renaissance role in leading the Irish to civility in the same manner that the Romans had saved the ancestors of the English from savagism. Inchoately the English expressed a theory of cultural development that eventually would explain how civil people had transcended the savage state. At the time, it was enough that they had laid out the lines of demarcation between themselves and the savages of Ireland and America.[36]

The Irish exhibited the major traits associated with savagism.

They were a hostile though scarcely competent people: "voyed of hospitalitie . . . uncivil and cruel, & therefore unapt for war-like affrayes . . ." Francis Bacon referred to "their customs of revenge and blood and of dissolute life and of theft and rapine . . ." Spenser seemed most taken by their "salvage bruttishnes and [loathlie] fylthynes . . ."[37] In the summer many of the Irish followed their herds, and the English took this practice as proof of nomadism and the absence of settled social arrangements. The sparse population, loose social organization, and dispersal of public authority offered further evidence of savagism among the Irish. Their personal habits appalled the English. They dressed in primitive cloaks or sometimes hardly dressed at all, disgusted the English at table, and led licentious, incestuous lives. Although the Irish had been Christian for centuries, pagan vestiges remained, which the English took as signs of idolatry. In addition, Irish resistance to the reformed religion attested to their kinship with the devil. Finally, the English accused the Irish of cannibalism. In a conflict of such extraordinary brutality, it was inevitable that this quintessential mark of savagism would be claimed. The English encountered in Ireland the kind of society they expected; it conformed to the universal pattern of savagism.[38]

Englishmen assumed that ignoble savagism was synonymous with violence. Lacking the moderating influence and discipline of society, savages engaged in violence as a normal activity. Thus Ralegh identified their manner of conflict with "the mere state of nature, of men out of community, where all have an equal right to all things; and I shall enjoy my life, my substance, or what is dear to me, no longer than he that has more cunning, or is stronger than I, will give me leave: for natural conscience is not a sufficient curb to the violent passions of men out of the laws of society." Ancient Greece offered an instructive illustration of the consequences of savagism. The inhabitants were "chased from place to place by the captains of greater tribes; and no man thinking the ground whereon he dwelt his own longer than he could hold it by strong hands." Hence towns were few and small; people had few permanent possessions. Nevertheless, "robberies by land and sea were common, and without shame; and to steal horses or kine was the usual exercise of their great men." In the "infancy" of society, turbulence occupied the affairs of men.[39]

Englishmen could scarcely claim that the creation of society had pacified the human spirit. Ralegh admitted that "the ordinary theme and argument of history is war . . ." War demanded as much of Europe's attention and resources in the sixteenth century as it did in any other age. Yet Ralegh distinguished savage war from conflict among civilized nations. Savages were "friends or foes by custom, rather than by judgment." They "acknowledge no such virtue in leagues, or formal conclusions of peace, as ought to hinder them from using their advantage, or taking revenge of injuries when they return to mind." When asked why they fought their neighbors, West Indians replied, "It hath still been the custom for us and them to fight one against the other." By custom, Ralegh meant the condition of nature as distinguished from existence ruled by intellect and conscious human decision. Savages fought for the same reason that beasts did: It was natural to their makeup. Civilized men engaged in war purposefully, as a matter of deliberate choice, for specific objects.[40]

Still, the argument that identified Indians with an undifferentiated and purposeless nature was difficult to sustain. Indians did possess the attributes of humanity; they could not act without some semblance of human motivation. Vespucci confronted the problem and devised the accepted solution. "They fyght not for the enlargeing of theyr dominion, forasmuche as they have no Magistrates: not yet for th[e] increase of riches, because thei are contente with their owne commodities: but onely to revenge the death of theyr predicessours." Later in the century Andrew Thevet thought he observed the same basis for conflict among the natives of Brazil.

> If you ask me why these wild men make warre one against
> an other, seeing that they are not greater Lords one than
> another, also for ẏ they do not estime worldly riches, & that
> the earth bringeth forth more than serueth their necessitie,
> you shal understad that the cause of their warre is euill
> ynough grounded, it is onely a desire of vengeance, that

they haue without any other reason or cause, but euen like
brute beasts, that cannot agree one ẇ another by no honest
meane: & to conclude, they say that they haue bene always
their mortall enimies.

Lescarbot cited the importance of revenge in native conflict,
and then added that the Indians made "war as Alexander the
Great did make it, that they may say I haue beaten you . . ."
Smith agreed that revenge was the major motive for war among
savages, but thought that they sometimes fought to capture
women and children. Any of these motives—revenge, jealousy,
or the desire for captives—satisfied the demands of human in-
centive. Civil people might be impelled to act by such induce-
ments. For the Indians, however, these were the inspirations of
nature, instinctual impulses worthy of savages and quite distinct
from the freely chosen principles that incited warfare among
civilized men.[41]

A people so inured to violence fought constantly. Savages
would surely oppose intruders from another continent, if only
because conflict was a way of life. They also fought among themselves. "They are cunning and crafty," wrote d'Avity, "and do
naturally loue war and reuenge; for they alwaies are in war one
countrie against another, killing all men they can take . . ."[42]
When neighboring tribes no longer served as outlets for their
violence, savages fell to fighting among themselves. Although
some observers noted the prohibition against killing women
and children, others stressed the unlimited character of savage
war. Not even the bonds of kinship kept the American natives
from engaging in the pandemic slaughter that afflicted the continent.[43] European explorers and settlers came to believe that
the native population had been substantially reduced because
of the Indians' inveterate fighting. "The people," wrote Arthur
Barlowe, "are marvelously wasted, and in some places, the
Country left desolate."[44]

White men held a variety of views on the manner of savage
war. Ralegh envisioned "naked savages fighting disorderly with
stones," but most commentators supported a more complex
conception of savagism. "Strategems, trecheries, or surprisals"
conformed to the stereotype of the savage as untutored in the
rules of manly conflict. The Indians, observed Thomas Hariot,

commonly attacked "about the dawning of the day, or moone light or els by ambushes, or some suttle deuises." They seldom fought formal battles, and then only when the forest afforded protection. Thevet noted that the natives spent a good deal of time threatening each other before engaging in actual combat. Savage cunning might well have been simply cowardice. Hariot contended that in conflict with the English the Indians found their best defense in turning up their heels.[45] Spenser, however, led his readers to expect a more formidable savage enemy:

> And in his hand a bended bow was seene,
> And many arrowes vnder his right side,
> All deadly daungerous, all cruell keene,
> Headed with flint, and feathers bloudie dide,
> Such as the *Indians* in their quiuers hide;
> Those could he well direct and streight as line,
> And bid them strike the marke, which he had eyde.
> Ne was their salue, ne was their medicine,
> That mote recure their wounds: so inly they did tine.

Reports from Canada told of a deadly kind of savage war. The Algonquins had lost some 200 people in an attack by their enemies from the south. The natives surrounded a fort, set it on fire, and cut down those who tried to escape. Only five people survived. Perhaps remembering his adventures in eastern Europe, Smith described a war game played by Powhatan's Indians. Disciplined companies of warriors simulated a battle between themselves and the Monacans. Although the scene testified to the similarity between war in Europe and America, Smith thought he detected a savage touch. The Indians released "horrible shouts and screeches, as though so many infernall hellbounds could not have made them more terrible." "All their actions, voices & gestures, both in charging and retiring were so strained to the hight of their quallitie and nature, that the strangenes thereof made it seem very delightfull."[46]

War among ignoble savages could be expected to be pervasive and destructive, though savages could also be wily, treacherous, and even craven. Most important, they did not play by European rules. Despite European practices equally as bloody, the Indians' habit of scalping a slain enemy as a token of victory impressed many observers as a singularly savage way

of proclaiming triumph. Early in the English experience in the
New World, the practice was noted in Florida, Virginia, and
Canada, and soon took on the character of a distinctive savage
trait.[47] By most accounts, the Indians were "butcherly minded."
They tortured captives in a most horrible manner. The Virginia
colonists believed that George Cassen and John Ratcliffe, among
others, had been tortured to death by the Indians. Smith offered
Powhatan as a particularly bloody example of savage brutality.
He treated his own people with the same ferocity he visited
upon his enemies, and ordered transgressors of his law to be
thrust alive into hot coals. Smith detailed several of his puni-
tive practices:

> Sometimes he causeth the heads of them that offend him,
> to be laid vpon the altar or sacrificing stone, and one with
> clubbes beats out their braines. When he would punish any
> notorious enemy or malefactor, he causeth him to be tyed
> to a tree, and with Mussell shels or reeds, the executioner
> cutteth off his ioynts one after another, ever casting what
> they cut of into the fire; then doth he proceed with shels
> and reeds to case the skinne from his head and face; then
> do they rip his belly and so burne him with the tree and all.

Clearly, in Smith's mind, the inhumanity of savage war revealed
only one aspect of the brutality that permeated native life.[48]

Europeans suspected virtually every American Indian of har-
boring a taste for human flesh. In fact, few of the peoples of the
New World practiced cannibalism, though the doctrine of ignoble savagism established at least a presumption of such a
practice. Ignoble savagism, after all, was more than an attack
on civil order. It shattered the very bounds of human existence.
Pushed to its logical limits, ignoble savagism was an assault on
the integrity of the human species, on the civility that had been
slowly nurtured over the centuries, and on the very physical
being of humanity. No more striking violation of humanity
could be committed than to devour the substance of another
human being. Europeans remained an aggressive people, but
they had managed to sublimate the impulse to cannibalism, the
most aggressive of all human tendencies. They recoiled with
such horror from it because they had long dreaded the reap-

pearance of anthropophagi and the danger of savage annihilation. They projected these atavistic fears on the people of the New World.[49]

Cannibalism became an immediate threat when starvation drove Europeans to devour their own. The New World had always held out the danger of a fall from civility. For colonists to emulate savage ways by resorting to the most degraded of all behavior gave stark evidence of the fragility of the civil order and the ubiquitous menace of savagism. Smith made light of an early incident at Jamestown, in which a colonist murdered and ate his wife, though he admitted the justice of the punishment. A later account, even though recognizing the provocation of the Starving Times, recorded that the guilty colonist "was for soe barbarouse a fact and cruelty justly executed." Purchas expressed no shock when he noted that the Indians themselves would have killed the stragglers from the Narvaez expedition if they had known that the Spaniards had eaten their own. To Laudonnière an incident of murder and cannibalism among the French was "a thing so pitifull to recite, that my pen is loth to write it." Under the circumstances, European cannibalism might have been excusable if it had not revealed the anthropophagic potential in all men.[50]

Columbus had returned from his first voyage with the earliest news of cannibals in the New World. Natives on Hispaniola told him of Indians who roamed the Caribbean seeking people to take captive and devour. Henceforth the European imagination held full sway. Virtually every voyage after that encountered signs of man-eaters, even in the northern regions where few existed. Much of the interest was pictorial. Maps of the new discoveries were frequently adorned with grisly portraits of Indians feeding on other humans. Many accounts of European experiences in the new lands were accompanied by scenes of cannibals enjoying their favorite repast. Engravings by de Bry, published in the 1590s, showed panoramic views of Indians engaged in a variety of cannibalistic activities. Many of the pictures were curiously clinical, drained of the gruesome message they were meant to communicate.[51]

What little the visual images lacked in hideousness the

printed word supplied. Writers scoured the world in search of
man-eaters, and found what they were looking for on every
continent. Yet no part of the world could compete with America. If a given group of natives did not actually eat human
flesh, it was rumored that their near neighbors did. Peter Martyr
communicated a sense of the terror that the thought of cannibals inspired. "There is no man," he wrote, "able to behowlde
them, but he shall feele his bowelles grate with a certain hor-
roure, nature hathe endewed them with so terrible menacynge,
and cruell aspecte."[52] One text will serve to illustrate the fate
that Europeans feared awaited them in America if they fell into
the wrong hands. Anthony Knivet, an English sailor, told of
his capture, along with twelve Portuguese, by Brazilian natives.
One of the Portuguese was brought before an old man who instructed him to bid the world farewell. Then a younger man
appeared, his face and arms dyed red, who announced that he
had killed many of the sailor's countrymen and intended to
kill him.

> After he had spoke all this, he came behinde the Portugall,
> and strooke him on the nape of the necke, that he felled
> him to the ground, and after hee was down gave him an-
> other that he killed him; then he tooke the tooth of a
> Conie and opened all the upper skinne, so they tooke by
> the head and the feete, and held him in the flame of the
> fire: after that, rubbing him with their hands, all the upper
> skin came of, and the flesh remained white, then they cut
> off his head, and gave it to him: they tooke the guts, and
> gave them to the women, after which they jointed him
> joint by joint, first hands, then elbowes, and so all the
> body. After which they sent to every house a peece, then
> they fell a dancing, and all the women made great store of
> Wine: the next day they boiled every joint in a great pot
> of water, because their wives and children might eate of
> the broth; for the space of three days they did nothing but
> dance and drinke day and night: after that they killed an-
> other in the same manner . . . , and so served all but my
> selfe.

Knivet expected the same treatment and so, doubtless, did
everyone who read his account.[53]

Cannibals exhausted the possibilities of ignoble savagism. To the Elizabethan mind cannibalism represented the inversion of civility and humane values. Civility set a protective screen around human beings that defended them from their own worst inclinations and from the forces in the world that worked to release those destructive impulses. No aspect of savagism seemed more perfectly designed to breach the barrier of civility than the eating of human flesh.

Ignoble savagism explained as little about native society as had the paradisaic conception. The outlines of the image had been drawn long before Europeans encountered the American natives, and nothing essential changed as a consequence of actual contact. But the relevance of ignoble savagism lay not in the inaccuracy of the picture it drew of the Indians or even in the wholly unpleasant conception of the American natives it communicated. The major significance of ignoble savagism was that it interpreted native life through a set of rigid formulas, abstract and lifeless, that afforded no promise of successful depiction. Ignoble savagism began with the assumption that Europeans confronted a people bereft of the ordinary acquirements of humanity. They lacked a civil order, engaged in violence without compunction, tortured their enemies, sacrificed captives and their own children, ate human flesh, and exhibited manners that would embarrass a barbarian. Furthermore, they had allied themselves with Satan against all God-fearing people. Ignoble savagism led the colonists to expect the worst from the Indians and gave them no means with which to bring their vision of native life closer to reality. It predicted and at the same time justified the violence that erupted between Englishmen and Indians. In some measure, at least, it caused the violence. In time it provided a handy explanation of the failure of English civility to transform the native people. Ignoble savages made poor converts. Moreover, ignoble savagism blinded the English to the significance of the gradual acculturative process that began once the two societies met. The English suspected from the beginning that civility would be vulnerable to the lure of savagism, and hence they interpreted any move of their countrymen toward native ways as a threat to civil order.

In the sense that ignoble savagism attributed to the American natives vices common to all men, it did not deny their humanity. All human beings were to some degree brutal, treacherous, and unpredictable. They could be expected occasionally to fall afoul of the best side of their nature. But ignoble savagism carried the accusation against the Indian a step further. It not only magnified the usual degree of human depravity, it created an Indian who had perfected the art of villainy. Evil emerged from the very substance of the ignoble savage's character. As a consequence the image of the native people tended to slip out of the human category. Their rage to destroy, to inflict pain, began to appear more bestial than human.

3

BESTIALITY

The Spaniards were the first to grapple with the question of the Indians' humanity. With the promulgation in 1537 of Paul III's bull *Sublimis Deus*, which declared the Indians to be "true men," Catholic Europe appeared to have settled the issue. Later in the sixteenth century, Las Casas and Sepúlveda revived it in their controversy over natural slavery, but the triumph of Las Casas confirmed the pope's decision. Certainly the Spanish crown demonstrated repeatedly that it acted under the formal assumption that the native people who lived under its suzerainty possessed all the endowments of humanity. Similarly, the missionaries devoted their energies to making Christians and Europeans out of native Americans because they believed them capable of transcending savagism and forming a civil order, a condition of life reserved for human beings.[1]

And yet the issue remained alive precisely because Europeans saw Indians as savages. The English never emulated the Spaniards in the making of formal pronouncements, but they entertained similar ideas about savages, and they followed the conventional European practice of referring to the Indians in language that tended to compromise their humanity. A savage might be either virtuous or vicious, which implied at least a presumption of humanity, but closer observation revealed that he could lay claim to few of the usual signs of human existence. His social order was minimal or nonexistent. He built no monuments; he left no mark on the world for others to trace his history. Few lamented his passing. Because the native people failed to replicate the civil order characteristic of European life, their humanity, in a rhetorical sense, remained open to question. Even travelers and colonists who had met real Indians, and hence must certainly have known that they were human, not only portrayed them as men with bestial habits but also often came precariously close to describing them as beasts who wore the masks of men. No Englishman formally proposed that Indians be driven from the ranks of humanity, but most Englishmen who wrote about them used language that in effect relegated Indians to a mesozone between animals and men.

Although Christianity brooked no dissent concerning the integrity of the human species, sixteenth- and early seventeenth-century writers, in their search for suitable way to describe the newly found people of America, confronted a bewildering array of myths, legends, literary motifs, and equivocal anthropological categories that obscured the distinction between man and animal. The Middle Ages had bequeathed a belief in various creatures whose natures spanned more than one of the accepted classifications of life. Animals had long been gifted with qualities distinctively human, as had human beings been judged by the degree to which they manifested the properties of animals. Christian moralists continued the biblical practice of equating sin with a descent into bestiality. Moreover, it was not uncommon for social critics to employ the language of bestiality to account for the failure of the lower classes to live up to the standards of their betters. Thus, the doctrine of savagism, and its inherent tendency to imperil the humanity of the Indians, represented only one of the prevalent modes of speaking and writing that blurred mankind's claim to special status in the universe.[2]

The earliest accounts of experiences in the New World available to Englishmen linked savagism and bestiality. The English versions of Sebastian Brant's *Ship of Fools*, which appeared in 1509, reported that in the New World the Spaniards had found people "which lyved as beestes." The English translation of excerpts from Vespucci's letters, which Jan van Doersborch brought out in Antwerp before 1522, contained a particularly apt identification of the bestial implications of savagism. Vespucci named the new land "Armenica," where he "sawe meny wonders of beestes and fowles." The people fitted the typical description of savages, in this instance a mixture of noble and ignoble traits. They had no king, lord, or god, went naked, and held property in common.

> The wymen be also as comon. And the men hath conuersacyon with the wymen who that they ben or who they fyrst mete is she his syster his mother his daughter or any other kyndred. And the wymen be very hoote and dysposed to lecherdnes. And they ete also on[e] a nother. The man etethe his wyfe his chylderne as we also have seen and they hange also the bodyes or persons fleeshe in the smoke as men do with vs swynes fleshe. And that lande is ryght full of folke for they lyue commonly. iii C. [300] yere and more as with sykeneesse they dye nat . . .

Vespucci reported that the natives were great fishermen and warriors. Mainly, they appeared to fight among themselves. The losers were killed and some eaten. The victors enjoyed long lives because they possessed "costely spyces and rotes." As it stood, his portrait touched on the major signs of savagism. Nakedness, promiscuity, the absence of public order, and common property made the natives noble. Violence and cannibalism revealed their ignoble side. Then, in the midst of his description, Vespucci dropped a telling line: "These folke lyven lyke bestes without any resonableness . . ."[3] The relationship was drawn with a simile. The Indians lived like beasts; they were not actually beasts. But once the connection had been made between savage existence and animality, Europeans who wrote about the New World fell into the habit of conceiving of the Indians as people who possessed their humanity in an imperfect way.

The association of the savage state with bestiality had classical origins. The English may not have pursued the problem of the Indian's humanity with the thoroughness of the Spanish debate, but they were equally familiar with the Aristotelian dictum that equated savagism with bestiality and natural slavery. In his translation of Ovid's *Metamorphoses*, George Sandys discussed the savagism of the "Cyclops" and the natives of the West Indies in unmistakably Aristotelian terms. Both these people were "lawlesse," "subiect to no government" or "bond of society." "They therefore are to bee numbered among beasts who renounce society, whereby they are destitute of lawes, the ordination of civility." In Aristotelian conception, men were by nature social and political creatures. To deny these human imperatives was to seriously impair one's claim to humanity. The English translation of Pierre d'Avity's survey of the peoples of the world offered an account of the savage practices of the American natives and recommended instruction in virtue and Christianity, for "Aristotle saith, that such men should be taken as beasts, and tamed by force." The Virginia Company's favorite expert on silk held similar views about the Indians of Virginia. He supported the Aristotelian remedy for people "that know no industry, no Art, no culture, nor no good vse of this blessed Country heere, but are meere ignorance, sloth, and brutishnesse, and an vnprofitable burthen onely of the earth." European writers used Aristotle to put the stamp of antiquity on the pervasive tendency to draw a close identification between the savage condition and animality.[4]

The habit of attributing bestial qualities to native Americans sprang from the very substance of the savage dogma. Savages established no stable relations among themselves and left no decisive mark on their environment. They rejected the eternal laws of religion. Like animals, their grip on the world was sensate. They did not reason; they only felt and acted. Noble savages, in fact, did precious little of the latter. The typical description that portrayed Indians as "wild and brutish people, without Fayth, without Religion, and without any ciuilitie" concluded that they lived "like brute beasts."[5] With remarkable consistency, comments on the New World pictured the Indians as wandering troops of savage beasts. Robert Gray caught the image in his *A Good Speed to Virginia,* a pamphlet designed to attract settlers and to assure them that the Indians had established no permanent attachments to the land. "Some affirme," he wrote, "and it is likely to be true, that these Savages have no particular proprietie in any part or parcell of that Country, but only a generall recidencie there, as wild beasts have in the forest, for they range and wander vp and downe the County, without any law or government, being led only by their owne lusts and sensualitie, there is not *meum* & *tuum* amongst them . . ." Gray had ulterior motives, but he adopted a conception of native life drawn directly from savagism and couched in language that came naturally to Englishmen when they contemplated the condition of life in America. A pamphlet published in 1610 to justify English activities in Virginia cautioned against the "fidelitie of humane beasts." One might as well, asserted the author, "make league, with Lions, Bears, and Crocodiles." Savagism and animality forged an inseparable link in the minds of European observers.[6]

As a consequence, virtually any native trait could be made to supply evidence of bestiality. Indians ate food the way beasts did, "as the cattell that feedeth in the fields," a reference that prompted Purchas to note in the margin "Beast in humane shape." They frequently cried out "like wild beasts or men out of their wyts." One sailor described them approaching his ship "throwing dust in the ayre, leaping and running like brute beasts, having vizards on their faces like dogs faces, or else they are dogs faces indeed." Lescarbot represented the Canadian natives "sitting on their tails like apes." The marriage and childrearing practices of the Mexicans convinced Martin Perez that "they live like beasts." "In all secrete actes of nature," commented a popular geography, the Indians were "comparable to brute beasts." Even in a context that seemed tailored to objectivity, the language of bestiality proved irresistible. Witness John Smith's comment (repeated verbatim by William Strachey) on the consequences of the cycle of native agriculture. "It is strange," he wrote, "to see how their bodies alter with their dyet, even as the deere and wilde beasts they seeme fat and leane, strong and weake." Smith knew intuitively that savagism brought the Indians perilously close to the animal condition.[7]

And yet animality was not irrevocable. Savages could be brought to civility; beasts, or men like beasts, might shed their animality, accept civility, and be reckoned real men. That the language of bestiality did not exclude amelioration was made clear by Louis Le Roy, whose work was published in England in 1594. Le Roy followed Jean Bodin in attempting to impose pattern on history. He inferred a cyclical process of decay and regeneration that fell short of authentic progressivism but allowed room for human improvement. "At the beginning," he wrote, "men were very simple and rude in all thinges, little differing from beastes." They subsisted by gathering herbs, fruits, and roots and by eating the raw flesh of animals, "which the earth brought foorth of his owe[n] accorde." They clothed themselves in animal skins and lived in "great holow trees; or vnder their thick leaued branches; or into low dyches, hideous caues, holow vautes, cabins, and lodges of wood . . ." They possessed vigorous bodies, ate strong meat, and survived to an old age. But this arduous existence soon took its toll. Men found that they could no longer digest raw meat "or dwell in the open aire naked, and uncouered." They sought "to soften the wild and sauage manner" by cultivating crops and orchards and by gathering "themselues in companies, that they might live the more safely, and commodiously. In such manner were they reduced, from the brutish life which they led, to this sweetnes and civilitie."[8] The equation of primal life with bestiality formed the basis of Le Roy's commitment to cyclic development and his belief in the capacity of human beings to wrench themselves free from the bondage of savagery. He saw no contradiction in language that called into question the humanity of early man and that at the same time plotted the process by which he would cease to be bestial.

Samuel Purchas printed one of Garcilaso de la Vega's stories that predicted a similar future for primitive men who began life in a bestial condition. The legend told of the son and daughter of the sun, who were sent to the people of Cuzco to lead them "from brutish life to civilitie." From these messengers of the sun, the Incas received a mandate to spread civil life to all the neighboring peoples, which they accomplished with an enthusiasm fully equal to that exhibited by the Spaniards centuries later. The feat was no less startling for the Incas than for those who benefited from their ministrations. All began at a very low state indeed.

> In old times all this region was untilled and overgrowne with bushes, and the people of those times lived as wilde beasts without religion or policie, without towne or house, without tilling or sowing the ground, without raiment, for they knew not how to worke Cotten or Wooll to make them garments. They lived by two and two, or three and

three, in caves and holes of the ground, eating grasse like beasts, and rootes of trees, and wilde fruits, and mans flesh. They covered themselves with leaves, and barkes of trees, and skins of Beasts, and others in leather. Once they lived as wilde beasts, and their women were in common and brutish.

After they had raised themselves from this humble condition, the Incas invaded the land of the Chirihuanas, where the "Naturals" were "brutish worse then beasts without Religion . . . , without Law, Townes, or Houses, and eating mans flesh . . ."[9] The Incas failed in their mission to the Chirihuanas, but other peoples equally primitive succumbed to their efforts. Like the Europeans, the Incas did not find that bestiality crippled the development of civilization.

The credulity that led European observers to confuse beast and man stemmed in part from the newness of the continent, which led to a reliance on the lore of many generations of travel literature. Europeans had been told of strange sights before, and the idea of a bestial Indian, half man and half animal, struck them as curious but fully within reach of their expectations. Sixteenth- and seventeenth-century Englishmen read Pliny and Mandeville, from whom they obtained a full store of legend concerning the assortment of preposterous creatures that inhabited distant lands. Reminiscent of the older writers, the *Treatyse of the Newe India* by Sebastian Munster recorded the existence of a wide variety of monsters and associated the cannibals of the New World with the anthropophagi of ancient times. Munster followed the inclinations of the vast majority of European observers who saw the New World through the lenses of ancient legend. This commitment troubled Richard Eden when he prepared Munster's book for publication in English, but he was at a loss to offer the reader a more satisfactory explanation. "It shall suffise al good and honest wittes," he wrote, "that whatsoeuer the Lorde hath pleased, that hath he done in heauen and in earth, and in the Sea, and in all depe places." Concerning the "strange workes of nature," Hakluyt admitted that he could not "cease to maruell and confesse with Plinie, that nothing is in her impossible, the least part of whose power is not yet knowen to men."[10] Monsters were noteworthy phenomena, as were bestial Indians, and both were fully consistent with the natural order God had seen fit to create and the ancients to describe.

Distant seas and the New World contained no shortage of marvels. Trees that bore oysters, a serpent with three heads and four feet, "a monstrous venemous worme with two heads: his body as bigge as a mans arme, and a yard long," sea monsters of various shapes, unicorns, and mermaids turned up regularly in the accounts of Elizabethan travelers. More significant was the tendency of creaturely categories to become mixed. Edward Webbe claimed to have seen a monster at the court of Prester John "having 4 heades, they are in shape like a wilde Cat, and are of the height of a great mastic Dog." Peter Martyr described an anomalous figure "in which nature hath endeuoured to shewe her cunnyng. This beaste is as bygge as an oxe, armed with a longe snoute lyke an Elephant, and yet no Elephant. Of the colour of an oxe and yet noo oxe. With the houfe of a horse, and yet noo horse. With eares also much lyke vnto an Elephant, but not soo open nor soo much hangyng downe: yet much wyder then the eares of any other beaste." It appeared, commented George Abbot, that nature had "studied to expresse a great many seuerall creatures in one."[11]

Similarly, the boundary between animal and human showed a certain flexibility. Edward Topsell included a picture of a monster – partly human, partly animal – in his *Historie of Forre-Footed Beastes*. In 1610 Richard Whitbourne encountered a "Mermaid or a Merman" in St. John's harbor. At first the creature appeared to be a woman: "By the face, eyes, nose, mouth, chin, eares, necke, and forehead, it seemed to bee so beautifull, and in those parts so well proportioned, having round about the head many blue streakes, resembling haire, but certainly was not haire . . ." Later he "beheld the shoulders & back of a man; and from the middle to the hinder part it was poynting in proportion somthing like a broad hooded Arrow . . ." Off Bermuda, English sailors sighted a sea monster that showed its upper portion on three occasions. To the amazement of the onlookers, the monster was "proportioned like a man, of the complexion of a Mulato, or tawny Indian." The experience was replicated for Thomas Glover on the Rappahannock River late in the seventeenth century. He sighted "a very strange Fish or rather a Monster," "a most prodigious Creature, much resembling a man." "His skin was tawney much like that of an Indian."[12]

The tale spread by Pliny and Mandeville–that in distant lands could be found men whose faces peeked out of their chests –was confirmed in the New World. Ralegh and Kemys returned from Guiana with news of the existence of such people. Neither had seen them, but Indian and Spanish accounts seemed dependable. Abbot was satisfied that the English testimony supported the ancient writers. "No sober man," he insisted, "should any way doubt the trueth thereof." Purchas expressed uncertainty but agreed to suspend judgment until reliable evidence could be obtained. Marc Lescarbot manifested only mild surprise when he heard such reports from the native people in New France.[13]

Perhaps the most persistent legends feeding the European appetite for monsters were those of Amazons and giants. Opinion on the existence of Amazons was split. Some refused to give any credence to stories of their existence; others devised ingenious schemes to explain their manner of life. They appeared to be less monsters than curious women who lived a disordered existence.[14] Giants, however, were genuine monsters and evidence that nature countenanced extraordinary creatures. In the New World they were first sighted in Brazil in 1500 by Vincente Pinzon. Sailors from Magellan's ships found them in Patagonia later in the century. Thereafter, Spanish colonists recognized traces of them in Mexico and Peru. According to Genesis, giants were the progeny of the sons of God and the daughters of men, the results of misalliances that provoked God to destroy the world in a flood. Apparently the flood failed to accomplish its purpose, for Ralegh believed that the first people to appear after it receded were of gigantic stature–the first primitive men–and as savage and hostile as the natives of America. Moreover, giants were monstrous–human in some peculiar way but constructed on a scale out of proportion to the usual human dimensions.[15]

The same uncertainty concerning the identity of his species attached to the wild man, who, according to legend, inhabited the forests of Europe during the Middle Ages. Throughout that period wild men were depicted sometimes as human, sometimes as beast, and frequently as both. The body generally appeared to be of human shape, but it was invariably covered with a coat of animallike hair. Formal thought in the Middle Ages made a clear demarcation between man and animal, and this sort of gradation proved to be a difficult problem. As a consequence no clear consensus emerged on the species of the wild man. The ambiguity persisted into the early modern period. At the same time that many of the old certainties disintegrated, the human category tended to become more fluid. In the hierarchy of life, men were both the highest of animals and the lowest of intellectual beings. This scale allowed room for high aspiration, but it also posed the possibility for slippage into the realm below. Creatures who appeared to be men in one context might be interpreted as animals or near-animals in another.[16]

Typically, the wild man was thought to have been born into a normal human situation, and, through some misfortune, nurtured in the wilderness. Conditions of life in the wild–extreme hardship, loss of intellectual stimulation, upbringing among beasts–tended to reduce the wild man to a subhuman level. Because the degeneration began when he was at the human stage, hope remained that the decline was reversible. The descent was nonetheless real, and the wild man acquired from it many characteristics of the beast. Although often lord of the beasts, his position of leadership could not save him from the accusation that his human credentials were impaired. As Spenser put it in the *Faerie Queene*: "He noursled vp in life and manners wilde,/Emongst wild beasts and woods, from lawes of men exilde."[17]

The wild man lacked the mental capacity essential to humane existence. Because he could neither conceive of nor recognize divinity, he was neither infidel nor idolater. He was incapable of engaging in the usual processes of mind. Of course, he could not speak. He was impelled to action only by instinct. Wild men lived alone in distant lands or deep in the wilderness. They could neither farm nor work metals, so lived by gathering and hunting. Self-preservation came readily, for wild men possessed great strength and aggressiveness. They fought constantly among themselves. For others the proximity of wild men created constant danger. The actions of wild men derived from impulses normal men had learned to temper. "The wild man's existence," explains one author, "is therefore a life of bestial self-fulfillment, directed by instinct rather than volition, and devoid of all acquired tastes and patterns of behavior which are part of our adjustment to civilization. He embodies a negative ideal in all its harshness and one-sidedness." [18]

The image of the wild man began a gradual process of change in the fourteenth and fifteenth centuries. He became less threatening, and Europeans managed to hold him at a greater psychological distance. As a result, two contrary tendencies developed. Because men ceased to fear the wild man, they found it easy to condemn his degraded condition and to mock his grotesqueness. At the same time they witnessed a transformation of their own world that generated profound anxiety and impelled them to seek security, at least symbolically, in the primeval forest of the wild men. In the Renaissance the wild man was usually considered a noble savage whose way of life offered an alternative to a corrupt world. Yet the wild man never lost his fearful potential for mayhem and violence—for doing the work of the ignoble savage. In the 1590s in England, contrary to the tendency of the age, the wild man became more brutal and monstrous. Needless to say, whether in his pacific or pugnacious form, the wild man did not acquire the full complement of human qualities.[19]

The wild man's violence sprang from his hostile environment, which he was required to tame without technology, and also from his instinctive nature, which commanded that he act from impulse. Without insight of mind or discipline of will, wild men lived in a state of total war of all against all. They fought fiercely, without rules, seeking the total destruction of their opponents. Civil people identified wild men with rapine and with storm, when the elements of nature seemed unbounded in their destructive force. To some, the formless character of the wild man made him seem insane, even though granting him this trait established for him a tenuous link to humanity. To others, he appeared to be demonic, which seemed more in keeping with his constitution. Yet the wild man was

not so much insane or the creature of the devil as he was the embodiment of the many primordial urges to which men had fallen heir. Because the wild man represented the darker impulses of the human spirit, Europeans tended to ignore his distinctively human qualities and to find, in his brutality, evidence of his essential brutishness.[20]

Spenser's *Faerie Queene* was the first serious effort in English to wrestle with the problem of the wild man and the broader issues of bestiality and savagism. It resolves the issues in favor of civil order. In the poem, Spenser praises the golden age and compares untouched nature with the corruption of his own time, but he believed that man's true end could be reached only through civility. The principal virtue of civil life he defines as courtesy, whereby men "beare themselues aright/To all of each degree, as doth behoue." For Spenser, primitive existence took on value only in the sense that men strove to overcome it or reach beyond it; civility did not rise from the primitive condition, but from an effort to surmount it through the exercise of courtesy. Wild men and savages might possess laudable attributes, but they lacked courtesy and hence were incapable of civil order.[21]

Spenser furnishes his poem with a variety of beasts, only one of which can be construed as benevolent. All the rest are hostile to man. Beastliness in Spenser's conception arises from the concupiscible faculty, which tends to act without restraint unless curbed and disciplined by the other faculties. The most dangerous of these brutish creatures is the Blatant Beast, whom Spenser associates with spite and slander. He inflicts incurable wounds not upon the body, as do most other beasts, but upon the soul. Hence the Blatant Beast typifies the potential for degradation contained in nature, the very substance of the anti-principle in life. He represents the destructive impulses that, in the human condition, are held in check by courtesy and civil order. He "is a Monster bred of hellish race," wrote Spenser. "Of *Cerberus* whilome he was begot,/And fell *Chimaera* in her darksome den,/Through fowle commixture of his filthy blot;/Where he was fostred long in Stygian fen,/Till he to perfect ripeness grew." This depraved creature roams the world, "the plague and scourge of wretched men:/Whom with vile tongue and venemous intent/He sore doth wound, and bite, and cruelly torment." Spenser strained his inventive genius to heap obloquy on the Blatant Beast. As described by one critic, he is "the totality of hostile elements in man's environment." He embodies the plenitude of personal viciousness, and threatens the stability of society. Spenser compares his behavior to the gnatlike perturbations that torment humankind in the struggle for life. Bestiality, for Spenser, menaces virtue, order, and human well-being.[22]

Spenser's wilderness ménage also includes the Salvage Man, a character more complex than the Blatant Beast but tied similarly to primal nature. Salvage Man represents the benign side of nature and hence might serve as a guide for a civilization corrupted by false principles or fallen into decay. The savage's principal virtues appear to be strength and steadiness, which civilized men need but sometimes lack. Although Salvage Man draws his power from the primal forces of life, Spenser makes it clear that civilized men would have to partake of the same endowments in order to survive. Whatever the savage's virtues, they are severely limited. He lives at a rudimentary level. He owns some of the means to make courtesy possible and possesses the strength to defend civil order against its enemies, but he cannot fully exhibit a courteous manner or participate completely in civil society. Salvage Man lives alone in the forest; his is lean, Spartan existence. He wears no clothes, nor does he possess any tools or weapons save an oak staff. His dwelling and furniture are made from moss and shrubs, and he gathers what food he can find in the woods. He knows the lore of the forest instinctively, not in a critical way. Without speech, he can communicate only by signs and gestures. Through the power of magic, he is invulnerable; when wounded, he does not bleed. Spenser saw the Salvage Man's major defect in his heedlessness, his inability to manage his environment. Nevertheless, he reveals a capacity to learn. To defend the lady in distress, he dons the armor of the wounded knight, though the knight has hidden his sword and the Salvage Man seems not to miss it. He discards the armor when it becomes an encumbrance. He also recognizes the magnificence of Arthur, the most impressive of Spenser's knightly characters. When he finds civility threatened, he shows pity and gentleness, virtues he has never known before. But these signs of nobility spring from the Salvage Man's noble birth, not from his training in the wilderness. Ultimately his limitations are more salient. He can heal the physical wounds of men, but he stands helpless before the real complexities of life. The inner wounds of human beings—for example, the bite of the Blatant Beast—remain exempt from his healing powers.[23]

Spenser does not directly question the humanity of Salvage Man. The name itself is ambiguous, but Spenser notes his gentle birth, which should put the matter to rest. Still, the language employed in *Faerie Queene* carries far-reaching implications. Spenser writes of one group of savages (clearly ignoble) who inhabited "wylde deserts," ate their neighbors, engaged in no farming, grazing, or trade, and survived by "stealth and spoile." At the same time he connects savagism with bestiality by referring to "the savage hart/Of many a Lyon, and of many a Beare." When Salvage Man falls into conflict with an errant knight, Spenser depicts his rage in similar language: "Like to a Tygre that hath mist his pray." Perhaps more revealing is his description of the relationship between the Salvage Man and Serena, whom he has saved from the same wicked knight. At first Serena fears him, but she soon learns that he means her no harm. He "Came to her creeping like a fawning hound," "Kissing his hands, and crouching to the ground;/For other language had he none nor speach,/But a soft murmure, and confused sound/Of senselesse words, which nature did he teach,/T'expresse his passions, which his reason did empeach." It is difficult to avoid the bestial connotations of excessive passion and speechlessness. Or, more likely, the problem arises from the paradoxical term "Salvage Man." Once the properties of savagism become attached to man, his image inevitably shades off into bestiality.[24]

The major English zoological treatise of the day, Topsell's *Historie of Fovre-Footed Beastes*, supplied striking evidence of the uncertain boundaries between man and animal. Although Topsell accepted the obligation to classify creatures as either human or animal, time after time his descriptions, and the accompanying pictures, fell between the two categories. Animal-like creatures possessed the qualities of human beings, and quasi-human creatures exhibited an animal component. Wild men, satyrs, monsters, and apes were the traditional representatives of this mixed classification. Topsell included all of them, with appropriate analyses of structure and behavior to point out the anomalous character of God's creation. "Some have doubted," he concluded in reference to a monkeylike specimen, "what kinde of creature this should be, which is in part a man, and yet a Foure-footed beast . . ." He found Pygmies especially troublesome. They possessed many of the physical characteristics of humans, yet earlier writers had excluded them from the ranks of men. Topsell followed the traditional practice. He determined that they were not men "bycause they have no perfect vse of reason, no modesty, no honesty, nor iustice of government, and although they speak yet is their language imperfect; and above all they cannot bee men because they have no Religion, which (*Plato* saith truely) is propper to euery man." Topsell's volume argued for the fluidity of creaturely boundaries at the same time that it asserted an unmistakable relationship between savagism and animality.[25]

So also did the writings of Montaigne. In his *Essays*, published in England in 1603 by John Florio, he formulated the classic definition of the savage[26] and went on to draw an elaborate comparison between man and beast. He wished above all to deflate human vanity, which he accomplished by praising the virtues of pristine savagism and by comparing humans unfavorably with animals. In "An Apologie of *Raymond Sebond*," he argued against the claims of human beings to a superior position in creation. He raised beasts above their accepted station and reduced humankind below its accustomed position. The result was an interpretation of nature that brought all creatures within a single classification. Men and animals were equal in Montaigne's view. No doubt he intended to say less about animals than about men, but by associating men and animals he may have said more than he intended. The effect of his argument was to obscure the distinction between man and beast and to stress the bestial character of man.[27]

Montaigne denied that man's ability to reason raised him above the beasts. He much preferred the instinctive powers of animals. Their natural sense enabled them to act as men did on the basis of reason, but more moderately and with superior acumen. Animals communicated among themselves and with human beings. If men did not understand them, the fault could as well be with the men as with the animals. Men often did not understand each other; hence, it was not surprising that they failed to understand animals. Gesture was "the proper and peculiar speech of humane nature," and men employed this mode, as did beasts. Animals who taught each other also taught men. They exercised memory and imagination the way human beings did. Both men and animals lived in society, required rules of order and mutual respect, engaged in defensive war, and used stratagems. Self-preservation animated beast as well as man. "*Nature,*" Montaigne contended, "*hath generally imbraced all her creatures.*" [28]

Montaigne exhibited more than an appetite for tall tales. He wished to leave no doubt that men and animals drew their beings from the same nature and did so in equal measure. Animals were as likely to see men as beasts as men were to see animals as beasts. The truth was that greater differences could be found between man and man than between man and beast. Given an opportunity, animals and men lived together in respect and equality. According to Montaigne, misunderstanding of the relationship between animals and humanity stemmed from the supposition that animals acted "by a natural inclination and forced inclination and forced genuitie" and that men acted from free will and industry. In fact, the actions of both derived from the same source. "Of the very same effects we must conclude alike faculties, and consequently acknowledge, that the same discourse and way, we hold in working, the very same, or perhaps some other better, doe beasts hold." Furthermore, lest humanity miss the point, he made it clear what that better source of activity might be. He believed it more honorable to act through a natural, unavoidable condition than through rash liberty. When Montaigne claimed that his object was "to maintaine the coherency and resemblance, that is in all humane things, and to bring them under the same general throng," he seemed more inclined to level humanity than to elevate the beast, though he did both in the course of his essay. Hostility to humanity loomed larger than his sympathy for the animal world. He preferred a man with the virtues of a beast to an animal with the endowments of humanity.[29]

In celebrating bestiality, Montaigne had in mind the American natives he had praised so highly. The attributes of the beast were similar to the savage virtues that separated the people of the New World from those of Europe. He saw little need for human beings to dress themselves so elaborately. For animals, hide provided ample protection against the elements, and savages seemed content to remain naked. The primitive Gauls wore few clothes, as did the contemporary Irish. Both men and animals were required to make provision against the lean season, but for the most part the earth yielded plenty without the interference of human hands, a truth discovered by the natives of America. Montaigne's implication was that men might learn these lessons from beasts, or they could turn to the New World for more explicit evidence. "The nations, that have lately bin discovered, so plenteously stored with all manner of naturall meat and drinke, without care or labor, teach us, that bread is not our onely food: And that without toyling, our common mother nature, hath with great plentie stored us with whatsoever should be needfull for us, yea, as it is most likely, more richly and amply, than nowadaies she doth, that we have added so much art to it." In the past, Montaigne claimed, civil men were too quick to condemn the ways of these new people because they were different. They were called brutish and savage, or stupid and beastly, because they dressed differently, possessed strange manners, and could not make themselves understood. "Whatsoever seemeth strange unto us, and we understand not, we blame and condemne. The like befalleth us in our judging of beasts."

The powerful strain of quietism that informed Montaigne's writing united beast and noble savage in close alliance.

Beasts doe manifestly declare unto us how many infirmities our minds agitation bring us. That which is told us of those that inhabit *Bresill*, who die onely through age, which some impute to the clearenesse and calmenesse of their aire, I rather ascribe to the calmenesse and clearnesse of their minds, void and free from all passions, cares, toiling, and

unpleasant labours, as a people that passe their life in a
wonderfull kind of simplicitie and ignorance, without letters, or lawes, and without Kings, or any Religion.[30]

Beasts and savage Americans carried on the same sort of passive
existence. Both drew their subsistence and virtues from nature.
But most important, both lived in a setting that contained none
of the obstructions and limitations of society.

Montaigne wrote subtle social criticism. Because he was
neither a biologist nor an anthropologist, he did not equate
man and beast in any technical sense. Yet, in diminishing the
claims of civilized men, he celebrated values that linked savage
men with beasts. He saw the same qualities in animals that he
perceived in savage men, and he compared civility unfavorably
with those qualities. The result was to countenance the tendency
in European thinking that associated the savage condition with
an impaired humanity.

Montaigne's strictures were received by an Elizabethan audience long accustomed to the practice of associating virtue with
animals. Aesop's *Fables*, the model for this form of moralizing,
had been published in English in 1485 by William Caxton and
was followed by fifteen editions in the next century.[31] Thomas
Chaloner credited Aesop when he advised sixteenth-century
Englishmen to observe "how amongest brute beastes, and burdes
also those lyue most wealthily, that have least to dooe with
disciplines." Sir Thomas Wilson's *Arte of Rhetorique* found
animal life a rich store of moral examples for humankind.
"Brute beastes . . . ," he concluded, "have shewed unto vs, the
paterns and Images of divers vertues." In his monumental compilation of zoological information, Topsell was careful to offer
a moral justification of his work. He reasoned that men and
beasts descended from a common parent, nature, and hence
"many and most excellent rules for publike and private affaires,
both for preseruing a good Conscience and avoiding an euill
daunger, are gathered from Beasts." By implicating human
beings in the lives of beasts, Elizabethan writers tended to reduce the distance between God's creatures.[32]

Although the image of the beast as exemplar for man was
pervasive, it should be noted that European thinking was

sharply divided. Just as savagism appeared in two forms—noble and ignoble—bestiality expressed a profound ambivalence in the European perception of animals. Besides representing nature and pristine virtue, beasts stood for man's fall from grace. Deeply embedded in Christian thinking was the notion that sin violated the integrity of the human condition. By sinning, men denied their nature, fell from their proper human status, and became like beasts. Human beings held a unique place in nature. They were the only creatures granted the capacity to overcome their passions and to live by the dictates of reason. Insofar as they failed to obey this injunction, they denied their nature, diminished their claims to humanity, and became beastlike. Men who behaved like beasts offended the very order of the universe. Writers of the day were obsessed with the danger of disorder and found the language of bestiality irresistible in describing its causes. They used references to animals and bestial behavior to evoke the special sense of doom and degeneration they felt in the late sixteenth and early seventeenth centuries.[33]

Thus, in the bestial analogy, moralists found a powerful rebuke for human iniquity. Of course they could always invoke the precedents of Satan's animallike qualities and the Beast of Revelation, who represented the sum of evil in the world.[34] Sin denied reason and reduced men to infancy, a time when they were incapable of governing their passions. What was "an Infant, but a brute, having the shape of a man?" Without reason, human beings in infancy were animated by "certaine violent motion, Like vnto bruit beasts, which are deuoid of reason and vnderstanding."[35] As adults they remained enslaved to the "delights and pleasures" of the flesh. As one preacher put it: "I make myselfe earthlie: and change my selfe from a reasonable man into a brute beast." Every possible offense against the laws of God and man, from frivolity to the sin against the Holy Ghost, prompted the use of the animal analogy.[36] Men were commanded to be holy the way Christ was holy. To do less was to "ioyne prophane & unholy members, to our holy head Christ, then we make Christ a monster. As if a man should ioyne, vnto the head of a Lyon, the necke of a Beare, the body of a Wolfe, and the legges of a Foxe; were it not a monstrous thing? Would it not make a mo[n]strous creature?"[37] Sin made animals of men and monsters of animals.

In his treatise on physiology, which appeared in 1613, Thomas Hill revealed the consequences of breaching the wall between man and beast and associating moral depravity with animality. Hill assumed that without Christianity men would inevitably behave like animals. Only the regeneration obtained from God's grace curbed the beast that dwelled within every man. Despite God's efforts, men continued to yield to the beastly urges of the flesh, a fact Hill found revealed in their physiognomies. The inward disposition to sin could not be hidden because the human body carried visible traces of the underlying unity between man and beast. Hill inferred human vices from the structure of the human body. Small ears like an ape's implied the apish vice of deceit; large ears supposed the dullness of the ass; ears formed like a dog's denoted meanness. Although his purpose was ostensibly moral–to release human beings from an addiction to their lowest instincts–the effect of Hill's work was to break down the differentiation between man and animal. Furthermore, he ascribed to animals and men the same personal qualities. The more he dwelled on the infinite variety of human vices, the more it became evident that men acted like beasts because both were molded from the same clay.[38]

In *The Tempest* Shakespeare explores the interrelations of man and beast together with the corresponding problem of savagism and civility. At issue almost immediately is Caliban's humanity. Shakespeare never settles the matter. In Caliban's character the savage manner partakes of powerful animal attributes, which transforms him into a curious amalgam of man and beast. The play was performed at court in 1611 and again in the winter of 1612–13 to honor the marriage of the king's daughter to the Elector Palatine, a celebration that, as mentioned in Chapter 1, also witnessed Chapman's masque. Virginia was the topic of the day, no doubt because of the recent wreck of the Virginia Company's ships on Bermuda (from which Shakespeare took his title), but also because Virginia hinted of such antithetical possibilities as paradise and a savage condition that bordered on bestial degradation.[39]

The play unfolds on a Mediterranean island that seems more like the New World than the Old and that possesses the characteristics of paradise. The island may be merely a projection of the imagination of Prospero, a deposed duke who has failed in the real world but who, on his island paradise, can exercise the dominion he craves. Through magic he manipulates the activities of the island's inhabitants. That this paradisaic dreamworld is Prospero's and not Shakespeare's becomes evident from the playwright's treatment of Gonzalo, a sage but fanciful counselor who promotes a paradisaic vision lifted from Florio's English version of Montaigne's *Essays*. Moreover, at the conclusion of the play, Shakespeare has Prospero abandon the island, forsake the false promises of magic, and return to a life of worldly responsibility. Shakespeare may have flirted with the possibilities of the earthly paradise, but ultimately he did not think it a fitting place to carry on the business of the world.[40]

Shakespeare's doubts about the feasibility of paradise should have been apparent from the beginning. When Prospero arrives on the island he finds two inhabitants, Caliban and Ariel. Caliban is the dubious offspring of an incubus and a witch named Sycorax, who has imprisoned Ariel. Prospero releases Ariel to be the agent of his magic and begins his unfortunate relationship with Caliban. Although they get on well in the beginning, Prospero soon finds Caliban a most unpleasant companion. He shows Prospero the resources of the island, and the magician reciprocates by attempting to teach him language. Caliban at first fails to learn, and then learns only to curse. But his shortcomings as a pupil are not the main cause of the dissension. Prospero makes Caliban a slave and torments him with magical powers after he attacks Miranda, Prospero's daughter. He is, says Prospero, "capable of all ill" and hence deserves the treatment he receives. Shakespeare does not explain why Prospero, who knows of Caliban's origins, should expect better of him, although this early confidence does prove the magician's naivete. Indeed Caliban makes a curious inhabitant of paradise unless Shakespeare intended to stress the ambiguities of the paradisaic vision.

By every account in the play, Caliban is something less than a man. Most often his fellow islanders call him a monster, a name that befits his parentage. Devils and witches were thought to bring forth beings with grotesque features that violated conventional human standards, though the category of monster did not exclude certain human characteristics. Caliban is a "man monster," a "drunken," "brave," "servant," and "most poor credulous" monster. He is also a "villian," a "slave," and a "savage." None of these appellations do him honor, but they do retain his tie to humanity. But such descriptions as "A freckled whelp, hag born, not honour'd with/A Human shape," "a thing most brutish," "a moon-calf," a "puppy headed monster," and "half a fish and half a monster" prove that Caliban evokes bestial images in the minds of those who see him. The fusion of types is not arbitrary. Caliban is both man and beast because he is savage. Trinculo, the jester, a low creature, recognizes him immediately:

What have we here?
a man or a fish? . . . A strange fish! Were I
in England now (as once I was) and had but this fish
painted, not a holiday fool there but would give a piece
of silver. There would this monster make a man;
any strange beast there makes a man. When they will
not give a doit to relieve a lame beggar,
they will lay
out ten to see a dead Indian. Legg'd like a man; and his fins
   like arms! Warm, o'my troth! I do now let
loose my opinion, hold it no longer: this is no fish,
but an islander . . .

When, a moment later, the drunk Stephano stumbles upon Caliban, he experiences the same instant recognition. "Have we devils here? Do you put tricks upon 's with salvages and men of Inde?" To Trinculo and Stephano the monster Caliban is an Indian, the same sort of creature they and Shakespeare had seen exhibited more than once in London.[41]

If Shakespeare created Caliban after the design of the New World (the name bears a striking resemblance to the words Carib and cannibal), his character derives from an older tradition. Caliban possesses all the marks of beast and wild man. His nature cannot rise above the sensate. "A devil, a born devil, on whose nature/Nurture can never stick; on whom my pains,/. . . all lost, quite lost . . ./So his mind cankers."[42] Though he enjoys a certain cunning and rudimentary understanding of his situation, he manifests no intellectual power. Music pleases him; he dreams of riches falling from heaven. He is imaginative, but lacks judgment. After taking Stephano for a god, he debases himself by worshiping one of the least worthy characters in the play. By conspiring with Stephano and Trinculo, he becomes implicated in the special immorality of civilization. Caliban's body is hairy or scaly like a wild man's. He spends his days eating, sleeping, and performing the simple tasks set for him by Prospero. Although he claims to seek freedom, it is plain that he can live with others only as a slave. He expects to be tied like an animal or to be turned into an ape. When Prospero and the other characters leave the island to take up the responsibilities of civility, Caliban remains because his endowments fit him only for life in Prospero's dreamworld. Prospero, after all, acknowledges Caliban as his own. His vices alone would not exclude him from the real world, for cruelty, lust, and rebellion can be found in civil life. Caliban stays on the island because his character falls short of the attributes necessary for humane existence. He is an American savage, clearly humanoid though not fully human.[43]

Caliban attests to how easily the American Indians could fall victim to the European tendency to measure the New World and its people through the concept of savagism and to how readily savagism slipped into bestiality. That the English never believed the Indians to be actual beasts was less significant than the overbearing compulsion of Englishmen and other Europeans to incorporate Indians into time-honored categories. Without an alternative to the savagism–civility division, Englishmen were virtually compelled by the habitual drift of language to begin speaking of Indians as though they were animals. This habit of speech found support in the persistence, into the modern era, of ancient and medieval traditions that obscured the demarcation between men and animals, equated the early stages of human development with bestiality, and interpreted sin as a fall from the human to the animal condition. Even the apparently benign conception of noble savagism lent itself to a bestial perception of American natives, though ignoble savagism seemed more compatible with the major implications of bestiality. As a consequence, when Englishmen came to believe that the savages of America threatened civil order in Virginia, they possessed a ready-made rhetorical instrument that excluded Indians from the benefits of civility and cast doubt on their humanity.

4

DEPENDENCE

Inevitably, savagism clashed with the English experience in the New World. In the sense that Englishmen acquired any generalized conception of native life, they were dependent on the doctrine of savagism. They might praise the noble savage, a surrogate for the white man's better self, or endorse the Indians' progress on a scale of development that culminated in civility, but they could never admit the inherent integrity of native culture. Nevertheless, English colonists came to Virginia and settled down to the task of dealing with real Indians who were organized into traditional societies and who possessed a powerful sense of ethnic loyalty. They came to value aspects of native culture, found more than one native trait worthy of emulation, and leaned heavily on the Indians for survival. At the same time, their belief in savagism persisted, with the result that dependence and imitation took on the appearance of genuine threats to civil order. Regardless of the attractiveness of aspects of native life and the usefulness of the Indians as producers of food, to Englishmen they remained savage and hence a potential menace.

Despite their inclination to be hostile to strangers, Europeans made no necessary connection between foreignness and incivility. Barbarians obtained their nefarious reputations not because they were alien but because they imperiled civilized society. Societies that posed no immediate danger to Europeans could boast the attributes of civility, and travelers returned from Asia and Africa with news of such people. The Chinese, in particular, seemed worthy of praise for their accomplishments. A Portuguese explorer, whose account was translated into English, reported that the Chinese were endowed "with so great wisedome and discretion in naturall thinges and in the government of their common wealthes, that no other nations ... seeme to pass the[m], or have therein the advantage of them, nor yet to have the like wittes, for all maner of Artes." Europe itself could not measure up to the greatness of China, though it might benefit from comparison with the rest of the world. The Chinese imitated the Greeks in claiming that they possessed two eyes, the Europeans one, "and that all the rest of other Nations are starke blinde."[1]

The Spaniards recognized signs of civility in Mexico and Peru and distinguished those two great southern empires from the rest of America. Nothing would better answer the charge that the Mexicans were a "grose and brutish people," wrote Acosta, than to "relat[e] their order and maner, whenas they lived under their owne lawes . . ." The Mexicans possessed "a certaine settled state, which was kept within compasse, by some decrees and customes of their owne . . ." Europeans were not of one mind concerning the existence of civility in America. They were more inclined to associate the new continent with savagism, but they found in the New World, especially in Mexico and Peru, societies with large populations, impressive technology, and formidable public organization. They could not help but perceive some of the traces of the civil order they identified with their own manner of life.[2]

Spanish reports from Mexico described a physically imposing society. Though the English encountered nothing comparable in the North, they hoped they would, and the Spanish accounts tended to color their experiences. Peter Martyr pictured cities on the Yucatán Peninsula where the Spaniards "marveyled to behold the houses buylded lyke towres, magnifycall temples, streates well paved, and great exercise of bying and sellyng by exchaunge of ware for ware. Their houses are eyther bylte of stone, or of bricke and lyme, and artificially wrought." In his preface to Peter Martyr's *Decades*, Richard Eden predicted that in the northern regions, which he confused with Mexico, the English would find "cities and towres so well buylded and people of such ciuilitie, that this part of the worlde seemeth lyttle inferiour to owre Europe . . ." Other news from the New World told of towns of 10,000 with houses four stories high and of provinces populated with as many as 40,000 people. Mexico prompted Spaniards and Englishmen to anticipate greater worlds to conquer. "It is to be thought, that the things not yet seene, doe surmount all that hitherunto ye have playnely seene." At first, David Ingram's report that on his legendary trek across the continent he had spied "a towne halfe a myle longe, and hath many streates farre broader than any streat in London"[3] sounded quite plausible.

On the northern continent, the English settled in 1607 amidst a native grouping that, at least in one major sense, manifested the signs of civility. Between the Northern Neck and what would become the Carolina border, the native leader Powhatan held sway over some 12,000 Indians in thirty different tribal groupings. The English were little inclined to concede to the Indians any of the qualities of civil order. They expected to find savages, and in their own minds they were not disappointed. But they could not ignore the forceful personality of Powhatan or the extensive power he exercised over his people. In his case the easy tendency to bestow European titles upon American leaders seemed fitting. He held his position over all but six of the thirty tribes by right of conquest, and he wielded power with what appeared to be the arbitrary will of a mighty despot.[4] When Englishmen did not associate Powhatan culture with savagism, they tended to invest it with the civil qualities of their own mode of living. Neither conception supplied the means for an accurate portrayal of native society.

According to Smith, Powhatan ruled by custom, apparently a less effective base of power than written law. "Yet when he listeth his will is a law and must be obeyed: not only as a king but as half a God they esteeme him." His inferior kings enjoyed powers no less effective. They commanded life and death over their subjects. Strachey called Powhatan a "great Emperour" and drew a luminous sketch of the native leader. He portrayed him as an elderly man (a little less than eighty, although he was probably twenty years younger), weather-beaten, tall, with "cleane lymbes" and a "sad aspect." He had struggled patiently over the years "to make his name and famely great." "He hath bene a strong and able saluadge, synowie, active, and a daring spiritt, vigilant, ambitious, subtile to enlarge his dominions . . ."

Despite evidence to the contrary, Strachey remained convinced that Powhatan was a savage and a tyrant. How explain, then, the majesty that seemed to attach to his personality? He found the solution in an "infused kynd of divinenes" given by God to those "who are his ymediate Instruments on earth," even to infidels who have no knowledge of God. Strachey established Powhatan's kinship with all civil rulers, but only by sidestepping the issue of savagism.[5]

Although most Englishmen could never quite shake off the belief that Powhatan ruled with brutal and despotic force, experience brought to light a different native leader with a nearly avuncular relationship to his people. Once, on his annual progress among the various villages that owed him allegiance or over which he exercised influence (the English monarchs made similar tours), Powhatan was entertained by the Potomac Indians. The young warriors of the tribe came before him to boast of their deeds of valor against their enemies, the "Massoamacks and the wilde Beastes of theire fforest." The stories became more spectacular as each warrior sought to impress the great chieftain. Finally the last of the warriors appeared, made the proper homage to Powhatan, and described his exploit. "And I my Lorde went this morninge into a great Marshe and there valientlye killed six Muske Ratts, wch though itt be no more then the boyes do dailye this my Liege is true and most of the rest but fables." The assembled Indians broke into laughter and Powhatan was so taken with the resourceful warrior that he assigned the highest award to the least achievement. Wisdom and benignity are not the virtues of savage tyrants.[6]

Powhatan's bucolic empire manifested other signs of civility. "Although the Country people be very barbarous," wrote Smith, "yet have they amongst them such government, as that their Magistrates for good commanding, and their people for due subiection and obeying, excell many places that would be counted very civill." It was "a rude kinde of Common-wealth, and rough governement, wherein they both honour and obey their Kings, Parents, and Governours . . . ," agreed Alexander Whitaker, the propagandist for colonization.[7] Some of Powhatan's underlings struck the English as a bit too stately for their own good, but most maintained considerable dignity.

The werowance of the Rapahannocks behaved "as though he had beene a Prince of civil government." A chieftain from the Eastern Shore "was the comliest, proper, civill Salvage we incountered." The admission that Indian behavior could resemble manners appropriate to the civil state came with some reluctance from the white man. Nevertheless, it was clear that the acknowledgment of such a being as a "civill Savage" represented a monumental concession from an ideology that insisted upon the strictest differentiation between civil life and the ways of the savage.[8]

Perhaps the weightiest evidence that the Powhatan Indians enjoyed a manner of life with more substance than the doctrine of savagism allowed came from the recognition that they were organized into distinct social groupings. Hariot noted that the Carolina Indians spoke different languages and that distance widened the differentiation among them. He recognized also that separate languages contributed to the political divisions among the Indians. Although Powhatan appeared to exercise vast power in Virginia, it soon became clear that the people under his jurisdiction retained separate identities. The various tributary chiefs knew the territorial bounds of their authority and apparently they were fully conscious of their political relationship to Powhatan. The arrangements reminded Strachey of the social and political divisions "amongst Christians," "some being great people, as the Saquesahanoughs [not a Powhatan tribe], some very little as the Wicocomocoes, some speaking likewise, more articulate and plaine, and some more inward and hollow . . . , some curteous and more civill, others cruell and bloudy." Powhatan ruled broad territories and had many petty kings subordinate to him. Other Indian leaders exercised a far more limited jurisdiction. By stressing the heterogeneity of native life, Englishmen edged closer to the realities of existence in the New World and further from the rigid definitions of savagism.[9]

The doctrine of savagism offered no explanation of the differentiation of sexual roles in native life. Europeans perceived that Indian men and women performed distinct functions and that they arranged their sexual lives in ways that set them off from conventional European behavior. Generally, European commentators disapproved, probably more for ethnocentric reasons than because of any conviction that sexual division stemmed from the savage mode. Smith registered a strong censure: "The men bestowe their times in fishing, hunting, wars and such manlike exercises, scorning to be seene in any woman like exercise, which is the cause that the women be verie painefull and the men often idle. The women and children do the rest of the worke. They make mats, baskets, pots, morters, pound their corne, make their bread, prepare their victuals, plant their corne, gather their corne, beare all kind of burdens and such like." The Powhatans, whose division of labor persisted until late in the seventeenth century, answered in kind. John Clayton observed the natives' customs at that time, and recorded that they "call the Inglish men fools in working themselves and keeping their wives idle." Lescarbot referred to similar arrangements among the northern people, but he was less censorious. It seemed that the women were "neither forced nor tormented" to carry out their onerous tasks.[10] Most observers agreed that sexual conventions were somewhat looser than in Europe, yet the system clearly operated according to a body of rules. Unbounded promiscuity was not pervasive. Homosexuality existed, though even this seemed to be hemmed in by certain customs. Whatever their opinions of the shortcomings of native domestic life, white men recognized some faint traces of the actuality.[11]

Class division among the Indians presented a similar problem for Europeans. Although the doctrine of savagism assumed a leveling of social status in native society, most observers noted the existence of class as though they were commenting on the inevitable hierarchical distribution of social power in any society. References to the "common sort" and the "better sort" were frequent in contemporary writings about the native peoples. John Smith disclosed the tension between idea and reality when he described his first formal audience with Powhatan. The native leader received Smith in state, his concubines and subchiefs arrayed in appropriate order. Smith presented gifts and Powhatan responded with an oration delivered by three of his "Nobles," about whom Smith commented: "if there be any amongst Saluages." In Virginia, it seemed, the better sort possessed more personal property, adorned themselves accordingly, and could expect immortality; the common natives owned little, dressed poorly, and had no hope for an afterlife. Males of the upper caste in Guiana covered their genitalia and took more than one wife, revealing that the signs of social class elevated some natives above the nakedness of the savage state.[12]

Surprisingly, Smith discovered something like private property in Virginia. The noble savage motif dictated the absence of "mine and thine" and that idea found corroboration in many ways in the communal customs of the native tribes. Private property, in the sense that modern Europeans had come to know it, did not exist among the Indians, though many of the native tribes did practice a species of separate usage. Its existence among the Virginia Indians struck Smith's eye. He noted that the tribal groupings held separate properties for farming, hunting, and fishing. Moreover, "each houshold knoweth their owne lands, and gardens, and most hire of their owne laborers." Whitaker contended that "they observe the limits of their owne possessions, and incroach not upon their neighbours dwellings" The link between private ownership and public power among the Indians should have become apparent to the English when the native chieftains delivered up vast stores of food on demand. A major portion of the product of native farming and hunting found its way into the hands of the native leadership. Hence Englishmen did recognize some aspects of the complexities of native life, and learned that Indians were not utterly ruled by the simplicities of savagism.[13]

Savagism, of course, persisted as the conventional generalization employed by Europeans in explaining the nature of native societies. Perceptions of the actualities of Indian culture remained dim, scattered, tentative, and invariably ethnocentric. But such insights did appear and testified to the capacity of some observers to see through a powerful and coercive ideology. More important, the drift toward more realistic perceptions of the native people revealed the strength of the relations established between white and Indian. Soon after landing in the New World, Europeans began learning from natives, and they were tutored not by the savages of their imaginations but by real Indians. In Virginia the colonists became dependent on the neighboring people for their very survival, and this dependence continued long after the permanence of the colony had been assured. Savages, noble or ignoble, could not have done for the English what Indians did do. The tragedy was that the English never quite saw the actuality; they never quite realized that they had become enmeshed in a relationship with a traditional society made up of real people. In the end savagism dominated the English perception of native life–with disastrous consequences for the Indians.

Although few Europeans expressed any explicit inclination to adopt the Indians' ways, many showed a genuine interest in learning about how they lived. Fernando Alarchon pressed an elderly Indian on the west coast of Mexico so closely for information that when he suggested that the Indian spend the night on his ship, he received a response that has been the bane of anthropologists since. The native replied that "he would not goe with mee because I would wearie him with asking him questions of so many matters . . ."[14] That many explorers, conquerors, and settlers asked questions and received answers was borne out by the rich ethnological materials contained in the collections of Eden, Hakluyt, and Purchas, and in the separate works of Hariot, Smith, and Strachey. The meticulous attention to ethnological detail evidenced in the drawings of White and Le Moyne testified to their insatiable curiosity about the minutiae of native life. Savagism constituted an insurmountable obstacle to any accurate generalizations about the nature of native society, but it did not inhibit the accumulation of a wealth of detailed knowledge about Indian culture.

Practicality stimulated much interest in native culture. Communication by signs and gestures seldom proved satisfactory. Europeans heard what they wanted to hear, especially about the riches they expected to find. Missionary activity could proceed when the whites learned the Indians' languages or when the Indians began to speak the white man's. In his "Discourse on Western Planting," Hakluyt recommended a knowledge of native languages. Indian visitors to England and the Continent helped and learned something about European languages themselves. Hariot apparently obtained a working knowledge of Carolina Algonquin speech from Manteo and Wanchese, the two Indians who returned with him to England in 1586. Later, in Virginia, Gabriel Archer and George Thorpe, among other Englishmen, gained a certain proficiency in the native language. Laudonnière said that the Florida natives spoke to him incessantly, enabling him eventually to carry on a simple conversation with them. Thevet thought the language of the Brazilian natives "short and obscure" though easier to learn than Turkish or many of the languages of the East. Early in the sixteenth century Cartier took the time to compile a list of Indian words; Smith did the same in the next century. Although the white man's languages ultimately became the major means of communication between the two peoples, in the beginning Europeans felt the need to inquire into the native mode of speech.[15]

Knowledge of Indian herbs first entered England by way of the great manual of the Spanish physician Nicolás Monardes, which John Frampton translated in 1577. Monardes compiled a vast treasury of information concerning the medicinal value of New World plants, but his most significant contribution was a description of tobacco, an American importation that became a cause célèbre in the seventeenth century.[16] Views on tobacco varied, but a powerful body of opinion looked upon it as a filthy and injurious weed. Moreover, in the mind of its foremost opponent, James I, tobacco was associated with savagism and bestiality. To smoke it was to imitate "the barbarous and beastly manners of the wilde, godlesse, and slavish *Indians*, especially in so vile and stinking a custom." James thought it fitting that tobacco should be associated with the pox, even as an antidote. From the Indians "was first brought into Christendome, that most detestable disease, so from them likewise was brought this use of Tobacco . . ." Yet hatred of savagism and all its works could not dissuade Englishmen from making their "noses a chimney." Tobacco became a national addiction, an important new industry, and the hope of the colony in Virginia. It was clear that Englishmen could learn from Indians despite the inhibiting force of savagism.[17]

Although Monardes looked upon Indians as a "naughtie kinde of people" who were reluctant to reveal their medicinal secrets, he expressed no doubts about the efficacy of their therapies. If the Indians would not teach the Spaniards the new pharmacology, the "Mountaines and Desertes" of the New

World would unveil its mysteries. It would take only diligence "to profite oure selves of these marveilous effects . . ." "They doe bee admirable, for that their vertues are most mightie against all venome and Pestilent Agewes, and venemous humors." Doubtless the doctrine of specifics played an important part in this confidence in American pharmaceutics. Renaissance apothecaries postulated a close connection between the character or origin of the disease and its remedy. For example, disease of the heart could supposedly be cured by heart-shaped leaves, hemorrhages could be relieved by red juices, and brain powder could be obtained from the brain-shaped meat of the walnut. Similarly, it was believed that relief for venereal disease would be found in the New World. "Our Lorde God would from whence the evill of the Poxe came," wrote Monardes, "from thence should come the remedy for them."[18]

Despite the health disaster that resulted from the introduction of new diseases into the New World, Europeans gained a generally favorable impression of Indian medicine. If native therapy had been less closely linked to religion, Europeans might have held it in even higher regard. Lescarbot thought the appeal to witches and charms as worthless in the New World as it was in the Old. Yet he noted of native practitioners: "There are some of them which sometimes do make incredible cures, as to heal one that hath both arms cut off." Cartier had experienced a less spectacular though perhaps more practical success of Indian medicine. When his men suffered from severe scurvy in the winter of 1535–6, he found the cure in a drink brewed from the bark of white cedar by the Indians. At Roanoke, Hariot, a man of scientific credentials, praised tobacco, sassafras, and the "Sweet Gummes" of the region. Smith seemed less enthusiastic about Indian medicine, though he took the time to describe a number of obviously useful remedies. Gabriel Archer, at least, was convinced by the natives' claims for their healing arts. He referred to "apothecary drugges of diverse sortes, some knowne to be of good estimacion, some strange of whose vertue the salvages report wonders . . ." Less critically, John Clayton reported of the Virginia Indians that they "have great knowledge of the vertues of their mediceniall herbes, and perform extraordinary cures with them." Although critical of some of the Indians' nostrums, whites were ready to learn the secrets of American pharmacology.[19]

The most striking disparity between reality and the doctrine of savagism arose from the obvious devotion of the Powhatan Indians to farming. Savages should have been gatherers who survived on the bounty of nature, or, at best, hunters who slaughtered game indiscriminately. They did not cultivate the soil because, it was thought, they had not yet risen to the level of sedentary life traditionally linked to the immemorial ritual of planting, cultivation, and harvest. When a people did cultivate the land, of course, they ceased to be savage and took a critical step in the arduous ascent from hunting to pasturage, to agriculture, and finally to commerce.[20] Ironically, the Indians engaged in three of these pursuits—hunting, farming, and trade—but they remained savages in the white man's eyes. It was not that Europeans were ignorant of the native economy. The first contacts, and virtually every one that followed, involved an exchange of goods. Few commentators failed to note the existence of Indian fields and to describe the crops raised in them. Native agriculture may not have conformed to the European ideal. By European standards, the variety of plants was limited. The methods seemed slipshod; fields were neither fenced nor carefully cultivated as in Europe; crops were not neatly segregated but planted intermixed in one field. Most important, among the eastern woodland peoples found by the English, it was the women who did the agricultural work, whereas the men hunted, fought, and appeared to waste their time in interminable discussions with fellow tribesmen. Even if the existence of farming provided evidence of an advance out of the savage state, the warriors' attachment to hunting and fighting revealed the truth about native society. Yet the fact was that white men seldom examined the problem seriously. They were content to remain gripped by the savage dogma and at the same time to trade with Indians, watch them raise a substantial portion of their food, and, in Virginia, to live off the Indians' agricultural achievements.

Most eastern native peoples practiced slash-and-burn agriculture. They cleared fields by girdling the trees and burning the underbrush. Land was planted for only a few years and then allowed to lie fallow for a long period. The limited population and the abundance of land made this system appropriate for aboriginal North America. The long fallow period maintained the fertility of the soil and frequent burnings added nutrients. Considering the Powhatan Indians' investment of time and energy, this method of farming was extraordinarily productive, though it supplied less than half their food. They gained the major portion through hunting, fishing, and gathering. Altogether their economy yielded an ample though scarcely abundant livelihood.[21]

The English settlers in Virginia developed an immediate interest in native agriculture. They had been instructed to choose a site for their colony by observing the native people. "If the naturals be strong and clean made, it is a true sign of a wholesome soil." It soon became obvious that they had selected wisely, for the neighboring tribes engaged in extensive farming and supplied the English with the wherewithal for survival. Although for two-thirds of the year the Powhatans depended on sources of food other than farming, a number of the surrounding peoples proved more affluent. The Accomac Indians planted enough corn to carry them through the year with a surplus. Fields of various sizes adjoined the native villages. Some were small plots 100 to 200 feet square, but others contained substantial acreage. The Pamunkey and the Appamattocks each had at least 100 acres under cultivation. Strachey reported that the Kecoughtans owned some 3,000 acres of cornfields. Smith remembered that the native plots ranged from 20 acres to over 200 acres. The men cleared the fields and the women and children did the planting. "Their manner is this," wrote Smith. "They make a hole in the earth with a sticke, and into it they put 4 graines of wheat and 2 of beanes. These holes they make 4 foote one from another. Their women and children do continually keepe it with weeding, and when it is growne midle high, they hill it about like a hop yard." The beans grew up the cornstalks. Often the native farmers put squash down as a ground cover, which solved the weeding problem. According to Hariot, the average yield for an acre planted with maize, beans, and pumpkins was 200 bushels.[22]

The native diet followed the seasons. In the spring, little of the previous harvest remained and the Indians survived on small game, such as turkeys and squirrels, and by fishing. When, in May and June, the time came to plant once again, they ate fish, acorns, and walnuts. When the season was particularly lean, the villages dispersed into small groups to gather crabs, oysters, land tortoises, wild fruits, and whatever game and fish were to be had. Through the summer, while the crops ripened, the Indians consumed berries, green corn, tuckahoe roots, and fish. The harvest came in the fall and the tribes celebrated their abundance. Once the crops had been picked and properly stored, the great hunting expedition was made to the falls of the rivers where game was more plentiful. Throughout the fall and winter seasons, the natives enjoyed the plenty obtained from their farming, hunting, and gathering: corn, squashes, beans, acorns, nuts, dried fruits and berries, and some game. They dried and smoked food to preserve it and knew how to store it through the winter. Sunflowers were probably raised by the Virginia Indians for bread and oil, and tobacco was grown for ceremonial and medicinal purposes.[23]

Once Europeans set foot in America they were at the mercy of supplies from across the Atlantic, which seldom arrived in time, or they faced the necessity of obtaining food from the native people. Growing their own crops required time and knowledge, which they were slow to acquire. When René Laudonnière established his Huguenot colony in the summer of 1564 on the St. Johns River in Florida, he brought enough supplies to last into the spring, when help was expected from Europe. He already knew something about the problem of food and the Indians. On a previous expedition to the New World, which landed on the Carolina coast, the French had run short and had appealed to the natives for help. The Indians proved generous, but in the off-season they could spare little. The French scoured the coast for twenty-five miles to the north and thereby brought in some food, though not enough to keep them from squabbling and finally abandoning their post. In 1564 Laudonnière stopped at the island of Dominica to fill his water casks and take on some fresh fruit. The first contact with the natives was peaceful, but the French became careless in picking bananas, trampled the Indian crops, and fell into a fight.

The lessons should have been obvious. Food in the New World was a precious commodity for the Indians as well as for the Europeans. Although the Indians would share it with remarkable generosity, they did not possess an unlimited supply. As a consequence the white man's voracious appetite became a source of endless provocation.[24]

French supplies dwindled in the least convenient season. By the spring of 1565 Laudonnière reported that his men "were constrained to indure extreme famine, which continued with us all the moneth of May: for in the latter season, neither Maiz nor Beanes, nor Mast was to be found in the villages, because they had employed all for to sowe their fields, insomuch that we were constrayned to eate rootes . . ." At first the Indans had been friendly, supplying the French with grain, fish, and a variety of other foods. As supplies ran low and the French importuned the Indians for more food, threatening to devour even the seed grain, relations grew tense and finally became hostile. When the need for provisions became acute, Laudonnière announced to the Indians that the French wished to trade. The natives recognized the plight of their visitors and drove hard bargains. Soon they owned all the trade goods and the French had yet to satisfy their hunger. In return for further aid, Laudonnière agreed to assist the neighboring Indians against their enemies. But no service rendered could quite fulfill the Frenchmen's needs. Moreover, in time the Indians did not possess enough to satisfy their own requirements. They proposed that the French adopt the methods long in use among the natives during seasons of scarcity. In these times the Indians dispersed in small groups through the forests, where they awaited the harvest and survived by gathering. The New World economy provided an adequate diet for the native inhabitants, but it could not stand the strain placed upon it by Europeans incapable of feeding themselves.[25]

In his desperation Laudonnière resolved on firm action. He took the local chief and his son prisoner and refused to release them unless the Indians agreed to supply the French with food. The results defied his expectations. The downfall of a prominent native leader aroused the ambitions of the neighboring tribes, who saw a possible advantage in the predicament of their enemy. They agreed to feed the French if they would murder the captive chieftain. The reaction of the chief's own people was even more surprising. They assumed that he would be killed because their own custom was to kill prisoners. The departure of their leader stimulated factionalism and a new tribal leadership came to power. Laudonnière finally abandoned the scheme and released the chieftain and his son. When he followed this gesture by once again requesting food, fighting erupted and a number of Frenchmen were killed–but no food was obtained. Hungry Frenchmen became a serious threat to the native food supply and disrupted the stability of Indian society.[26]

In a similar situation on Roanoke Island in 1585–6, the English repeated the French experience. Although news of the Huguenot effort in Florida had reached England, measures taken failed to make the colonists independent of the natives and hence avoid conflict over demands for food. Once again, the first contacts with the Indians were peaceful. The English constructed their fort adjacent to the native village on the island and may have built their dwellings among the Indian lodges. While English and Indians had food, relations remained amicable. But a mishap in landing had destroyed part of the English provisions and by the spring of 1586 the situation had become desperate. Resentment increased among the Indians as their own resources became tight. They raised prices and then cut off all trading with the English. When the Indians retreated into the wilderness to gather and hunt, Ralph Lane thought he detected a conspiracy to starve the colony. "The king [Wingina] was advised and of himselfe disposed, as a ready meane to have assuredly brought us to ruine in the moneth of March, 1586, himselfe also with all his Savages to have runne away from us, and to have left his ground in the Island unsowed, which if he had done, there had bene no possibilitie in common reason, (but by the immediate hand of God) that we could have bene preserved from starving out of hand." Lane led a hopeless expedition up to Roanoke River in search of food. He obtained little, but his determination seemed to have impressed the natives, for they agreed to plant corn and build fish weirs for the colonists. In May the Indians reestablished their boycott, and the English were forced to adopt the native custom of dispersing their numbers to search for food. The Indians saw their chance and laid plans to destroy them. Lane learned of the conspiracy and struck first. For the moment the Indians were subdued, though the source of tension between the two people remained. Because of the logistical problem of carrying supplies across the ocean, Europeans could survive in the New World only with the aid of the Indians. But the Indians did not possess the resources to feed both themselves and the newcomers.[27]

The relations between Indians and Englishmen in Virginia between 1607 and 1622 supplied ample evidence, first, of the incapacity of the English to feed themselves, and then, of their dependence on the Indians for food even after the colony was firmly established. The inability of the English to grapple successfully with the basic necessities of life in the New World became apparent soon after the arrival of the first wave of colonists. And nothing changed through the first generation of the colony. Dissension and incompetence among the leaders, the failure of the company to send a sufficient number of farmers, the presence of large numbers of people who either would not work or who did work of little use to the colony but who nevertheless required supplies, the astonishingly small amounts of work required of the colonists by the leadership—all these factors contributed to the failure of the colony to become self-sufficient.[28] Fortunately for the English, the colony had been established among a native people capable of supplying substantial amounts of food well into the second decade after its inception. That the native society could serve as an English granary and that the Indians often gave their food willingly should not mask the tension that English dependence generated in the relations between the two peoples.

The Virginia Company expected that, initially, the colonists would rely upon the natives for aid. "In all Your Passages you must have Great care not to Offend the naturals if You Can Eschew it and imploy some few of your Company to trade with them for Corn and all Other lasting Victuals if you [they?] have any of this you must Do before that they perceive you mean to plant among them for not being Sure how your own Seed Corn will prosper the first Year to avoid the Danger of famine use and Endeavour to Store yourselves of the Country Corn." The concession, once made, became a prophecy. Except for a short period after 1614 when the company distributed land to the first investors and the colonists produced a surplus to sell to the Indians, the English were "constrained yerely to buy Corne of the Indians." In 1621, long past the formative period, the London Council issued the usual instructions to the new governor, Sir Francis Wyatt, to suppress tobacco planting and encourage the planting of corn, "not depending continually to be supplied by the Salvages, but in case of necessity to trade with them, whom long ere this, it hath been promised and expected should have beene fed and relived by the English, not the English by them . . ."[29] In the council's view, reliance on the Indians was bad economics and bad Indian policy, but it was also an appalling blow to English self-esteem, a quality crucial to the triumph of civility over savagism.

Within weeks of their landing at Jamestown the English were a sorry sight. Great numbers fell sick, others wandered off only to be killed by the natives, fields lay untended, and the food supply shrunk. The Indians reacted as might be expected. They drove hard bargains for English goods and developed a powerful contempt for the incompetence of the people who had invaded their country. But they brought in supplies. "Bread, Corne, Fish, and Flesh in great plentie," wrote George Percy, "which was the setting up of our feeble men, otherwise we had all perished." The English came to expect plenty from the Indians. When Smith returned from captivity in the Powhatan villages, he described the considerable resources of native agriculture. Confidence grew that new arrivals, who invariably landed without adequate provisions, would be fed with native supplies. As the years went by the English traded regularly for food, required Indians to empty their stores, or stripped native fields by force of arms. If support could not be found locally, they combed the shores of Chesapeake Bay and moved up the rivers. Year after year the colonists went about their business with the assurance that their own lack of foresight would be rewarded by the industry of the Indians.[30]

Although the relationship was not without reciprocal advantage (the Indians often traded willingly and received goods that they valued), the constant demand for food constituted a major source of tension between the two peoples. The Indians sought to remedy the situation by teaching the English how to grow Indian corn and build weirs in the rivers. (The English were less successful as fishermen than as farmers.) The colonists regretted their dependence. Smith recalled the reliance of the Spaniards on the native people and how it had worked to their disadvantage. If English dependence persisted, he knew how serious would be the consequence should the Indians abandon their fields and retreat into the wilderness. The chief of the Paspahegh offered a starkly realistic analysis of the problem. "We perceive & well know," he told Smith, "you intend to destroy us, that are here to intreat and desire your friendship, and to enjoy our houses and plant our fields, of whose fruit you shall participate, otherwise you will have the worst by our absence, for we can plant anywhere, though with more labour, and we know you cannot live if you want our harvest, and that reliefe wee bring you; if you promise us peace we will beleeve you, if you proceed in revenge, we will abandon the countrie."[31] Powhatan made a similar threat. But the Indians neither abandoned the country nor obtained quite the peace they wanted. Perhaps the threat was not merely idle, but one can only wonder where the Powhatans would have retreated. Their lands were hemmed in on all sides by other native peoples, most of them enemies. Although supplying the English with food weighed heavily on the natives, they were willing to do so in return for some assurance that the English would be less aggressive.

For the English the reliance on the Indians became a way of life. Tobacco brought a certain prosperity, but it threw the colonists into even deeper dependence on the Indians for food. Land that might have grown corn produced tobacco instead. The authorities railed but achieved little. "Nothing can be more dishonorable to O^r nation," proclaimed the governor in 1623, "then to stand in need of supplies of O^r most necessarie food from these base Salvages nor more dangerous, then to have O^r lives, and the life of the colony it self, to depend uppon the uncertaine hope of trade wth them."[32] The Indians stopped planting tobacco, thus ratifying the division of labor between the two peoples. After the company's change in leadership in 1618, great numbers of new colonists appeared in Virginia, poorly supplied as usual, and the colonial authorities were forced to appeal to the Indians for food. Even after the massacre of 1622, the colony took measures to ensure a supply of Indian corn before it mounted its campaign of retaliation.[33]

Although the English in Virginia recognized the necessity of depending on the Indians for food, they never reconciled that reality with the ideological necessities of the doctrine of savagism. The noble savage could make some claim to abundance, though not to the kind of plenty that derived from an economy based upon agricultural exploitation of the land. Of course, ignoble savagism postulated a native people of insufferable poverty and certainly with no interest in the cultivation of crops. In treatments of the New World economy, the theme of scarcity linked native farmers with savage Indians. When the burden of native affluence became too heavy for Europeans to bear, they pointed to the improvidence of Indians who expended their meager resources with no apparent concern for tomorrow and to the scarcity that seemed a recurrent part of native life. Doubtless the observation possessed some anthropological accuracy. Even Indians as well-off as the Powhatan tribes and their neighbors lived through a period of dearth in the cyclic round of farming, hunting, fishing, and gathering. Many native peoples were not nearly as opulent as the Indians of the Virginia Tidewater and had become inured to exiguous seasons in the rhythm of their lives. For Europeans the discovery of scarcity among the Indians supported the contention that savage people were inept, irresponsible, and childlike.

From various parts of the New World came reports of native people who hovered at the lowest level of subsistence. Alvaro Nuñez described natives on the Gulf Coast who lived on tuna for three months of the year and virtually starved for six. According to Lescarbot, the Florida Indians were often reduced to eating "a thousand filths, even to the swallowing down the coals, and to put earth in their spoon meat." In the cold winters of the North the natives "sometimes endure so great extremity, that they are almost constrained to eate one another . . ." Reckless savagism, it was believed, lay behind this scant mode of life.

Even Indians tolerably well-provided with the world's goods seemed bereft of any serious thought to what the next day might bring. The natives of Brazil "eateth at all times by night and by day, and everie houre and moment, and when they have any meate they keepe it no long time, for they have no providence for the future . . ." Tribes less well-provided for were equally improvident and, it seemed, equally generous to European visitors. The Canadian Indians lived "from hande to mouth" and in the cold winter they "fell into some scarcities of victuals; yet did they not refuse to serve the Frenchmen, with any thing they had all the winter long . . ." Savages worked little, ate when they could, and starved when food grew scarce.[34]

The English in Virginia kept a particularly sharp eye for scarcity among the Indians. They had good reason to, for they knew how heavily their own survival rested on the prosperity of the Indians. But the context of such observations was more than practical. Starving Indians supplied evidence of savagism in the New World and assuaged the misgivings of a civil society whose shortcomings forced it to depend on people supposedly less advanced on the scale of social development.

Smith found some Indians more competent than others. He contrasted the agricultural proficiency of the Eastern Shore natives with the ability of the mainland tribes. The Accomacs grew enough corn to keep them the whole year, whereas "the other not for halfe the years . . ." The mainland tribes lived on nuts and berries for a substantial part of the year and often were forced to scatter through the forest in order to survive. In 1610, when the English deserted the colony, they had not traded with the Indians for many months. "The trothe is they had nothinge to trade withall but mulberries." Yet the plight of the Indians did not prevent the English from filling their own needs. In the winter of 1607–8 the English ran short of corn and Smith was forced to tell the colonists that Powhatan had no corn to give. He added the assurance that if the corn had been available he would have obtained it. The Chickahominies were less fortunate. Their corn supply was greatly diminished and "they complained extreamly of their owne wants, yet fraughted our boats with 100 bushels of corns." On a later occasion Smith returned and again found their corn supply low, "yet loding the barge, I returned to our fort: our store being now indifferently wel provided with corne . . ."[35] In Smith's economy, Indian privation became English abundance—at least for the moment.

The English expected the savage Indians to be improvident. Even "at their best," commented Strachey, "they had but from hand to mouth." Savages lived for the moment, either violently or in idyllic passivity. With only a limited perception of time, they gorged themselves in times of plenty—"they be all of them huge eaters"—and went hungry when food was scarce. They neither husbanded their resources nor planned for the future. Nor did they bequeath reserves to future generations. Although they inhabited a fertile region, Smith doubted that the Virginia Indians could support even the 5,000 people who lived within sixty miles of Jamestown. They made "so small a benefit of their land." He envied the "*Spanyards* good hap to happen in those parts where were infinite numbers of people, who had manured the ground[,] with that providence, it affoorded victualls at all times." If the Spaniards had landed in a country "as salvage, as barbarous, as ill peopled, as little planted, laboured, and manured, as *Virginia*," they would have been as little rewarded as the English. "Except it be a little corne at some time of the yeere is to be had, I would not give twenty pound for the pillage is to be got amongst the Salvages in twenty yeeres . . ."[36] For Smith and his compatriots the problem was not so much the ill grace that accompanied their acceptance of charity, but the almost perverse insistence, in defiance of reality, that only savagism could explain the nature of native society.

Apparently only Powhatan looked to the future. He kept a huge storehouse which he packed by assessing eighty percent of the goods produced by his people. Strachey interpreted Powhatan's exaction as evidence of the despotism exercised by a barbarous potentate. In fact, the English benefited from the native practice. The high price placed on corn by the Indians testified to its scarcity. "Had it been gold," exclaimed Smith, "with more ease we might have got it." By centralizing the major portion of native resources in his own hands, Powhatan facilitated the process by which the English filled their storehouses with the product of native labor. What appeared to the English to be evidence of savage tyranny or simply a convenient method of supplying their wants was in fact an important mechanism in the storing and redistribution of resources among the Powhatan people. Powhatan and other native leaders used the goods exacted in tribute in a variety of public functions and in the dispersal of provisions throughout the area of tribal dominion. In an economy that hovered close to subsistence, the Indians had organized the means to supply the immediate future and to support a life rich in public ceremony. English observers found Powhatan's wealth impressive, but they missed the significance of its accumulation.[37]

The issue of savagism became particularly acute when individual colonists abandoned the Jamestown settlement and threw in their lot with the Indians. It was possible to repress acknowledgment of the colony's dependence on the food-producing skills of the Indians, to attribute it to a passing aberration, or to stress the episodic character of native abundance. But when Englishmen deliberately chose to renounce the loyalties of a lifetime, native society became more than a challenge to the proficiency of English technical skills—it became a threat to the existence of European society in the New World. More important, Englishmen who deserted the colony reverted, by definition, to a lower order of existence. They ceded their claims to civility and sank to the savage level. A people as sensitive to their place in the world as the English were bound to react strongly to such an assault on the integrity of their society.

The literature of exploration and colonization abounded with stories of white men who had fallen in with the natives, often as a result of shipwreck, but sometimes because they preferred life among the savages.[38] The Spanish authorities thought the matter serious enough to order that all white men found in Indian towns be sent back to Spain. Whatever the social preferences of these fugitives, it was clear that their lives changed once they came under the influence of native culture. Given the opportunity, most seemed willing to return—and to regret their behavior among the savages[39]—but others forged new and stronger loyalties. Two Spaniards wrecked on the Mexican coast in 1511 were found by Cortez. One returned willingly, but the other had acquired an Indian family and therefore refused, though his real reason may have been shame. "He had his nose ful boared of holes, & his eares fagged, hys face & handes painted according to the use of y countrey . . ." Laudonnière came upon two Spaniards in Florida in 1564. They were naked, wore their hair long, and "found our manner of apparell strange." They reported that three or four women who had survived a wreck some fifteen years before lived as wives among the Indians. These stories disclosed the susceptibility of civilized men to the ways of savagism.[40]

How deeply Englishmen felt the lure of savagism was revealed on the Bermudas in 1609–10, when the Somers expedition foundered on those vacant islands. Dissension developed soon after the English landed. A group of colonists expressed their disagreement with the established authority, then "like outlaws retired into the woods to make a settlement and habitation there," and finally threatened to move to one of the other islands. The leader of this little rebellion was John Want, "a sectary in points of religion" who was suspected of being a Brownist. He apparently felt little respect for the constraints of civil order. This episode had hardly concluded when one Stephen Hopkins, "a fellow who had much knowledge in the Scriptures and could reason well therein," assailed the very basis of legitimate authority. He argued "that it was no breach of honesty, conscience, nor religion to decline from the obedience of the governor or refuse to go any further led by his authority (except it so pleased themselves), since the authority ceased when the wreck was committed, and, with it, they were all men freed from the government of any man, and for a matter of conscience it was not unknown to the meanest how much we were therein bound each one to provide for himself and his own family." Two of the dissidents who had "fled into the woods" remained in Bermuda when the colonists continued their voyage to Virginia.[41] The Bermuda experience demonstrated the frailty of the civil bond among the English colonists and thus illustrated how dangerous the attractions of savagism might prove to be in Virginia.

The English knew the importance of learning about the Indians and delegated certain individuals to live with them in order to acquire the native languages. One of the most celebrated of these was Thomas Savage, who arrived in Virginia in January 1608 at age thirteen. The following month he accompanied Newport and Smith to the first important public conference with Powhatan. Newport exchanged Savage for Namontack, the Indian leader's adviser. Savage lived with the Indians for three years, learned to speak the language "naturally," and was trusted by Powhatan. For many years he served the colony as translator. He was instrumental in opening the Eastern Shore for trade and English settlement and was granted land there by the Laughing King. Savage managed to acquire knowledge of native culture and to retain the Indians' sympathy while avoiding any suspicion that he had betrayed the civil order. But Powhatan detected his fundamental loyalties almost immediately. After he had been with the Indians only a short time, he was sent back to Jamestown because he failed to exhibit sufficient empathy with the Indian interest. Powhatan eventually came to think better of the boy, but Savage remained an Englishman with a specialized knowledge of Indian ways. Another young colonist, Henry Fleet, was captured by the Potomacs in 1621, spent five years with them, and became "better proficient in the Indian language than mine own." He became an Indian trader, but showed no loss of loyalty to the English.[42]

Not so Captain Henry Spelman. He landed at Jamestown in 1609 and soon afterward was taken by Smith to negotiate with the Indians at the falls of the James. Smith planned to make him an interpreter and exchanged him for an Indian village (at least so Spelman believed). He stayed with the Indians for only a short period, and then turned up again in Jamestown. This time George Percy sent him off to Powhatan, with whom by his own account he remained six months. He played a dangerous game among the Indians. Powhatan used him to deliver a message to Jamestown that resulted in the slaughter of some thirty Englishmen. On one occasion Pocahontas interceded for his life. Before his luck ran out (it did later), he fled to the Potomacs, where life was less precarious. He had been living with them for more than a year when Samuel Argall stopped by and offered a ransom for his return to Jamestown. These months among the Indians were apparently formative. He became "the best linguist of the Indian Tongue of this Countrys" and spent a good portion of his time living, trading, and negotiating with the natives. Though his services were of undoubted value, he seemed to arouse animosity among his fellow Virginians. In 1619 the General Assembly tried him on the charge of casting dishonor upon the colony in conversation with Opechancanough. He was convicted, degraded in rank, and condemned to serve as the governor's interpreter for seven years. John Pory, the assembly speaker, disliked his attitude when the sentence was read and claimed that Spelman "had in him more of the savage then of the Christian." Spelman had served the colony too well. By learning to deal with the Indians, he had edged too close to the savage world.[43]

Few prisoners who returned from the native villages failed to carry some mark of savagism. Indians usually killed male prisoners, though they welcomed women and children. Some led arduous lives for a period, but most were eventually admitted into native society. Spenser described the captivity of Pastorella among the Satyrs: "With them as housewife ever to abide,/To milk their gotes, and make them cheese and bred." The situation was little different among the Indians. Manners gradually adapted to circumstances; dress and hairstyle conformed to the native pattern; attachments formed, and some whites, especially the young, preferred their new situation. The process of acculturation proved effective with some prisoners. But often the procedure was forced, for in their own villages the Indians were ardent proselytizers. For the English such transformations, forced or voluntary, were unforgivable not only because they implied a betrayal of one's family, friends, and social loyalties, but also because to become an Indian was to embrace savagism—to fall from grace.[44]

Desertion of the colony for life in the Indian villages became a problem almost immediately, and it continued to plague the Jamestown authorities until the massacre of 1622. As soon as food ran short, the colony's small complement began to drift toward the Indians. The Spanish minister reported in 1612 that some forty or fifty Englishmen had married and lived with the Indians. Doubtless many more had made the transit and were never heard from again. In 1621 the company noted that 120 persons either died in passage or ran away. Obviously the num-

bers fluctuated with the health and tranquility of the settlement, but defection remained a critical problem—so much so
that in 1610 the colony made flight to the Indians an offense
punishable by death. The leadership repeated the stricture in
1611, adding that anyone who was captured by Indians and did
not take an opportunity to escape would be subject to the same
penalty. Often enough Indians welcomed these English rene-
gades, though not always. In 1619 an Englishman named Poule,
"in a manner turned heathen," lived among the Potomacs. Between 1616 and 1621 a fugitive named Robert Marcum resided
with the Eastern Shore natives. Some of the earliest who fled,
desperate for food, were humiliated by the natives and put to
menial tasks. In 1609 Smith reported with a certain pleasure
that the Indians had adopted the same rules governing work
that he had initiated at Jamestown. Visitors who did not work
did not eat. The Indians returned the runaways to Smith's jurisdiction, where they were duly punished. On another occasion
the Jamestown authorities employed the tribesmen to track
down a band of colonists who had fled south. Yet the leakage
of population continued, leading to the conclusion that, in comparison to the dismal existence in Jamestown, savagism possessed certain charms.[45]

It clearly did for the two German artisans (Adam and Frantz)
Smith dispatched to Werowocomoco in 1608 to build a house
for Powhatan. Their behavior revealed to Smith the acute danger posed to the colony by the attractions of savagism. They
agreed to "live with Powhatan as his chiefe affected: free from
those miseries that would happen the Colony," advised him to
withdraw into the wilderness, and, on another occasion, recommended that he attack the English. They also sought allies in
Jamestown (one of them infiltrating the colony in Indian dress
for that purpose) and arms and metal tools for their new countrymen. Powhatan had them murdered in the winter of 1609–10
because he feared they would betray him as they had Smith.[46]

Obviously some Englishmen either failed to perceive the
menace of savagism or calculated only the immediate advantage
of alliance with the Indians for survival in the New World.
Others, no doubt, joined the Indians or adopted their ways
fully intending to discard civil restraint and to enjoy the reputed

freedom of the savage condition. For the leadership of the colony, for those who made its laws and directed its affairs, and for those who wrote about it, any hint, even under the pressure of necessity, that Englishmen might find life among the Indians superior to the measured existence of the settlements risked the triumph of savagism over civility. The irony that savagism worked both ways was lost on them. Englishmen who joined the Indians seeking release from the burdens of European society were as much animated by the doctrine of savagism as were those who feared the demise of civil order.

The coercive power of the doctrine was amply demonstrated by the failure of the colonists to perceive the nature of native society despite their continued dependence on that society. They recognized particular aspects of native culture, and even adopted some of them, but the theoretical structure of savagism remained intact. Had the colonists not drawn freely upon the output of native farming they could not have survived, yet they continued to see Indians as savages, immature and incompetent people who lived in a blighted world of endemic scarcity.

5

CONVERSION

Despite the implications of savagism, Englishmen were fully persuaded that their settlement in the New World would effect the transformation of native society. Whether noble savages required instruction in morality and the art of living–or whether ignoble savages could benefit from either–seemed less pertinent than the conviction that Christ commanded Englishmen to spread his religion among the heathens and that savage people ought to be thankful for the gifts of Christianity and civility. Many Englishmen went to the New World as conscious proselytizers, and native society endured monumental changes as a result of their coming. Yet the English failed in their missionary effort and enjoyed only limited success in inculcating the values of civility among the Indians. The reshaping of native society came gradually, as a consequence of disease, war, the loss of land, and the adjustments induced by the infiltration of European artifacts. In the years before 1622 all these processes had begun, but none were consummated until later in the century. Without the theoretical means with which to recognize the subtle processes of social change, the English attributed their failure to the Indians' rejection of civility. They expected spectacular results; they found instead the obdurate persistence of savagism.

More than a generation ago, Louis B. Wright argued convincingly that religion played an important role in the creation of the first English empire. Modern distinctions between piety and mammon carried little weight in the sixteenth and seventeenth centuries. Even when such distinctions did wield influence, Englishmen found no difficulty in discerning the uses of piety in spreading English influence and reaping the rewards of colonial exploitation. Perry Miller has pointed out that the celebrated religious enthusiasm of New England was by no means singular among New World colonies. The leaders and supporters of Virginia expressed the same commitment to Christianity and accepted the same obligations for the transmission of that commitment to the native inhabitants. Neither Virginians nor New Englanders enjoyed much success, but this disappointment was scarcely an indictment of the sincerity of their convictions. They held them honestly, though the Virginians may have found them a burden and the New Englanders a source of worry when their futility became evident.[1]

At the same time that Englishmen chafed over a "wretched and more than disastrous age" that fed their appetite for a primitive ideal, they entertained visions of extraordinary future accomplishments. The New World served both those needs. "Up then," Hakluyt incited Ralegh, "go on as you have begun, leave to posterity an imperishable monument of your name and fame, such as age will never obliterate. For to posterity no greater glory can be handed down than to conquer the barbarian, to recall the savage and the pagan to civility, to draw the ignorant within the orbit of reason, and to fill with reverence for divinity the godless and the ungodly." "Those who have any forward mindes in well doing to the generalitie of mankind," write Christopher Carleill of colonization, will perceive the merit "of reducing the savage people to Christianitie and civilitie. . ." "The children of Adam" require learning, argued William Kempe. "Look upon the barbarous nations, which are without it; compare their estate with ours. . . They for want of learning can have no laws, no civil policy, no honest means to live by, no knowledge of God's mercy and favour, and consequently no salvation and hope of comfort." Even in the unregenerate, wrote Henry Parry, discipline and respect for the commandments of God were necessary in order to avoid the punishments due to sinners and to preserve the peace of society. The impulse to convert the Indians drew on the deepest instincts of Europeans to do good, to eradicate savagism, and to form the world to their own liking. A learned Spaniard said of

Columbus's second voyage that the adventurer had set out "to unite the world and give to those strange lands the form of our own."[2]

Until 1622 public pronouncements from England and Virginia were virtually unanimous on the morality and expediency of bringing Christianity to the Indians of Virginia. They echoed Cortez in maintaining that "the chiefe and principall cause of our coming into this country, was to set forth the faith of Jesu Christ, & therewithal doth folow honour & profite which seldome times do dwell together."[3] Sermons, propagandistic literature, instructions to the colony's leaders, and histories of the colony announced the policy over and over again. Colonization demanded conversion of the Indians to Christianity. All other goals were subordinate to that overriding objective. In his "Discourse on Western Planting," Hakluyt counseled the queen to fulfill her obligations as defender of the faith by sending preachers to "those poore people wch have sitten so longe in darkness and in the shadowe of deathe. . ." This work, he insisted, should be "the principall and chefe of all others, accordinge to the comaundemente of our Saviour Christe."[4] Clergymen such as William Crashaw, William Symonds, Alexander Whitaker, and John Donne exhorted the Virginia Company to ship the Gospel to the Indians.[5] Yet the company scarcely required the reminder. From the beginning, company policy promoted missionary work "as the most pious and noble end of this plantacon. . ."[6] After years of colonial experience that should have drained him of illusions, if he had any to begin with, John Smith could write of the colonist: "If hee have any graine of faith or zeale in Religion, what can hee doe lesse hurtfull to any: or more agreeable to God, then to seeke to convert those poore Salvages to know Christ, and humanitie. . ."[7]

The conviction that the Indians must be converted allowed Englishmen to make sense out of the discovery of the New World. How could a continent have remained concealed for millennia and then been suddenly revealed if God had not intended it to happen in that way? Englishmen in the New World believed they played a role in God's providential plan. "Time doth new worlds display,/That Christ a church, o'er all the Earth may have. . ." God communicated to his people through

direct commands, as in the Gospels, but he also unfolded h
plan for the world through the instrumentality of secondary
cause. He enjoined Christians to spread his message, and the
discovery of the New World disclosed a vast field for its dissemi-
nation. "Consider also," wrote Dionyse Settle of Frobisher's
second voyage, "that Christians have discovered these countries
and people, which so long have byen unknowne, and they not
us: which plainly may argue, that it is Gods good will and
pleasure, that they should be instructed in his divine service
and religion, whiche from the beginning, have beene nouzeled
and nourished in Atheisme, grosse ignorance, and barbarous
behavior." Converting the Indians was more than an exercise
in English ethnocentrism. It made the English agents of a universal scheme ordained by God.[8]

Savagism posed small obstacle to the realization of the Christian mission in America. In fact, the more degraded the portrayal of the Indian the more persistent the determination to
raise him from ignorance and enlighten him with God's message. America should be settled "for the gaining and winning
to Christ his fold, and the reducing vnto a ciuill societie . . . of
so many thousands of those sillie, brutish, and ignorant soules,
now fast bound with the chaines of error and ignorance, vnder
the bondage and slavery of the Diuell." For Thomas Church-
yard, the benighted savage presented an extraordinary opportunity to combine material advantage with conversion. "And
surely this is a true testimonie of greate goodnesse intended,
that our Nation in suche a Christian sorte and maner, refuseth
no hazarde nor daunger, to bryng Infidelles too the knowledge
of the omnipotente God, yea, albeit great wealth and commoditie maie rise to us of their labours, yet the purpose of mani-
festyng Gods mightie woorde and maiestie among those that
feed like monsters (and rather live like dogges then men) doeth
argue not onely a blessed successe, but perswadeth a prosperous
and beneficiall retourne."[9] Savagism deserved abomination, but
at the same time it represented an occasion for the Christian to
realize the proper end of God's providential plan.

Despite the problem of savagism and the difficulties of converting Indians, the divine promise supplied reassurance of
success. Men would not have been directed to preach the Chris-

tian message if savage people were incapable of hearing it or were permitted to resist it. "As farre forth as we coulde perceive and understand by these people," observed John Florio of the Canadian Indians, "it were a very easie thing to bring them to some familiaritie and civilitie, and make them learne what one woulde. The Lord GOD for his mercies sake sette thereunto his helping hande when he seeth cause." Nature itself conspired to fulfill the divine plan, and every nation possessed the inner ability to throw off barbarism. "God hath sowen the seedes of every ones heart: which groweth more or lesse according to the pleasure of the seedeman, manifested in the proportioning of nature, whereof every climate hath severall stroke, as being an instrument whereby God frameth capabilitie more or less to comprehend the same." Englishmen needed only to look at themselves for evidence of the unity of mankind and the process by which the Indians might be rescued from the savage state. "One God created us," affirmed Whitaker, "they have reasonable soules and intellectual faculties as well as wee; we all have *Adam* for our common parent: yea, by nature the condition of us both is all one, the servant of sinne and slaves of the divell." Englishmen were asked to recall the condition of their own souls before they received the Gospel.[10]

History testified that the process had occurred before. Ancient Muscovites, Lacedaemonians, Germans, Gauls, Picts, Scotsmen, and an assortment of nearly forgotten people had once resembled the natives of the New World in their manner of life. Most had long since abandoned their savagism and accepted Christianity and civil manners. The experience of the ancient Britons held special meaning for sixteenth- and seventeenth-century Englishmen eager to sweep the New World clear of savagism. Doubts about the advantages to the Indians of conversion would be answered by comparing the "present happiness" of Englishmen "with our former ancient miseries wherein we had continued brutish, poor, and naked Britains to this day if Julius Caesar, with his Roman legions (or some other) had not laid the ground to make us tame and civil." William Strachey asked rhetorically: "Were not Caesars Britaines as brutish as Virginians?" Apparently he took satisfaction from the answer: "The Romane swords were best teachers of civilitie to this & other countries neere us." The precedents were clear. Indians could be expected to make the same progress that had brought the English to their present enviable position.[11]

The Indians' savage condition conspired to aid the Europeans in fulfilling their missionary obligations. To be sure, they were capable enough despite savagism. Hakluyt announced that the natives of the northern continent were "of better wittes then those of Mexico and Peru, as hath bene found by those that have had some triall of them: forsaking their idolatrie . . ."[12] More commonly, Englishmen prefaced comments about native abilities with the notation that the Indians were a "simple and rude" people, without laws or the knowledge of God. Yet precisely because these native qualities were seen as limitations they posed no obstacle to the conversion of the Indians. "Gentle and tractable" Indians were "most apt to receive the Christian Religion and to subject themselves to some good government." The less the natives knew, the fewer their cultural encumbrances, and the more readily they would be formed anew in the white man's image. Columbus believed that Indians would be converted easily because they showed no signs of religion. When he proposed to teach them Spanish, he spoke as though the process would be akin to teaching them to speak. He hypothesized that they possessed the human potential for speech, but that they utterly lacked any semblance of culture and hence had nothing to say. Peter Martyr caught his meaning succinctly: "For lyke as rased or unpaynted tables, are apte to receaue what formes soo ever are fyrst drawn thereon by the hande of the paynter, even soo these naked and simple people, doo soone receaue the customes of oure Religion, and by conversation with oure men, shake of theyr fierce and native barbarousnes." Marc Lescarbot used a similar image—a blank tablet that awaited the addition of color—to support his own optimism concerning the prospects for converting the Indians.[13]

Englishmen saw hope for conversion even when it became clear that the Indians professed a rival religion. The Virginia Company took the precaution of instructing Thomas Gates to annihilate the priestly class in order to make way for conversion to Christianity. Worship of the devil had to be eliminated before Indians could be expected to accept the Christian message. At the same time, despite the assumptions of savagism about the absence of religion among natives, Englishmen found it difficult to believe that a people could be devoid of the religious impulse. Regardless of appearances, "no Nation vnder the sunne [was] so barberous . . . but aymed at the worshippe of God, and either worshipped him or some thing els in his place." This "religious affection . . . doth remaine written by the finger of God, in the harts and consciences of all men living, howe rude sauage or barberous soeuer they be." Whether savages lacked the primal religious instinct or manifested traces of religious inclination natural to all men, their conversion to Christianity was expected momentarily.[14]

Even though American natives seemed more likely to comply with than to resist the friendly efforts of the English to convert them, the question remained open and company policy beginning in 1609 expressed a willingness to adopt other means if the Indians proved recalcitrant. In 1616 Francis Bacon issued some free advice that revealed how close to the surface was the temptation to resort to compulsion. He cautioned the Duke of Buckingham that the English should "make no extirpation of the natives under pretence of planting Religion: God surely will no way be pleased with such sacrifices."[15] Doubtless, Englishmen believed in this principle. Their strongest expectations supported it. Yet misgivings persisted. Ignoble savages could not be fully trusted to conform to God's plan. Englishmen knew that circumstances might require a resort to more forceful methods.

The Spaniards provided substantial testimony to the willingness of the native people to abandon the old religion and conform to the beliefs and practices of Christianity. If Englishmen were to believe Peter Martyr, it was only necessary to condemn native idolatry, preach the doctrine of one God, and give the Indians a picture of the Virgin. Without protest the Indians supposedly smashed their idols, cleaned the dried blood from their altars, placed the Virgin in an honored position, and erected a cross on the roof of their temple. In Mexico, according to Gómara, the native leaders expressed a willingness to follow the Spanish religion, though they were troubled by the need to forsake many generations of belief and feared the reaction of the populace. But to Acosta the solution was straightforward: "When they shew the Indians their blind errors by lively and plaine reasons, they are presently perswaded and yeelde admirabley to the trueth." The Spaniards had enjoyed striking successes in establishing their religion in the New World, and the English could not help but admire them for it, though they feared Catholicism and condemned Spanish cruelty.[16]

The English knew very well that the Spaniards often employed duress in gathering converts in the New World. Translations of Martyr, Gómara, Las Casas, Oviedo, and Acosta had all appeared by the time the English settled in Jamestown, and had recorded in rich detail the Spanish campaign to rid the New World of idolatry and enforce a new Christian dispensation. The English disapproved of Spanish methods, especially late in the sixteenth century after the two countries went to war.[17] But they learned from the Spanish experience. As they admired Spanish success when the Indians willingly accepted Christianity, they also noted that the Spaniards often found it necessary to appeal to force in doing God's work. The English themselves had done the same thing in Ireland.[18] When affairs in America turned nasty, when the Indians proved reluctant or insincere converts, the English would propose a more vigorous policy of proselytization. Robert Gray communicated English ambivalence on the subject. He was convinced that men by nature craved correct principles. If they believed otherwise it was the consequence of faulty education, which English missionaries would soon correct. Yet he was not quite as certain as he seemed. "A wise man, but much more a Christian, ought to trie all meanes before they undertake warre: divastation and depopulation ought to be the last thing which Christians should put in practise, yet forasmuch as everie example in the scripture . . . is a precept, we are warranted by this direction of Joshua, to destroy wilfull and convicted Idolaters, rather then to let them live, if by no other means they can be reclaimed."

In his later years, Smith, who had never been very enthusiastic about the plan to convert the Virginia Indians, came to question its very feasibility. He quoted a bitter letter from Jonas Stockam, a clergyman who had discovered little response to God's message in the Virginia colony. Every attempt to convert the Indians by "faire meanes" had failed. They "devoure" the gifts offered to them, "and so they would the givers if they could." Efforts to convert them with kindness were met with "derision and ridiculous answers." Young English boys sent to learn their language and gain knowledge of their society "returne worse than they went." "I can finde no probability by this course to draw them to goodnesse: and I am perswaded if *Mars* and *Minerva* goe hand in hand, they will effect more good in an houre, then those verball Mercurians in their lives. . ." He saw slight hope of accomplishment until the "Priests and Ancients have their throats cut. . ."[19]

The object of this sanguinary policy was as much the infusion of civility into native life as the conversion of Indians to Christianity. Englishmen, as did other Europeans, distinguished Christianity from civility–though they seldom separated the two. Long experience had taught that non-Christians could be civil; it was equally plain that the process of transcending savagism required conversion to Christianity and the adoption of civil manners. Discussions of the Indians' future invariably combined Christianity and civility. Both were essential ingredients for the transformation of native culture. Neither held priority over the other. As Crashaw phrased the prescription: "We give the Savages what they most need. 1. Civilitie for their bodies. 2. Christianitie for their soules." "For what more pleasant Sacrifyce can we offer in this life, unto our GOD," wrote John Frampton in a subtle interweaving of the two themes, "than to labour in all that ever wee may, to bring the Barbarous to Civilitie, the Rude to knowledge, the superstitious to the true & lively worship of his name, to win them from vanitie to veritie, from death unto life?" Common humanity and Christian charity, maintained Purchas, obliged Englishmen "to recover if it be possible, as by Religion, from the power of Sathan to God; so by humanity and civility from Barbarisme and Savagenesse to good manners and humaine polity." To make the Indians Christian implied making them civil. No one proposed the establishment of civility without Christianity.[20]

The direct method of conversion appeared most appropriate to Englishmen who trusted in the receptivity of the Indians and the persuasiveness of the Christian message. At Roanoke, Hariot proceeded to deliver his message with little deviousness. "Manie times and in every towne where I came, according as I was able, I made declaration of the contentes of the Bible; that therein was set foorth the true and onelie GOD, and his mightie workes, that therein was contayned the true doctrine of salvation through Christ, with manie particularities of Miracles and chiefe poyntes of religion. . ." Though he clearly distinguished the doctrine from the book, the Indians found the latter more attractive. They were "glad to touch it, to embrace it, to kisse it, to hold it to their brests and heades, and stroke over all their bodie with it . . ."[21] The direct approach yielded scarcely better results in Virginia, but a Protestant culture was bound to rely heavily on the preaching of the word. Clergymen were encouraged to go to the New World to strengthen the faltering defenses of Christian civility among English settlers and to bring the Gospel to the unwashed savages. In 1618 the company instructed Governor Yeardley to set aside glebe lands to furnish an annual salary of £200 for each clergyman. In order "to allure the Heathen people to submit themselves to the Scepter of Gods most righteous and blessed Kingdome," in 1620 the colony required every borough to provide for a minister. Little came of the effort. Many of the clergymen died soon after reaching Virginia. Not all were dedicated to the task of bearing "the name of God to the Gentiles." The colonists and their ministers were usually too fearful or too harassed to promulgate the word, and the Indians too pleased with the old ways to listen.[22]

The English attempt to transform native society was not without subtlety. From the beginning they realized that more would be required to convert the Indians than formal presentation of Christian principles. It was widely assumed that all Englishmen would be missionaries who would bring civil ways to America and convert the Indian by example. George Thorpe, the company's agent for the college lands, recommended gentleness in approaching the conversion of the natives. He "was so tender over them, that whosoever under his authority had given them but the least displeasure or discontent, he punished them severely." When the Indians complained of the fierce mastiffs owned by the colony, Thorpe had some of them killed in their presence. He reported to the company in 1621 that the

Indians "affect English ffassions" and would be "alured" into more extensive imitation of English ways by gifts of "apparell & househouldestufe." For Opechancanough he constructed an English-style house. After the massacre, many Englishmen became convinced that the hospitality shown to the Indians had been a critical factor in the heavy toll of dead. The population of the colony was widely dispersed because of the desire for more tobacco lands, but also because the colonial authorities hoped that Englishmen living among the Indians would further the growth of civility. By opening their homes to the Indians, exchanging goods and knowledge, and exposing the natives to the proficiency of the white man's world, the English thought that native society would gradually be recast.[23] John Rolfe hoped by "piety, clemency, courtysie and civill demeanor (by which meanes som are wonn to us already) to convert and bring to the knowledge and true worshipp of Jesus Christ 1000:s of poore, wretched and mysbeleiving people . . ." Of course this indirect approach assumed the cooperation of the white populace and a level of piety that the Indians would find attractive. The company ordered "that the people in Virginia bee trayned up in true religion, god lives and vertue, that ther example may be a meanes to winn the Infidells to God. . ."[24]

For English virtue to prove effective in transforming native society, systematic and intimate relationships would have to be established. Robert Johnson formulated a twofold plan: "Take their children, train them up with gentleness, teach them our English tongue and the principles of religion; win the elder sort by wisdom and discretion, make them equal with your English in case of protection, wealth, and habitation, doing justice on such as shall do them wrong." "Instead of iron and steel, you must have patience and humanity to manage their crooked nature to your form of civility. . ." Repeatedly the company pressed the colonists to bring native children into their homes in order to teach them English and the manners and attitudes of civility. Indian children captured in war might be apprenticed and thus serve a useful purpose while they were freed from the bondage of savagism. Others, more favored, would be sent to England to be educated.[25] Adults presented a more difficult problem. They too might benefit from closer contact with English culture, and they could serve the English in countless ways—"in killing Deere, fishing, beatting of Corne and other workes. . ." But having Indians in close proximity always presented a danger, and it was therefore decided that they should be admitted into English territory only in small numbers and in heavily populated areas. A good guard was to be kept on them at night, no Englishman was to entertain them alone, and they were to be housed separately from the whites.[26] Children would be welcomed, but adults could enter the English world only with prudent safeguards.

The formalization of these plans came with the establishment of a college at Henrico to dispense education to the children of the Indians. In 1617 the king ordered the bishops to support a special collection throughout the realm. The next year the company set aside 10,000 acres to support the college. Bequests in various amounts added to a growing endowment. Soon tenants arrived to work the land, buildings were erected, and a school rector was sent to direct the affairs of the college. In addition, the company accepted donations to establish a collegiate school at Charles City which would offer elementary education to Indians and then send them on to the college. It was an ambitious scheme cut short by the massacre. Not until late in the century did a college come into existence with an Indian school attached to carry out in part the original plan.[27]

The English scheme failed to transform native life. Although money flowed into the colony for missionary purposes and much preparation went into the new college, instructions from London were never sufficiently compelling to make either whites or Indians do what they chose not to do. The Henrico college itself never existed and hence educated no Indians; few became Christians or acquired the special skills that would have admitted them to the sacred precincts of civility. Doubtless the major reason lay in the inherent obduracy of culture. Without powerful reasons to change, the Indians clung to the old ways. The English, of course, sought nothing less than a total transformation of native society, a cataclysmic change that could have come about only in the most extraordinary circumstances and that probably would have spelled the disintegration of the Indians as a people. Within a century, as war, disease, and the pressure of English settlements became more destructive, native society did suffer such a calamitous breakdown. But in the immediate situation the English failed as missionaries because the Indians preferred not to cooperate with the collapse of their way of life, and many colonists could see little advantage in making white men out of Indians. For example, the colonial authorities charged with the task of attracting converts soon found that the "Indians are in noe sort willinge to sell or by fayer meanes to part with their children. . ." As for the colonists, George Thorpe quickly discovered the truth: "There is scarce any man amongst us that doth soe much as afforde them a good thought in his hart and most men wth theire mouthes give them nothinge but maledictions and bitter execrations beinge thereunto falslye caried wth a violent misp[er]swation . . . that these poore people have done unto us all the wronge and iniurie that the malice of the Devill or man cann affoord. . ."[28] Thorpe represented the views of the company and the few committed to its plan; he did not reflect the prevailing opinion among the colonists.

The case of Pocahontas, who represented the only notable success in the English attempt to lure the Indians from savagism, revealed some of the reasons for the failure to attract more. Pocahontas had demonstrated an early attachment to the English. She had visited Jamestown often and had taken the English part in her father's village. Why she should have found the English so attractive—in view of the fact that her father and her countrymen did not—remains a mystery. Nevertheless she was a virtually ideal subject for the English to tutor in the ways of civility. Not only was she a willing convert, but the fact of her relationship to Powhatan promised to breach the wall of savagism that obstructed all English efforts to spread European manners. Of course no such breach occurred. Pocahontas remained a singular specimen of what the English wished to accomplish in the New World.

For all her apparent interest in the English, Pocahontas went over to their camp only after Samuel Argall abducted her in April 1613. She had not visited Jamestown in three years and in the meantime she had married an Indian. Argall took her prisoner as a matter of state policy. He gave no hint that he intended her conversion. Once she was in his hands, he dispatched a runner to Powhatan with terms that revealed his intentions. Powhatan was instructed to "send home the Englishmen (whom he deteined in slaverie, with such armes and tooles, as the Indians had gotten, and stolne) and also a great quantitie of corne. . ." Doubtless her conversion was on some English minds, but it did not enter into the kidnapping scheme as formulated by Argall and Governor Dale. Once she had arrived at Jamestown, Pocahontas renewed her affection for the English–in part because she began to doubt the affection of her father. Powhatan did not immediately respond to the English demands. When he did, Pocahontas became a hostage who would remain with the English as a token of peace. By 1613 Powhatan was ready for an end to hostilities with the English. They had more than proven their military capacity, and he saw clearly the need to moderate their hostility and demands for food. Hence he determined to use his daughter's presence in their town as an opportunity to come to an agreement. Pocahontas stayed at Jamestown, was placed under the care of Alexander Whitaker, a clergyman of Puritan bent, and met John Rolfe. Within a year she had accepted Christianity and agreed to become Rolfe's wife. Thus, the most important of the English conversions occurred as a secondary consequence to the conflict between whites and Indians. Moreover, it took place only after Pocahontas had become alienated from her own family, had developed an affection for Rolfe, and had been subjected to the intensive proselytization of the Reverend Whitaker.[29]

Rolfe's struggle with himself over his libidinal fancy for the attractive Indian revealed an important aspect of the problem of conversion. He was determined to grasp any justification but "the unbridled desire of carnall affection" for his marriage to Pocahontas. He would marry her "for the good of this plantation, for the honour of our countrie, for the glory of God, for my own salvation, and for the converting to the true knowledge of God and Jesus Christ, an unbeleeving creature . . . ," but not because he loved her. The problem was savagism–and with a special puritanical twist. Rolfe interpreted his affection for Pocahontas as a "diabolical assault," against which he struggled mightily. He feared that he would incur God's displeasure as had "the sonnes of Levie and Israel for marrying strange wives." It was because Pocahontas's "education hath bin rude, her manners barbarous, her generation accursed, and so discrepant in all nurtriture from my selfe" that Rolfe trembled when he thought of her. In his mind libidinal fantasies, biblical prohibitions, and fear of Satan had become entwined with the doctrine of savagism. He appeased his anxieties only by resolving to convert Pocahontas and thus purify his sexual urges and obliterate the vestiges of savagism.[30]

Englishmen tended to view conversion as an attack on savagism, and consequently as a method of assuaging their own apprehensions about the preservation of civility. The doctrine of savagism had presented subtle obstacles to the implementation of a formal program. Savages might be saved from their woeful condition—indeed, it was imperative that this be done—but Englishmen still seemed to shrink from a concerted effort to convert them. Rolfe's internal quandary was symptomatic of the larger issues of savagism that confronted all Englishmen. Satan made a better enemy than he did a candidate for conversion. Ignoble savages may not have been beyond redemption, but the state of relations with them never seemed settled enough to warrant hope that they would cease their hostility. At a terrible expenditure of psychic energy, Rolfe had managed to surmount the problem of savagism and to bring Pocahontas within the fold of civility, but as time went on most Virginians entertained little expectation of bringing in the rest of the native population.

Pocahontas went to England in 1616, as did many other Indians before and after her. She had learned her lessons, having been "taught to speake such *English* as might well be understood, well instructed in Christianitie, and was become very formall and civill after our English manner . . ."[31] In one sense the trip was a success. Pocahontas was received widely in English society and enjoyed her day at court. The company took the opportunity to show off the fruits of its efforts in America. But the visit ended badly—precisely as the vast majority of such voyages did end. As the homeward-bound ship moved down the Thames, she became ill, disembarked at Gravesend, and died soon afterward. For hundreds of Indians who found the white man's world attractive and made the expedition to Europe, the end was the same.[32]

Of course not all Indians went to Europe willingly. From the time that Columbus returned to Spain in 1493 with eight Arawaks from Hispaniola, Europeans regularly abducted and enticed Indians to come to the Old World. After 1501, when Cabot landed three Eskimos (or perhaps Micmacs), a steady stream of American natives visited England. They were at first a great curiosity, an exotic testimony to the discovery of new lands. "The like of this strange infidel was never seen, read, nor hearde of before," wrote a contemporary about the Eskimo who returned with Frobisher from his first voyage. "His arrival was a wonder never known to city or realm. Never like a great matter happened to any man's knowledge." Every voyage began with instructions, or with the intention, to bring back a human exhibit from the New World. Visitors were often received at court, made a splash in society, and toured the fairs and public entertainments where the curious gawked at them for a price. Elizabeth satisfied her own appetite for the exotic by instructing Frobisher: "You shall not bring above three or four persons of that country, the which shall be of divers ages, and shall be taken in such sort as you may best avoid offence of that people." Frobisher fulfilled only part of the queen's request. He brought back a specimen, but not without exciting the antagonism of the natives.[33]

By the time the English became active in exploration and colonization, the Indians had long since been alerted and antagonized by this practice. Spanish, Portuguese, and French ships coasted the eastern shore of the American continent picking up Indians at random and selling them as slaves in other parts of the New World and in Europe. A noted example was Don Luis de Velasco, the Indian responsible for the destruction of the Spanish mission on the York River in 1571. He had been captured some years before and brought to Spain for training. Usually, Indians were plucked from the continent a few at a time, but occasionally substantial numbers were taken. For example, some fifty Indians from Brazil took part in a pageant at Rouen in 1550, and in 1586 Francis Drake picked up 300 natives in the Caribbean and carried them to Roanoke and perhaps to England.[34] The most notorious English case involved a Captain Hunt who captured twenty-four Indians in New England in 1611 and sold them at the Straits. Almost a century of kidnapping instilled in the coastal tribes a spirit of caution in dealing with the Europeans, and in many districts open hostility to the landing of any strangers. According to Smith, Hunt's exploit served "to moove their hate against our Nation, as well as to cause my proceedings to be so much more difficult." In the winter of 1607–8, when Smith fell into the hands of Opechancanough, the Indians suspected him of responsibility for a murder and an abduction that had occurred two or three years before on the Pamunkey River.[35]

Confronted with native hostility stemming from heedless marauding along the coast by European ships, some few traders and colonists perceived the significance of their actions.[36] Yet virtually no self-examination occurred. White men assumed that they were within their rights in snatching Indians from the New World and transporting them thousands of miles from their homes. Just as a tourist might arrive home with a trophy of his trip, white men regularly called at European ports with cargoes of American humanity. Savagism imposed no burden on the European, for savages could claim none of the rights or social attachments that accrued to a civil order. It could only be supposed that Indians would like nothing better than to escape the miseries of life in savage America. And, indeed, some Indians appeared to leave the New World voluntarily. At least many boarded ship willingly, though they could scarcely have been conscious of the implications of the act. Except by the slavers, the natives were well-treated. A few returned to America in good health. They had come to Europe as specimens to be prized, shown off, and swayed toward the ways of their captors.

From the beginning the practice involved more than the pillaging of the native population. If the captured Indians landed in reasonably good health, they were bound to be influenced by the new situation and hence to take on a special value to their keepers. That the process worked, at least in part, may be gleaned from Robert Fabyon's account of the natives brought to England by Cabot in 1501. "These were clothed in beastes skinnes, and ate rawe fleshe, and spake such speech that no man could understand them, and in their demeanour like to bruite beastes, whom the king kept a time after. Of which upon two yeeres past after I saw two apparelled after the manner of Englishmen, in Westminster pallace, which at the time I could not discerene from Englishmen, till I was learned what they were. But as for speech, I heard none of them utter one word."[37] Before long, speech became an essential part of the education of Indian visitors. They discarded their skins of beasts, gave Englishmen a short course in native language, and learned to communicate in English. Some who visited England returned to America to do the white man's work. Yet because their numbers remained small, and because even fewer survived, Indian visitors could form only a minor part of the acculturative process.

Doubtless the English expected more of their pupils. In September 1584 Manteo and Wanchese, from the Carolina coast, were landed in England by Philip Amadas. Ralegh made judicious use of them to promote his colonial enterprise. They were taught English, dressed in "brown taffeta," and quizzed about the character of their country. Thomas Hariot picked up some Algonquin from them. On this occasion both Indians remained in England for about eight months; in 1586–7 Manteo spent the better part of a year there before returning to America with John White. For unexplained reasons, Wanchese betrayed the English soon after his return to the New World, but Manteo proved more reliable. "He behaved himselfe toward us as a most faithful English man." After Manteo accepted baptism, White installed him as chief of the Roanoke and Croatoan Indians with the proviso that he should recognize the overlordship of Ralegh and the queen. Manteo found it impossible to exercise authority over the Roanoke Indians and finally retreated to his own people at Croatoan. It cannot be said whether his loyalty remained secure enough to aid the colonists left by White. The English learned something from their two guests, and they unquestionably added to the experience of the Indians. In what measure this interchange affected the Carolina natives can only be guessed. But most important, the policy of molding

Indians into agents of English colonization proved a failure.[38]

In Virginia the English hoped Namontack, Powhatan's adviser, would aid them in softening the savagism of the Virginia Indians. With Powhatan's permission, he accompanied Christopher Newport to England in April 1608 and returned in September. He appears to have made a later voyage to England with another native named Matchumps who, according to Smith, murdered him in Bermuda sometime in 1609 or 1610. Smith thought Namontack a shrewd fellow. For its own purposes the company passed him off in London as Powhatan's son. Smith believed that Powhatan sent Namontack to England "to know our strength and countries condition." When he returned, Smith continued to look upon him as an ally, though the brevity of his stay in England and his second departure and death a year later gave him little influence in the process of acculturation.[39] Powhatan dispatched another agent to England in 1616 to accompany Pocahontas, her husband, and a sizable native entourage. He seems to have discovered that he could not count the English population single-handedly but learned little more. Some of the Indian women who crossed the ocean with Pocahontas adopted English ways. After she died they were supported by the Virginia Company and two of them turned up in Bermuda in 1621 in search of husbands. The plan was to send them to Virginia where their presence might be useful in spreading Christianity and civility among their countrymen. The same role had been intended for Pocahontas.[40]

Indian visitors played a minor part in the acculturative process largely because so few returned to the New World to report their experiences in Europe. The vast majority died on shipboard or soon after they were exposed to life in a new land. The three Indians, possibly Powhatans, who demonstrated the use of the canoe in the Thames in September 1603, reached London in the midst of a raging plague. Some American natives survived and did not return; they faded into the European population, never to be heard from again. Some who did return were at best ambivalent in their loyalties. Exposure to the white man's world might have broadened perspectives, but it did not necessarily obliterate native loyalties. Englishmen tended to think that the sight of the Old World would purge the Indians of their savage prejudices and mold them into agents of civility. They were wrong for a variety of reasons, but in great measure because the rate of attrition among Indians in Europe was extraordinarily high. For most native people a free trip to the Old World meant death rather than acculturation.[41]

Of all the instruments of acculturation applied by Europeans to the New World, trade may ultimately have had the most profound effects. It started earliest. Every explorer or fisherman who plied the American coast engaged in a little commercial intercourse. When English settlement began in earnest in the early seventeenth century, Europeans and Americans had been exchanging goods for more than a hundred years. It was inevitable that the exchange should take place, if only because both peoples recognized commerce as an important human activity. As a consequence great changes were worked in the character of native society and new industries developed in Europe to support commerce with the American Indians. In exchange for furs and skins, the Europeans supplied a rich assortment of artifacts that introduced a stone age people to the age of iron and modern textiles. Yet the results were not immediately decisive. The Indians absorbed great quantities of European goods without losing the integrity of their society. No doubt acculturation induced strains in the native social fabric, but dependence and cultural collapse came later. In the early years the Indians engaged in trade with the English without obvious pathological consequences. They frequently did business on their own terms, and they managed to obtain one artifact—firearms—that proved immensely effective when the time came to resist English encroachments by force.[42]

The English expected much from the New World. It promised imperial prestige and economic relief through the reduction of Spanish power and the opening of new markets for English goods. But they learned very early that the Indians of the northern continent would not serve the economic purposes of English industry in the way many promoters of colonization had anticipated. The problem was savagism. In their rudimentary condition of life, the Indians could offer only simple products for exchange and consequently could absorb only limited quantities of what the English produced. The English believed that once the Indians were civilized, however, the situation would change. In his book on travelers, Sir Thomas Palmer defined the issue succinctly:

> For though there bee many Ilands in the World, that content themselves and live without the commodities of other places; neither have they other than a certaine naturall kinde of provision, distributed well and orderly alike to all Nations for the naturall support thereof: Yet being once brought into civilitie, and to the taste of the World, either to be equall to others, or to be engreatned; there is no Nation or Countrie, but standeth in necessarie neede and want of forraine things: the which being once tasted of generally, it is almost impossible to be left and forgotten.[43]

Until this transition occurred, the English would be content with the raw materials of the New World.

Hakluyt perceived the problem at least in its elementary form. If a people have an appetite for English cloth, he advised, "then are you to deuise what commodities they haue to purchase the same withall. If they be poore, then you are to consider of the soyle, and how by any possibilitie the same may be made to enrich the[m] that hereafter they may haue somthing to purchase the cloth withall." Perhaps most important, he instructed wandering agents of English enterprise to keep an eye out for the products of the forest—"all the natural comodities of their country." The economic arguments of his "Discourse on Western Planting" stressed the potential of the continent rather than its industrial achievements. Whatever he may have hoped for the future, for the present Hakluyt recognized that the wealth of America lay in its natural resources.[44]

As it turned out, the two major commodities obtained by white men from Indians were not entirely natural resources. The fur and skin trade rested on a complex process that began in the forest but ended with a finished product. Indians were not simply hunters; they were manufacturers of skins and furs for a sophisticated European market.[45] In Virginia, food quickly became the major item of exchange between the two peoples. Only because the native economy yielded ample supplies at certain times of the year were the English able to eke out a sparse existence in the early years of the colony. The doctrine of savagism led Englishmen to expect a trade in raw materials only—until that time when the native peoples would acquire the productive skills and the appetite to consume that accompanied civility. In addition, particularly in Virginia, savagism obscured the significance of the natives' talent in trading the products of their economy for the goods offered by the English.

Evidence of the Indians' commercial instincts appeared in Virginia almost immediately. The colonists' desperate need for food led to the opening of a brisk exchange of goods. Smith did his utmost to keep prices low by hard bargaining and the threat of force. But he could control neither the leadership of the colony nor the colonists themselves. The natives first bartered for the trinkets designed specifically for the Indian trade, and then demanded tools, guns and weapons, and copper. Competition among the colonists and a shortsighted generosity in the colonial leadership drove up prices of Indian food and put the colony at a serious commercial disadvantage. According to Strachey, Powhatan obtained English copper so cheaply that he could sell it to his neighbors at a hundredfold profit. Not until the colony forbade private trading and the native society began to disintegrate did the balance shift toward the English. Savagism could no more explain the dependence of the English on native supplies than it could the extraordinary commercial success of the Indians with their English customers.[46]

Yet the Indians' apparent business acumen masked an important strain in native character—a strain the Europeans found admirable though tainted by savagism. Indians were hard traders and at the same time remarkably generous. They seemed to view the commercial nexus as more than an exchange of goods; it held for them broad social implications that puzzled the colonists. Mystified Europeans experienced both their wily trading and their openhanded munificence. Hakluyt recorded a meeting between Eskimos and English explorers in Greenland in 1585 that serves as an example. At the outset the English had "sworne by the sunne" after what they thought to be the Eskimo fashion. They exchanged greetings and one of the Eskimos kissed an Englishman's hand. "We were in so great credit with them upon this single acquaintance, that we could have any thing they had. We bought five Canoas from them:

wee bought their clothes from their backs. . ." The Eskimos
went to great lengths to please the English. They "would give
us whatsoever we asked of them and would be satisfied with
whatsoever we gave them." Cartier traded with the Micmacs
"till they had nothing but their naked bodies, for they gave us
al whatsoever they had . . ." When Lescarbot encountered a
similar brand of prodigal generosity, he probed a little deeper
into its meaning. "For the savages," he wrote, "have that noble
quality, that they give liberally, casting at the feet of him whom
they will honour the present that they give him. But it is with
hope to receive some reciprocal kindness, which is a kind of
contract, which we call, without name: 'I give thee, to the end
thou shouldst give me.' " Lescarbot had stumbled upon the
native practice of gift giving, a custom that invested commerce
with profound social significance. To European observers, however, native generosity appeared to stem from the savagism of
a simple and untutored people who had not yet acquired the
wit to know the value of property.[47]

John Smith had no such illusions. He thought Powhatan
a cunning and treacherous savage who was to be managed by
force and superior cunning. He knew the Indians could be
crafty traders, and he had done his utmost to keep prices for
food within the reach of English resources. One can appreciate
his chagrin, therefore, when he witnessed Christopher Newport's effort to introduce magnanimity into the commerce between whites and Indians. Newport met Powhatan at Werowocomoco in early 1608. The native leader put on an impressive
show of feasting, dancing, and much ceremonial display before
getting down to a serious exchange of goods. Powhatan proposed that Newport should first lay out all his trade items so
that he might choose what pleased him before reciprocating.
Smith saw this as nothing more than a ruse to raise prices, for
he had experienced the same procedure with the Chickahominies. He was right. Newport received little for his goods and
Smith saved the day only by introducing beads of blue glass,
a new commodity that Powhatan craved inordinately.

On the surface the occasion had the appearance of a cultural
standoff. Two peoples of ingrained trading habits engaged each
other in barter and neither managed to come out ahead. But

Smith's description of the events hinted at another meaning, one closely bound up with the problem of savagism. *"Powhatan,"* he wrote, "carried himselfe so proudly, yet discreetly (in his salvage manner) as made us all admire his naturall gifts, considering his education." By his proposal to Newport, Powhatan seemed "to despise the nature of a Merchant, did scorne to sell, but we freely should give him, and he liberally would require us." To Smith, this was clever business and at the same time evidence of Powhatan's savagism. Actually, it revealed the traditional practice of gift giving. The goods traded were not to be separated from the characters of the men making the exchange. *"Captaine* Newport," announced Powhatan, *"it is not agreeable to my greatnesse, in this pedling manner to trade for trifles; and I esteeme you also a great Werowance."* The giving was an expression of esteem which demanded a compensating gesture. Smith saw it as mere business, when in fact it cut much more deeply into the cultural fabric. He could understand the business aspect well enough, but the ceremonial gesture struck him as a manifestation of Powhatan's savage temper.[48]

Whatever the meaning of commercial transactions between white and Indian, trade and the presence of Europeans in the New World had worked important changes in native life. No doubt Lescarbot engaged in a bit of wish fulfillment when he interpreted native interest in the French as "a beginning of voluntary subiection, from whence a hope may be conceived that these people will soon conform themselves to our manner of living."[49] The English of Jamestown were less sanguine, though they certainly wished for the same end. They wanted Indians to become Englishmen. They could see, however, that few Indians would accept the propriety of such a transformation. Savagism retained a powerful hold over the native character. In the meantime the evidence mounted that the native people enjoyed an extraordinary appetite for the artifacts of the white man's culture and that this craving might accomplish what English persuasions could not.

On the northern fishing grounds in 1602 Bartholomew Gosnold encountered Indians whose lives had been touched by the yearly visits of Europeans. The English vessel was boarded by eight natives from "a Baske-shallop with mast and saile, an iron grapple, and a kettle of Copper." "One that seemed to be their Commander wore a Wastecoate of black worke, a paire of Breeches, cloth Stockings, Shooes, Hat, and Band." The rest were dressed in the native fashion, though "one or two more had also a few things made by some Christians. . ." They drew a map of the coast and "they spake divers Christian words, and seemed to understand much more than we, for want of Language could comprehend." This was the most frequented portion of the Atlantic shore north of the Spanish settlements, with obvious consequences for the native inhabitants. Although in the white man's eyes they remained savages, they had incorporated an array of European artifacts and cultural traits.[50]

English ships bound for the New World set sail laden with the "slight Merchandizes thought fit to trade with the people of the Countrey." A Bristol vessel sailed in 1602 with a cargo of "Hats of divers colours, greene, blue and yellow, apparell of course Kersie and Canvasse readie made, Stockings and Shooes, Sawes, Pick-axes, Spades and Shovels, Axes, Hatchets, Hookes, Knives, Sizzers, Hammers, Nailes, Chissels, Fish-hookes, Bels, Beades, Bugles, Looking-glasses, Thimbles, Pinnes, Needles, Thread, and such like." Peter Martyr had expressed some surprise that "even these naked men doo perceyve that an axe is necessarye for a thousande veses. . ." The Indians valued iron axes more than "greate heapes of golde." Certainly the Eskimos who dismantled a pinnace being built in Greenland by John Davis in order to get at the nails testified to the strong desire among the natives of the New World for the artifacts of European culture. Thevet recorded that Brazilian natives paid a substantial price in silver for four hatchets, "for they are necessarie to cut their woodde, the which before they were constrained to cutte with stones . . ."[51] With abundant evidence that European material culture had made its way in America, the English had reason to hope that savagism would recede. The process of exchange, no doubt, introduced the Powhatan people to many new and useful artifacts and eventually made them dependent on the English. But in the short run, at least until the massacre, the commercial initiative remained in the hands of the Indians. The English required food more urgently than the Indians demanded English goods. Trade changed

much about native culture, but without the wasting consequences of dependence Powhatan society managed to exchange
goods with the English and retain its integrity.

The persistent demand for arms by the Powhatans was symptomatic of the strength of native society. The English themselves were to blame. Soon after landing in Virginia they fought
a pitched battle with the Indians in which firearms proved decisive; then, to overawe the natives, they staged public demon-
strations of the power of their guns.[52] If the Indians needed to
be convinced, they soon were. English arms were clearly superior to their own for hunting and fighting. Powhatan never
missed an occasion to demand swords and guns in return for
corn. Newport was disposed to give him his way, but Smith entertained a healthy fear of firearms and steel weapons in the
hands of people he sensed as his enemies. It was, he said, "an
ill example to sell swords to Salvages." No matter the prohibitions imposed by the company or the efforts of colonial authorities to halt the movement of improved weapons into the
forest, the Indians obtained arms and became proficient in using
them. Argall understood the menace, and after the capture of
Pocahontas he demanded the return of English prisoners and
weapons. A few of each were returned, but the Indians remained an armed and, as the English would soon learn, dangerous people.[53]

If the English had been able to predict the effects of their
diseases on the natives, they might have been less fearful. Even
an armed Indian was helpless before the wasting consequences
of European ailments. Because of their relative freedom, in the
precontact period, from the numerous maladies that afflicted
Europeans, Indians were extraordinarily susceptible once the
white man brought his diseases to the new continent. At Roanoke, disease contaminated the native people soon after the
arrival of the English, and with devastating results. The colonists no sooner left a native village than the Indians fell sick
and died—"in some townes about twentie, in some fourtie, in
some sixtie, & in one six score, which in trueth was very manie
in respect of their numbers." Drake brought more sickness with
him when he stopped at Roanoke to transport the first colony
home. The Spanish Jesuits who landed among the Powhatans

in 1570 reported that the Indians had recently endured six years of famine and a decline in population. It seems likely that the natives' misfortune was associated with the diseases deposited along the coast by European vessels in the course of the sixteenth century. Similarly, Powhatan may have been referring to more than the consequences of war when, in 1608, he told Smith of "having seene the death of all my people thrice, and not one living of those 3 generations, but my selfe." At Jamestown, illness erupted among the English almost immediately after the initial complement landed. Doubtless the affliction touched the Indians as well, for in 1608 Smith found smallpox among the Accomacs of the Eastern Shore. A major epidemic struck the Powhatans in the summer of 1617; it also infected the English. At the same time a malady spread among the deer of the region, constituting a serious blow to the hunting economy of the natives and perhaps to their own health. In the summer of 1619 both Indians and whites became ill once again. The English tended to view disease as the work of Providence, as a chastisement visited upon them because they failed to conform to the divine covenant and upon the Indians because of their stubborn attachment to savagism and the wiles of Satan. They were not above using for their own benefit the demoralization that disease propagated among the native peoples. The Florida Indians tainted by Drake's men were convinced that "it was the Inglisshe God that made them die so faste." Hariot implied that the English viewed disease as a weapon of civility in the war against savagism.[54] Ultimately disease was the major killer of the native peoples and a principal cause of the decline of their society. It began its work even before the English established a permanent settlement and had greatly reduced the native population by the end of the seventeenth century.

Englishmen expected that the conversion of native society would accomplish the destruction of savagism by creating a compliant and dependent Indian who would identify himself with the white man's way of life. Some few Indians adopted Christianity, took on European manners, and developed loyalties to Englishmen, but the vast majority remained attached to the old ways and loyal to the tribal order. Even the indirect

changes that, in the next generation, would spell the disintegration of native life did not signal for the colonists any marked
transformation in the native character. The Indians seemed capable of selecting a variety of European artifacts and traits without doing apparent damage to the integrity of their culture. In
the case of firearms, they became proficient in the use of the
one item from the arsenal of European technology scarcely
calculated to reassure the colonists that their program of conversion had been a success. Hence, nothing happened between
1607 and 1622 to reverse the English conviction that Indians
were the willing adherents of savagism.

6

MASSACRE

Relations between Englishmen and Indians in Virginia culminated in the massacre of 1622. The interplay of the two societies evidenced by the dependence of the English on the Indians and the real and promised changes in native culture failed to allay the deep hostility between white and Indian. Neither mutually advantageous trade nor the absence of open conflict could quite dispel the English conviction that the Indians were savages. Although each side often behaved amicably toward the other, neither could feel secure with potentially hostile neighbors. For the English the doctrine of savagism invested most relationships with the Indians with the threat of violence. Moreover, since the earliest contacts these theoretical expectations had been realized in the actual fighting between the English and the native warriors. In the wake of the massacre, Englishmen were fond of claiming that it came as a complete surprise. So salutary had been their treatment of the Indians, they claimed, that they could find no explanation for the attack other than divine displeasure or the reappearance of savagism. In fact the English came to the New World convinced of the danger of savagism and they continued to see it as the informing principle of native behavior. The massacre may have surprised some, but most Englishmen held beliefs about Indians that fully anticipated the assault and may well have made it inevitable.[1]

The surface friendliness of Indian-white relations in Virginia between 1614 and 1622 masked a deeper conviction among Englishmen that savage Indians would not cease to be savages and hence could not be trusted. John Smith never stopped believing in the observation he made in the first months in Virginia. The "saluages," he said, were "our enemies, whom we neither knew nor vnderstood." When Humphrey Blunt was killed near Point Comfort in 1610, Thomas Gates saw the need to alter his view that the Indians would be won over by moderate treatment. "He well perceived how little a fair and noble entreaty works upon a barbarous disposition." Samuel Purchas thought Gates's retaliation perfectly reasonable. "Can a leopard change his spots?" he commented. "Can a savage, remaining a savage, be civil?" Whatever the English might have done during the years of peace to save the Indians from the grip of savagism, they continued loyal to the doctrine. The massacre was no more than the fulfillment of their convictions.[2]

Although James I had done his utmost to usher in a new age of peace, Englishmen of the sixteenth and seventeenth centuries were not only accustomed to violence and turmoil, they were inclined to look upon war as the dominant force of their age. Englishmen fought both on the Continent and in Ireland during the Elizabethan period, and at sea they sustained intermittent hostilities with France and Spain. Soldiers who could not be satisfied with the formal conflicts in which their country engaged sought out wars in exotic lands in which to employ their talents. They wrote popular accounts of their exploits and invariably sang the praises of manly battle. When a more technical literature on the science of war and its social meaning began to appear toward the middle of the sixteenth century, Englishmen became more widely acquainted with the reality and significance of international conflict. Ralegh began his essay on the question with the announcement that "the ordinary theme and argument of history is war" and went on to distinguish it from mere violence and to explain how deeply embedded war had become in the vicissitudes of life. War, wrote Dudley Digges, was "sometimes lesse hurtfull, and more to be wisht in a well governed State than peace . . ." The Earl of Essex, that most pugnacious of English noblemen, expressed similar feelings about the uses of war and the hazards of peace when he discerned a movement toward a cessation of hostilities with Spain. He regretted that Englishmen had "growen generally unwarlike; in love with the name, and bewitched with the delights of peace." Enough of the generation that invaded America managed to resist the "delights of peace" and to expect armed conflict.[3]

English writers believed that war held special meaning for the relationship between savagism and civility. With the advent of the civil condition, conflict acquired a new character. It was invested with ethical limits and rules of procedure, though it continued to occupy a significant place in the balance of life. War alternated with peace in the cyclic round of human affairs. But for the savage state in its ignoble form, war was the very substance of life. According to Sir John Smythe, an old-fashioned and voluble late sixteenth-century commentator on the science of war, men formed themselves into "common wealths, or other civill societies" precisely "to defende them[selves] from the vnaturall rapines, violence and oppressions, of their domesticall malicious neighbours . . ." Furthermore, argued Thomas Procter in a popular treatise on war, history has demonstrated that civil men have used arms "seeing mē to live in disorder without gouernmēt neither comfortably to thē, nor cōmodiouslye one for another [.] They extēded their power & dominion over thē to refourme them into an happie & civil sorte of life." Englishmen not only had reason to anticipate the eruption of violence in America in order to defend themselves against savage Indians, but they also believed that they owned a license to initiate it should armed might be required to overcome the threat of savagism.[4]

The literature of exploration supplied ample evidence of the dangers of violence that awaited Englishmen in the New World. Defense was critical. Fortifications were to be constructed promptly and kept guarded. Francis Bacon warned colonists that "at the first planting, or as soon as they can, they must make themselves defensible both against the natives and against strangers . . ." In dealing with the savages, it was important to be alert to any hostile activity. "He that takes heede and shields him selfe from all men, maye happe to scape from some. . ." It was considered better to act first than to risk death at the hands of malignant savages. "Such was their brutishness and their treacherie, that they would have betrayed vs vnder a shew of amitie: but we espying their treason gave the first onset, and euery shot of vs chose his man. . ." Samuel Purchas detected, in the Spanish experience, reasons for caution in dealing with Indians. He recorded an incident in de Soto's exploration of the continent when, in retaliation for the threat of conspiracy, the Spaniards captured thirty Indians, cut off their right hands, and sent them back to their villages. Purchas noted in the margin: "The grand conspiracy of the Indians against the Christians. Note well." It seemed plain that the Spaniards had fared badly in the New World. Great numbers had died for a variety of reasons, many at the hands of the Indians. "So fatall hath Florida beene to Spaine," wrote Purchas, "that (I hope) Virginia may have the greater dowry for her English husband." Success hinged on the ability of the English to read the signs of the savage malevolence that they expected to encounter.[5]

From Roanoke the English received an uncertain message. Indeed, virtually every account presented testimony of native friendliness combined with reports of enmity and danger. Arthur Barlowe concealed information concerning an initial clash with the natives in order to preserve the propagandized image of the new colony.[6] Yet the accounts of the various expeditions and the mysterious fate of the colony afforded evidence that the Indians remained true to their savage reputations. From the beginning the Roanoke settlers feared the Indians. Simão Fernandes, the Portuguese pilot, remembered previous visits to the Chespeake Bay region in which the Indians had been unfriendly, and he refused to return there with John White or to linger long on the coast. White himself may well have accompanied Frobisher to Baffin Island and witnessed the conflict with the Eskimos, of which he made a famous picture. Although the initial relationship between whites and Indians at Roanoke may have been peaceful, the two sides soon fell into conflict which the English believed led to the destruction of the colony. At one point in his *Historie*, William Strachey seemed convinced that, on the basis of Roanoke, antagonism was inevitable at Jamestown. He counseled that the natives should be treated with "love and friendship, vntill for our good purposes towardes them, we shall fynd them practize vyolence, or treason against vs (as they haue done to our other Colony at *Roanoak*)." He also appeared to believe that the

Roanoke colonists somehow survived among the Indians, only to be murdered some twenty years later by Powhatan at the behest of his shamans. Purchas was satisfied to have Powhatan merely present at their deaths, but left no doubt that the "savages dealt perfidiously with them." Whatever may have happened at Roanoke, it put the English on guard in their later colonial endeavors.[7]

Hence at Jamestown the English expected antagonism and violence from the start. The instructions from the company cautioned against allowing the "natural people" to come between the English and the coast because "you Cannot Carry Your Selves so towards them but they will Grow Discontented with Your habitation" and give aid to enemies who might invade the colony. Furthermore, the colonists were advised to "never trust the Country people with the Carriage of their Weapons. . ." Before reaching Virginia the expedition stopped at Nevis to replenish supplies. The English landed "well fitted with Muskets and other convenient Armes, marched a mile into the Woods; being commanded to stand vpon their guard, fearing the treacherie of the Indians, which is an ordinary vse [of] them and all other Sauages on this Ile. . ." They were not attacked; the natives they did see ran away. Once they set foot in Virginia there was enough violence to reinforce English expectations, though the anticipation persisted even when the natives proved friendly. "They are naturally given to trechery," wrote Gabriel Archer after a survey of the villages along the James, "howbeit we could not finde it in *our* travell vp the river, but rather a most kind and loving people." The doctrine of ignoble savagism preceded the opening of conflict between Indian and white man.[8]

Nevertheless the prediction of hostility between white and Indian was not without substance. Besides the misunderstandings between the two cultures, the failures in communication, and the little irritations that erupted into violence, Indians and Englishmen possessed divergent interests. The English came to the New World first to subjugate the native people and then to dispossess them. The Indians divined the English intention almost immediately. They temporized and sought accommodations, but they also fought to protect their stake in the American land. Eventually, in 1622, they launched a full-scale assault to exterminate the English and restore native hegemony in Virginia.

Indian hostility was linked to the realization that the English proposed a permanent establishment in Virginia. "The [native] people vsed *our* men well," reported Sir Walter Cope, a member of the first council, "vntill they found they begann to plant fortefye, Then they fell to skyrmishing & kylled 3 of *our* people[.]" The English attempted to quiet native suspicions of their claims. In May 1607, at the falls of the James River, Christopher Newport erected a cross with the "inscriptyon Jacobus Rex 1607 and his owne name belowe," a symbolic act with obvious implications for the English. When the Indians inquired concerning the meaning of the cross, Newport evaded the question. He told them the arms of the cross represented himself and Powhatan and "the fastening of it in the myddest was their United Leaug." For the time this seemed to satisfy the natives. Some Indians caught on before others. At a town near the falls of the James, "the Sauages murmured at our planting in the Countrie, whereupon this Werowance made answere againe very wisely of a Sauage, Why should you bee offended with them as long as they hurt you not, nor take any thing away by force, they take but little waste ground which doth you nor any of vs any good." Although Powhatan saw potential allies in the English intruders, he soon divined their real intentions. He insisted that the English confine themselves to Jamestown and expressed fears that they had come to steal the Indians' lands.[9]

The actual situation was probably a good deal more complex. The Powhatans held enough land to support themselves and, at least in the early years, to accommodate the relatively small English population. The immediate consequence of English settlement was a decline in native population, which diminished the tribes' need for land. In fact none of the tribes was dispossessed until after the 1622 massacre. The problem was that the English impinged on specific native lands and competed for important resources. The English planted their settlements along the rivers, close to lands long occupied by the Indians and conveniently located for the exploration of water resources.

In addition, the small English population spread quickly up the rivers, disturbing areas used by the Indians for hunting and gathering. Because the English closely associated land with national sovereignty, they were inclined to anticipate antagonism when they moved in on the native domain. They granted the native people at least a minimal right of land ownership, but they did not consider this right to be strong enough to warrant resistance to English settlement. Savages, it was thought, were incapable of establishing the same kind of relationship to land as civil society made possible for Englishmen. In reality, of course, the Indians had a powerful sense of territorial space and were unlikely to accept the intrusion of the English into their area of control.[10]

The English encroachment on the native food supply was an important source of friction. Although both sides derived advantage from trade, the exchange was invariably a delicate procedure. Pressed too far, the Indians often reacted violently. When the English failed to satisfy their needs, they took extreme measures. At Roanoke the excessive demands for food made by the English provoked the Indians to retaliation. The same situation obtained in Virginia over a more extended period. In 1609, during a particularly difficult time, Smith sent a contingent of colonists to live off the largess of the Nansemonds. The Indians were unfriendly and the colonists fought among themselves and with Smith. Seventeen of them went to trade with the natives and disappeared. George Percy reported: "In all lykelyhood (they) weare cutt of and slayne by the salvages and wthin fewe dayes after Lieftenantt Sicklemore and dyvrs others weare found also slayne wth them mowthes stopped full of Breade beinge down as it seamethe in Contempte and skorne thatt others mighte expecte the Lyke when they shold come to seeke for breade and reliefe amongste them." Percy likened the incident to the fate of the Spaniard whose throat the Indians had filled with molten gold as just recompense for his avarice. The Virginia natives owned little gold, but they did have food which the English pursued with a lust equal to the Spanish craving for that precious metal.[11]

Besides the major issues of land and food, the everyday relations between whites and Indians bred hostility. Indians

coveted the artifacts of the white man's world and made a habit
of taking them at every opportunity. The native ethos did not
stress the sanctity of private ownership as did the European
value system. Explorers and colonists agreed universally that
"these Sauages are naturally great theeves." The stolen silver
cup at Roanoke was only one of many sources of unpleasantness
between whites and Indians, but the English took the incident
seriously enough to burn a village in reprisal. In Virginia the
English were always sensitive to the unauthorized presence of
their tools and guns in the native lodges. Smith favored firmness
and audacity in controlling the Indians. Cowardice and excessive amity, he thought, would only provoke them to hostility.
He knew how the natives would react to any signs of English
weakness. The periods of greatest danger occurred when the
English were least able to care for themselves. In an official promotional tract, Robert Johnson admitted that "our people
starved, and the poor Indians by wrongs and injuries were made
our enemies. . ."[12]

Would Indian and Englishmen have been hostile to each
other without the issues of land and food or the particular
grievances that set them apart? Very likely. Strangers, after all,
become enemies as often as they become friends. Knowledge of
a strange people serves as well to incite war as to prevent it.
Unquestionably, a century of European marauding along the
coast, coupled with the peculiar pugnacity of Elizabethan Englishmen, inspired conflict in Virginia.[13] Still, relations between
whites and Indians had not been consistently hostile. Europeans
could be as friendly and hospitable as Indians; Indians could
be as aggressive as Europeans. Both societies expended vast resources on warfare, and in both cultures prowess in war opened
doors to prestige and leadership. Conflict was as endemic to
America as it was to Europe. Sixteenth-century Englishmen
learned early that enemies surrounded them. Powhatan held
similar convictions about his own world. Both sides were right,
and it is not surprising that upon meeting they should eventually fit each other into the conventional schemes of their
lives. The English added the special conception of ignoble
savagism to fuel their belligerence. To the Indians the English
were a "people come from vnder the world, to take their world

from them."[14] Each side felt threatened by the other because each saw the other as an alien people. "It is clearly not easy for men to give up the satisfaction of this inclination to aggression," wrote Freud in another context. "They do not feel comfortable without it. The advantage which a comparatively small cultural group offers of allowing this instinct an outlet in the form of hostility against intruders is not to be despised. It is always possible to bind together a considerable number of people in love, so long as there are other people left over to receive the manifestations of their aggressiveness."[15] In one sense war between whites and Indians served both sides equally well. It permitted each to assert the integrity of its own way of life. But ultimately a disparity of force existed between the two, so that war that served the purposes of Englishmen contributed to the destruction of Indian life.

The fighting began immediately. On the evening of April 26, 1607, Indians, "creeping upon all foure, from the Hills like Beares," attacked a small party of Englishmen on the south shore of Chesapeake Bay. The Indians were probably Powhatan's men, who at the time were engaged in or had just completed the slaughter of the Chesapeakes (and perhaps of the remnants of the Roanoke colony).[16] Powhatan's shamans had prophesied that the Chesapeakes would destroy him if he did not attack first. He complied with the shamans' advice, only to be informed that yet another power would rise in the Chesapeake area to conquer his kingdom.[17] The English thrust themselves into the midst of this turmoil and suffered the consequences. Relations in the succeeding weeks varied according to the immediate circumstances and probably the effectiveness of Powhatan's control. Then, on May 26, 1607, the warriors assaulted the weak half-moon defense at Jamestown and were driven off by the ships' guns. Powhatan soon halted the direct attacks, and a state of armed enmity was established between the two peoples. Until 1614 whites and Indians killed and captured each other regularly, depended on each other for food and implements, and waited for a break in the tension. From 1614 to 1622 comparative peace reigned while the English acquired strength and the Indians became increasingly insecure and prepared for a last strike at their enemies.[18]

The English should have been prepared for the internecine conflict that greeted them in America. The doctrine of ignoble savagism claimed the inevitability of indiscriminate slaughter. Spanish and French reports and previous English experiences supported the description of a native population seriously divided and in a state of constant friction. George Peckham quoted David Ingram to the effect "that the Savages generally for the most part, are at continuall warres with their next adjoyning neighbours . . ." He could not have known the fallibility of his source, but he could have no doubt that it reflected the reality of life in the New World. Europeans generally came to expect internal conflict in America, and they were prepared to make the best use of it. Peckham went on to contend that the Christians were fully justified in supporting one group of natives against another in order to obtain land and to spread civilized ways.[19]

Accounts of Spanish exploration and settlement stressed the importance of conflict among the American natives. The Spaniards immediately exploited the animosity between Arawaks and Caribs by siding with the more tractable Arawaks. They blew up the cannibalistic proclivities of the Caribs into a monstrous tale of savagism that justified conquest and extermination. In Mexico and Peru the Spaniards frankly admitted that their success depended on the aid of Indian allies who joined them because of long-standing enmities among the native peoples. Acosta thought the divisions providential. It was foolish, he wrote, to believe that the Spaniards could subdue the Indians at will. Chile had yet to yield to their attacks, and the Chichimecas in northern Mexico remained fiercely independent. But in regions where the Indians were divided among themselves or where, as in Mexico and Peru, subjugated people yearned for revenge, the Spaniards could expect their arms to triumph.[20]

When the English arrived on the southern continent, they condemned the Spaniards for cruelty but followed the Spanish example in seeking allies, especially the Arawaks against the Caribs. Ralegh employed native aid against the Spaniards and became involved in the internal conflicts of the Guianian tribes. Later, at a time when the Virginia colony was struggling for survival, Robert Harcourt joined the Yaios in an attack on their enemies. "These things in time," he wrote, "will much auaile vs, being well observed, and rightly applied according to occasion." The Yaios were led by Leonard Ragapo, who had accompanied Ralegh to England, where he had then lived for three or four years. The English made every effort to manage the internal turmoil of life in Guiana to their own advantage.[21]

In Florida in 1564, René Laudonnière noticed that attentions offered to one native group were resented by another. When the Indians pressed him to join them in attacks on their enemies, he remembered that "the Spanyards when they were impolyed in their conquests, did alwayes enter into alliance with some one king to ruine another." Laudonnière took part in some small raids; Indians were killed, scalps and prisoners were taken. But not until the following year did the scope of his plans for Florida mature. News of a distant chieftain capable of fielding three to four thousand warriors stimulated his appetite for land and subjects. "If I would joyne and enter into league (with this Indian leader), we might be able to reduce all the rest of the inhabitauts unto our obedience. . ." His dream faded because food ran low and his men sickened and became sullen. In the end the French offered to fight for the Indians as mercenaries in return for food. The Indians saw no reason to support dependent white men who could not support themselves. Laudonnière perceived the potential in native divisiveness and enmity, but he lacked the resources to profit from the situation.[22]

Lescarbot reported a similar eagerness on the part of the Canadian Indians for help against their enemies. Three generations before, Cartier had resisted the importunate requests of the natives on the St. Lawrence to join them in attacking rivals and had cleverly managed to avoid hostilities. According to Lescarbot, a later French refusal to intervene in an Indian conflict brought down threats of annihilation on them. Yet the French were fully capable of exploiting the Indians' desire for alliance. Lescarbot's commander, Poutrincourt, entertained the Indians and listened with satisfaction to an oration delivered by Membertou, their leader. Membertou was desperate for aid. He spoke of the friendship of the French, of what the Indians hoped to receive from them in the future, "and how much their presence was profitable, yea, necessary unto them, because that

they did sleep in security and had no fear of their enemies, etc."
The French left before changing the balance among the native
peoples, but Lescarbot made clear the opportunities available
in America for Europeans bent on molding native life to their
own interests.[23]

The situation in Virginia appeared to be ideal for making
alliances and playing off one native people against another.
Powhatan, through force and guile, had extended his power
over some thirty tribes. Only the Chickahominies and the Chesapeakes in the Tidewater managed to maintain their indepen-
dence, the latter not for long. But the Algonquin Powhatans
were ringed by hostile people who threatened their existence.
To the west on the upper James and Rappahannock two Siouan
tribes, the Monacans and Manahoacs, presented the most immediate danger. The Oconeechi, also Siouan, occupied lands
on the upper Roànoke and the Iroquoian Nottaway and Me-
herrin tribes held the territory to the south. The English saw
the possibilities in this situation, but apparently so did Powhatan. He looked upon the intrusion of the English into his
domain as a threat to his power but also as an opportunity for
gaining new allies against his enemies.[24]

Initially the English pressed for a formal alliance with Powhatan, capped by the coronation ceremony in the fall of 1608
which the company designed to symbolize the subservience of
the Indian king to James I. Smith and Newport played on Powhatan's fear of the Monacans by offering to lend aid in attacking them. At first Powhatan was enthusiastic, but when Newport led an expedition in the direction of the Monacan country
he changed his mind. He distrusted the English and suspected
that they might join the Monacans against the Powhatans.
His intuition was correct, for in 1609 the company instructed
Thomas Dale to establish alliances with the western tribes as
a check to Powhatan. During the 1609–14 conflict, the English
established friendly relations with the Potomacs and the tribes
on the Eastern Shore, native groupings that had resisted inclu-
sion within Powhatan's domain. The English proved useless to
Powhatan. They could make agreements, but he soon realized
that they possessed little strength to fulfill them. In 1619 Opechancanough sought the aid of the English against his western

enemies who, he claimed, had murdered some of his women. Governor Yeardley agreed to send a small contingent in order to cement relations with Opechancanough, and because the expedition held out the hope of obtaining some native children who would make good servants or candidates for the college. In the diplomatic arena of the New World, the English employed the Machiavellian method in vogue in Europe. They concluded from the doctrine of savagism that in America the method would yield results even more impressive than it had in the Old World.[25]

Although the colonists failed to construct the system of alliances that would subject the native societies to English interests, they did play an active role in intertribal affairs, and they did affect the relations among the Virginia tribes. Smith boasted that at one time thirty-five (or thirty-nine) Indian kings paid tribute to the English in return for aid against their enemies. No doubt he exaggerated. However, the English did make one major diplomatic move. The establishment of the colony drove the Chickahominies, a semiindependent tribe, into Powhatan's camp. But when Powhatan determined on peace in 1614, the Chickahominies were forced to scramble for an English attachment. Governor Dale granted them the right to call themselves Englishmen, and they agreed to a yearly tribute. In 1616 the Chickahominies balked at the tribute, and Governor Yeardley marched into their country to ensure their subordination. Opechancanough, chief of the neighboring Pamunkies, remained aloof despite treaty obligations to the Chickahominies, hoping to gain from their humiliation. As a result the Chickahominies broke into factions that drifted toward Powhatan and away from the English.[26] The colonists did better in obtaining the allegiance of some of the tribes on the edges of the Powhatan territory by offering them aid against opponents to the north and west. Smith made agreements with the Potomacs and Susquehannocks, but these accords did little to change the diplomatic situation in the immediate vicinity of the colony. Only the Potomacs provided some leverage against the Powhatans. They did not participate in the massacre of 1622, though in its aftermath they clashed with the English. In these early years of settlement the English derived minimal benefit from the divisions in native societies.[27]

From the beginning the English cultivated the lesser Indian leaders in the hope of creating fissure in Powhatan's empire. One of these, Arahatec, entertained Newport in May 1607. Englishmen and Indians exchanged gifts, and much dancing and feasting took place. In the midst of the festivities the great chieftain Powhatan made his entrance, at which all the Indians rose "save the *kyng* Arahatec." The incident revealed the hierarchy of native life and the possibilities for the introduction of English duplicity. "There is a king in this land called great Pawatah," reported Archer, "under whose dominions are at least 20[ty] severall kindomes, yet each king potent as a prince in his owne territory." The English were convinced that they remained loyal only because Powhatan possessed the power to strike fear in their hearts. If the English were to break Powhatan's authority by imprisoning him or turning him into a tributary, the lesser chiefs would be free of his tyranny and would pay homage to the English as they had to Powhatan. The minor chieftains showed little interest in the arrangement, though tensions very likely did exist in their relations with Powhatan.[28]

Because the English recognized Powhatan's power and because they needed his good offices in obtaining food, in the beginning at least they treated him with the appearance of equality. Smith opposed the policy, but even he admitted that Powhatan wielded real authority and arrayed himself in the trappings of legitimate power. Newport visited the native leader in the manner of a royal ambassador greeting a minor but important potentate. Of course the English did not truly hold Powhatan in such high regard, for a savage could make no claims to legitimate authority. The truth of the matter was revealed in the coronation charade. Newport, prepared for a formal crowning of a king, arrived at Werowocomoco in the fall of 1608. Powhatan was suspicious. He told Smith that he needed no help against the Monacans, nor did he wish the English to explore beyond the mountains. As for a coronation, if Smith brought him presents from a king then he, Powhatan, must be a king in his own right. The presents were delivered and the copper crown placed on his head. Newport and the London council may have believed in the efficacy of the procedure but Smith did not and neither did Powhatan—"he neither knowing the maiestic, nor meaning of a crowne." Ironically, the coronation disclosed the cultural distance that separated the two peoples. Some months before, Powhatan had initiated the captive Smith into the tribal order in a ceremony that Smith found infinitely perplexing and not a little disquieting. Now Newport, in turn, was attempting to pacify Powhatan's savagism with a ritual equally foreign to native practice. As measures of control formal ceremonies or bogus coronations had little impact on the Indians.[29]

A number of observers recommended the advantages of friendly relations in achieving the ends of colonization, though seldom without noting that force and manipulation might be necessary. The elder Hakluyt, from the security of his study, maintained that "a gentle course without crueltie and tyrannie but answereth the profession of Christian, best planteth Christian religion; maketh our seating most void of blood, most profitable in trade of merchandise, most firme and least subiect wholly to remoove by practise of enemies." Laudonnière had more than once used force in Florida, but he did not cease to hope that more amicable relations might be established with the native peoples. He discovered an appropriate lesson in the experience of the Romans in the making and keeping of empires. They had employed force and suffered the consequences, their country bled white in constant wars. "These are the effects and rewards of al such as being pricked forward with this Romane and tyrannical ambition will goe about thus to subdue strange people. . ." It was left to Bacon to add a note of reality to the hope for tranquil relations with the American natives. He struck a nice balance among trade, amity, and caution. Not only should settlers entertain the Indians with "trifles and gingles," he counseled, but they should also "use them justly and graciously, with sufficient guard nevertheless."[30]

Sir George Peckham offered a similarly calibrated appraisal of the relations between Englishmen and Indians. First the natives were to be convinced by word and deed that the colonists had come "not to theyr hurt, but for theyr good, and to no other ende, but to dwell peaceably amongst them, and to trade and traficke with them for theyr owne commoditie, without molesting or greeving them any way." Moreover, because the "Savages be fearefull by nature," the English were to do their utmost to reassure them "by quiet peaceable conversation, and letting them live in securitie." This method would achieve results because "all straunge creatures, by consitution of nature, are rendered more tractable and easilier wunne for al assayes, by courtesie and myldnes, then by crueltie and roughnes. . ." Trifling gifts would help cement an alliance, but the Indians also had to be made to understand that they could depend on the English for aid against their foes. Thus the English would "mightely stirre and inflame theyr rude myndes gladly to embrace the loving companye of the Christians," and, most important of all, "by theyr francke consents, shall easily enjoy such competent quantity of Lande, as every way shall be correspondent to the Christians expectation. . ." If the Indians should "barbarously. . . goe about to practise violence" by either repelling an English landing or refusing to allow the English to enjoy their rights in the New World, then the English would be justified in doing what might be necessary to ensure their own safety. If the Indians persisted in opposition, "the Christians may issue out, and by strong hande pursue theyr enemies, subdue them, take possession of theyr Townes, Cities, or Villages . . . to use the Lawe of Armes. . ." As did most Europeans, Peckham favored amity, but he clearly knew the uses of violence.[31]

Even after the colonizing process began, Englishmen continued to speak of the importance of harmonious relations with the Indians. Robert Gray seemed shocked at the very thought of English violence. "Farre be it from the nature of the English," he wrote in 1609, "to exercise any bloudie crueltie amongst these people." Not everyone, it seemed, possessed Gray's confidence in the passivity of English colonists. Rules formulated for Roanoke assumed that the English would cause strife. Soldiers were explicitly forbidden to rape or steal, "stryke or mysuse" an Indian, or enter a native house uninvited. Indians could not be forced to labor unwillingly. Strachey's compilation of laws for Virginia testified to a similar interest in maintaining the peace between colonists and Indians by curbing the hostile activities of the colonists. Throughout the early years of the colony, company instructions enjoined that "all just, kind and charitable courses shall be holden with such of them, as shall conforme themselves to any good and sociable traffique and dealing with ye subjects of us. . ." This constant proscription of violent behavior unveiled the rift between wish and reality in the New World.[32]

Although relations between whites and Indians in Virginia were far from pacific even during the period of formal peace, certain Englishmen attempted to implement a policy of generosity and concord toward the Indians. Newport approached Powhatan with benevolence and did his utmost to establish harmonious relations. He was willing to play Powhatan's game in trade and to grant the native chieftain the attention appropriate to his station. A telling incident revealed the lengths to which he would go. On his visit to the village of Arahatec, Newport overheard the chief's brother tell Arahatec that one of the Indians had struck an Englishman. Newport misunderstood the identity of the offender, "understanding the proneness of his owne men to [inflict] such iniuryes." He had the Englishman bound to a tree in the presence of the Indians "and with a Cudgell soundly beate him." Arahatec stopped the beating and punished his own man in turn.[33] Later, George Thorpe was similarly well disposed toward the native people. He punished tenants who had offended them and accommodated them on the issue of the English mastiffs.[34]

But Thorpe made few friends among the colonists. Many thought it fitting that he should be killed in the massacre and his body mutilated. Smith never tired of pointing out the defects in Newport's policy of conciliation. He believed that it would only arouse the savagism of the Indians and work to the detriment of the colony. Smith represented the dominant feeling of the colonists—not that of Newport or Thorpe, or of the company in London—on the management of Indian affairs. In the *Generall Historie* he summarized his own approach to the problem.

The Salvages being acquainted, that by command from *England* we durst not hurt them, were much imboldned; that famine and their insolencies did force me to breake our Commission and instructions; cause *Powhatan* [to] fly his Countrey, and take the King of *Pamaunki* Prisoner; and also to keepe the King of *Paspahegh* in shackels, and put his men to double taskes in chaines, till nine and thirty of their Kings paied us contribution, and the offending Salvages sent to *James* towne to punish at our owne discretions: in the two last yeares I staied there, I had not a man slaine.[35]

Smith approached the Indians with complete self-confidence. He believed that they existed to serve English purposes, and attributed any sign that they differed with this interpretation to their savage natures. Conciliation impressed him as dangerous sentimentality.

Smith's success in dealing with the Indians rested on a number of factors, not the least of which was his extraordinary personality. But, perhaps most importantly, the Europeans held the edge in technical mastery. From the Indians they craved mainly land, food, and gold. From the Europeans the Indians obtained a wide variety of instruments that increased the proficiency of many activities necessary to their lives. In more than one way the Europeans exploited this disparity. They attempted to instill in the native mind the image of a vastly competent and overwhelmingly powerful European colonist whose knowledge of the universe and efficiency in the making of war guaranteed his triumph in the New World. Of course the facts often belied this image, and the Indians found no reason to tailor the interests of their own society to the demands of the white man. But often enough Europeans could make a convincing case for the superiority of their culture's artifacts and hence for the advantage to the natives in conforming to the white man's design for America.

The English believed that the Spaniards had established the precedents. They had been victorious in Mexico largely because they used metal weapons and armor against a native people who possessed no metal and who were virtually naked.

Moreover, the Spanish horses terrified the Mexicans, who had never seen such formidable creatures before. According to George Abbot, Cortez had not fared nearly as well against the Moors in North Africa. Richard Hakluyt's instructions to the Virginia colonists stressed the importance of maintaining this image of omnipotency. The English were to show no signs of weakness. If men were killed in clashes with the Indians, that fact must be kept from the enemy. If the Indians should realize that the English were merely "Common men" and that by suffering the loss of some of their own people they could diminish the numbers of the English, they would be tempted to attack the colony. It was essential that the appearance of invincibility be maintained.[36]

Firearms, more than any other item in the material culture of European civility, gave Englishmen a technical edge in the New World. Because the colonists depended on muskets and calivers for survival, they tended to identify them with the civil order. Savages owned no guns. The English kept firearms from the Indians not only because they saw the danger in giving efficient weapons to an enemy, but also because they recognized the irony of allowing the native warriors to defend savagism with an instrument distinctive of civility. The relative newness of guns in the English arsenal contributed to the tendency to identify them in a special way with civil life. For centuries the longbow had been the characteristic weapon of the English yeomanry, and a collective belief had developed concerning its significance for the English sense of national identification. Then, in the second half of the sixteenth century, technology outran myth. Despite much soul-searching and opposition, firearms replaced the longbow in the hands of English soldiers and became for many Englishmen symbols of modernity. In the New World the English discovered savage people who, dependent on bows and arrows, had failed to make similar progress. According to Humfrey Barwick, Englishmen who resisted the tide of improvement "have the like estmation of the Long Bow, as the Irish have of their Darts, the Dansker of their Hatchets, and as the Scotch men have had of their Speares: all which are more meeter for Sauadge people or poore Potentates, who are not able to maintain others of greater force, then for puissant

Princes." Thus the English invested firearms with profound meaning for the contest between savagism and civility.[37]

Hakluyt added some practical advice concerning the use of guns to ensure English preeminence. Whenever Englishmen fire weapons in sight of the Indians, he counseled, "be sure that they be Chosen out of your best Markesmen for if they See Your Learners miss what they aim at they will think the Weapon not so terrible and thereby will be bould. . . to Assailt You." The Indians immediately understood the significance of firearms in their dealings with the whites, and the Europeans took every opportunity to impress them with the tremendous power the gun afforded over the bow. Laudonnière in Florida and Poutrincourt in Canada both gave the natives a prompt and awe-inspiring demonstration of fire power. Newport spread reports of the effectiveness of firearms on his first exploration of Virginia. At Arahatec's village he terrified the natives by ordering a musket fired. He assured them "that wee never use this thunder but against our enemyes" and went on to offer the aid of firearms in an attack on Arahatec's enemies. "We found," commented Archer, "it bred a better affectyon in him towardes us." A similar demonstration at another village did not create quite the same stir. After a time the natives became accustomed to the Englishmen's guns. They obtained their own, though on occasion they tried to match the English with aboriginal weapons. An Englishman challenged an Indian to pierce a shield with an arrow. The Indian accepted the challenge and drove an arrow a foot through it, which much disconcerted the Englishman because he knew that a pistol shot would not penetrate the shield. The English then made their case by setting up a steel target which splintered the native arrow and reestablished the supremacy of European technology.[38]

On more than one occasion Smith matched firearms against Indian arrows in open conflict, but he could also be a crafty manipulator of his savage enemy. The instant that guns failed and he fell into native hands, he adopted a more subtle approach. He entranced his captors with a compass. (Hariot used the same trick at Roanoke.)

They marvailed at the playing of the Fly and Needle, which they could see so plainely, and yet not touch it because of the glass that covered them. But when he demonstrated by that Globe-like Jewell, the roundnesse of the earth, and skies, the spheare of the Sunne, Moone, and Starres, and how the Sunne did chase the night round about the world continually; the greatnesse of the Land and Sea, the diversitie of Nations, varietie of complexions, and how we were to them *Antipodes*, and many other such like matters, they all stood as amazed with admiration.

In the crisis of the moment he stressed the power of English ships, powder, and arms, but his object was clearly broader than the intimidation of superior force. He intended to introduce to the natives the meaning of civility and to impress on them the intellectual and technical poverty of savagism. Whether the Indians grasped that meaning was less significant than what the incident divulged about Smith's supreme confidence in his own way of life.[39]

European technology did more than impress the Indians with the white man's power. It bestowed on Europeans the aura of divinity. As the agents of impressive technological force, Europeans soon competed with the most successful of native spirits. Although Europeans attributed the native tendency to include them among the gods to savage naiveté, they were half convinced of its plausibility. "Let anyone but consider," wrote Bacon, "the immense difference between men's lives in the most polished countries of Europe, and in any wild and barbarous region of the new Indies, he will think it so great, that many may be said to be a god unto man, not only on account of mutual aids and benefits, but for their comparative states—the result of the arts, and not the soil or climate."[40] White men knew they were not gods, but they also believed that the gulf separating savagism and civility was wide enough to allow them to play the divine role in dealing with Indians.

The natives of the Caribbean took Columbus and his crew "to be men come from Heaven." According to Acosta the Peruvians stood transfixed at the sight of approaching ships. When they discovered the bearded men who walked on the decks, they believed them to be "gods or heavenly creatures." Few Europeans who came into contact with native people did not find themselves mistaken for divine beings of some sort. It seemed to take no more than the strangeness of the situation or a minor acquaintance with European tools for the Indians to treat "the Christians as if they had beene sent downe from heaven, and thinking them to bee immortal."[41] Needless to say, Europeans perceived the advantages of cultivating this attitude.

The English experience along the Atlantic coast was much the same. Thomas Hariot and Ralph Lane both recorded incidents in which the Indians, who more often were singularly unimpressed with the whites, attached divine meaning to a display of European science and technology. In 1605 George Weymouth used the lodestone, an instrument the native people apparently found compelling, to impress the New England Indians. "This we did to cause them to imagine some great power in us: and for that to love and feare us." According to Smith, the Susquehannocks he met in 1608 paid him the adoration due a god. After driving the French from their Maine settlement in 1613, Samuel Argall replaced them in the Indians' esteem. They had been in the habit of referring to the French as "Demy-Gods." The Indians added new gods to their pantheon with the same ease that the English accepted the homage they believed was due from savages.[42]

Indian attitudes toward religion conspired to aid the English in their effort to undermine native culture. The Indians took a strikingly instrumental view of their spirits. They were interested in results. Gods that failed would be replaced by deities more likely to succeed. As the English became more secure and as their power became evident to the Indians, their God also seemed more attractive. The native people showed little interest in accepting Christianity on its own terms, but they were often eager to enlist the Christian God in their contest with the elements. Hariot described how the native chieftain at Roanoke, Wingina, joined the English in prayer, "hoping thereby to bee partaker of the same effectes which wee by that meanes also expected." Later, when he fell ill and despaired of the power of his shamans to wrest a cure from the deities, Wingina appealed to the English to pray for him. The werowance of the Quiyoughcohonnocks showed a similar capacity for incorporating the Christian God into his own mode of religious petition.

Smith admitted his failure to divert the chieftain from his "blind Idolatry," but noted that "he did beleeve that our God as much exceeded theirs, as our Gunnes did their Bowes and Arrowes: and many times did send to me to *James* Towne, intreating me to pray to my God for raine, for their Gods would not send them any." The remarkable resilience native religion demonstrated by allying itself with Christianity should not obscure the reality of the situation. Native culture endured severe strain as a consequence of the pressure of English influence. As the native spirits lost their potency, native society slipped gradually within the orbit of the white man's world.[43]

Even Opechancanough, the organizer of native resistance to the English, succumbed to the vitality of the white man's God. George Thorpe made a monumental effort to convert the native leader. He failed and suffered the consequences. Yet his efforts had not been without effect. Opechancanough recognized the weakness of his own religious customs. In January 1622 the authorities in Virginia reported to London that "hee willinglye acknowledged that theirs was nott the right waye, desiringe to bee instructed in ours and confessed that god loved us better then them, and that he thought the cause of his Angre againste them was theire Custome of makinge their Children black boyes." As he was shortly to launch his warriors in a full-scale assault on the English, Opechancanough clearly remained loyal to the native way. Yet he had apparently lost his faith in the legitimacy of the huskanaw ceremony, the ritual by which the Indians filled the ranks of the priestly class, and he was groping for new and more facile methods of recruiting the divine power in support of the native cause.[44]

In securing their position in Virginia the English relied as much on force as on manipulation. Most of the leaders of the colony had fought in either the Low Countries or Ireland or both, and some, like Smith, had wandered strange lands in search of strife. When the Indians showed a tendency to resist, the English wasted no time in resorting to violence. Hakluyt advocated the use of "our old soldiours trained up in the Netherlands" to ensure the conversion of the natives. In retrospect Smith warned that the founders of great kingdoms "were no silvered idle golden *Pharises*, but industrious iron-steeled Publicans." The men who made Virginia a successful colony knew the uses of force, and they employed it with devastating effect and little compunction.[45]

The English regretted that unruly colonists often initiated the violence between whites and Indians. The experience at Roanoke proved that undisciplined settlers who behaved aggressively toward the Indians could be the cause of much unhappiness. Ralph Lane complained of the "wylde menn of myne owene nacione" over whom he attempted to exercise authority. Eventually the "hande of God came upon them for the crueltie, and outrages committed by some of them against the native inhabitantes of that Countrie." In the early history of the Jamestown settlement few colonists could muster the strength or initiative to spread havoc among the native people, but with the increasing security of the colony and the expansion of the settlement, Englishmen and natives fell into disputes and violence occurred. No doubt such scattered disorder took its toll in the relations between the two societies. The leadership attempted to curb the growing turbulence by forbidding unauthorized dealings with the Indians, but with little effect. Violence became as much a characteristic of relations between Indians and whites as was trade, diplomacy, or proselytization. But the real violence in Virginia was not the consequence of fortuitous conflict between people with different ways of life. It occurred, instead, because Englishmen would permit no slight to go unpunished. They insisted that every violation of their interests should be redressed, and they kept to this rule with the iron will of Elizabethans inured to the brutal conflicts of the time. After the massacre the English embarked on a conscious policy of terror; before, they had made violence the habitual method of suppressing the savage menace.[46]

The constant English demand for food inevitably provoked hostilities between whites and Indians. In 1609 the commercial balance leaned so heavily in favor of the Indians, and the colony had come to such a serious pass, that the company issued frank instructions for the use of force. Sir Thomas Gates was told that the Indians would "never feede you but for feare." If the Indians abandoned their lands, Gates was to "seise into yor custody half their corne and harvest and their Weroances and all other knowne successors. . ." The same year, when supplies had run seriously short, Gerge Percy sent Francis West to the Potomac to trade. A previous attempt had resulted in the death of a number of Englishmen, so West took no chances. "He in short tyme Loaded his penesse sufficyently yett used some harshe and Crewell dealinge by cutteinge of[f] towe of the Salvages heads and other extremetyse [.]" Tension persisted between the two sides even after the establishment of peace. When the English needed food, their custom was simply to take it. In 1619 Opechancanough complained of the activities of a certain Ensigne Harrison who did business in the English manner. According to Harrison, "the Indians refusing to sell Corne, those of the shallop entered the Canoa with armes and tooke it by force, measuring out the corne with a baskett they had into the Shallop and . . . giving them satisfaction in copper beades and other trucking stuffe." The method was Smith's. It brought success in Virginia and he recommended it for use in New England. "I durst undertake to have corne enough from the Salvages for 300 men, for a few trifles. And if they should be untoward (as it is most certaine they are) thirty or forty good men will be sufficient to bring them all in subiection, and make this provision. . ." Efforts to foster peace did not stifle the English penchant for violence.[47]

The English, assuming that savages should be subjected to the laws of civility, did not hesitate to punish Indians for violating the rules of the white man's world. Smith threw Indians into jail for stealing and threatened them with more serious punishments. At one point some sixteen or seventeen Indians inhabited the Jamestown jail. For conspiracy the English delivered a more summary form of justice. When he became convinced that Opechancanough plotted against the colony, Smith collared the Indian in his own village and intimidated him into protestations of friendship. A less fortunate Indian, who killed a colonist and was accused of spying for Powhatan, lost a hand before being sent back to his village. Thomas Gates tried to settle the question of Indian spying once and for all. Some of them he "cawsed to be Apprehended and executed for a Terrour to the Reste to cawse them to desiste from their subtell practyses." The natives who survived could be thankful that they did not suffer the treatment Gates accorded to his own people. "Some he appointed to be hanged Some burned Some to be broken upon wheles, others to be staked and some to be shott to deathe all their extreme and crewell tortures he used and inflicted upon them to terrify the reste. . ."[48]

It was a brutal age, and the English acted as might be expected. Yet, in their treatment of the native people, the doctrine of savagism seemed to release them from whatever inhibitions might have tempered their behavior toward people fortunate enough to claim civility. Faced with a savage enemy, the English demonstrated a startling capacity for savage behavior. George Percy's story of the Indian queen and her children reveals the somber facts about English brutality. In an attack on a Powhatan village in 1610, one of Percy's officers presented him with the "Quene" of the town, her children, and another Indian. When Percy censured the officer for having spared them, the soldier responded that as Percy now held them he could do with them as he wished. "Upon the same," remembered Percy, "I cawsed the Indians heade to be cutt of[f]." After burning the native crops, the party began the voyage home with its surviving prisoners. On shipboard a "Cowncell" determined to kill the children "wᶜh was effected by Throweinge them overboard and shoteinge owtt their Braynes in the water." Apparently this resort to barbarism did not satisfy the more sanguinary soldiers, and Percy was forced to defend the life of the queen. Back in Jamestown, Captain Davis informed Percy that Lord Delaware was displeased that the woman had not been killed. The governor recommended burning. Percy declared that he had seen enough blood for the day. Besides, he thought burning an inappropriate way to murder a queen. He told Davis "either by shott or Sworde to geve her A quicker dispatche. . ." Davis escorted the woman into the woods and put her to the sword. Percy expressed some misgivings about the episode but not enough to save any lives. To every Englishman involved it seemed altogether fitting that savages of all ages should be slaughtered.[49]

On March 22, 1622, the Indians rose in retaliation. Under the leadership of Opechancanough, they attacked the English settlements and killed over 300 people—nearly one-quarter of the settlement's population.⁵⁰ The assault exposed both the desperation of the Indians and their remarkable ability to co-ordinate and execute a plan with ruthless determination. For the English it confirmed their long-held conviction: The Indians were savages who should never have been trusted. This one brutal act released the English from the last vestiges of humane obligation. After the massacre of colonists by Indians, the colonists proceeded to the systematic subjugation of native society.

Opechancanough had laid his plans carefully. Soon after he assumed leadership of the Powhatans, rumors reached James-town of his hostile intentions. Apparently he played the double game effectively, for he managed to allay English suspicions. If a Christian Indian had not betrayed the plot on the night of the twenty-first, the toll of dead would surely have been higher.⁵¹ The precipitating event was the murder, some two weeks before the attack, of Nemattanew, a Pamunkey war chief who was close to Opechancanough and who had long been prominent in the opposition to the English. He killed a colonist named Mor-gan and was dispatched in turn by two of Morgan's retainers. Opechancanough reacted sharply to his death and shortly after sent his warriors against the English settlements. Superficially the picture seemed clear enough. Pushed to the limit by the ag-gressive English, Opechancanough made plans, bided his time, and struck the colony when he was ready. He seized on the murder of Nemattanew only as the immediate occasion for the attack, which was actually the result of a rational estimate of native interests.

Although only fragmentary evidence remains, it seems likely that the uprising of the Powhatans sprang from a deep sense of crisis and even helplessness. After fifteen years of close as-sociation with the English, native society had been driven to the point of collapse. Opechancanough and his people sought relief from this painful condition in the activities of Nematta-new, a prophetic figure who promised the Indians a restoration of the tranquil existence they enjoyed before the coming of the English. The colonists knew Nemattanew well. As early as 1611, they had recognized him as a leader in the Indian opposition to their expansion and more than once had accused him of conspiring against the colony. They noted that he wore a feathered cloak and hence named him Jack of the Feathers.[52] Nemattanew's customary apparel associated his behavior with Okee, the potent negative spirit who instilled great fear in the Indians and who demanded elaborate propitiations. For Powhatans Okee usually appeared in the form of a feathered being.[53] Feathers were also a prominent feature in the rituals of a death cult, perhaps of Spanish or Mexican origin, that had caught on among the native peoples of the Southeast after the middle of the sixteenth century and was probably a sign of social pathology.[54] Hence Nemattanew drew on powerful forces affecting native culture. The warriors were likely to believe him when he claimed to possess a magical ointment that would shield them from English bullets. Before succumbing to a gunshot wound himself, he requested an English burial so that the manner of his death would be concealed from his own people. There would seem to be little doubt that he was deeply implicated in Opechancanough's plans. According to one Englishman, he "drew the plot."[55] Opechancanough launched the assault soon after Nemattanew's death, at a time of the year when the Indians were unaccustomed to fighting, in order to avenge Nemattanew's murder and to fulfill his prophetic role.

The English perceived most of these facts but invested them with meanings that conformed to their habitual way of thinking about Indians. They sensed, for example, that the uprising had some connection with strange stirrings among the native gods. After the horrible events, one of the Indians had blurted out "that their God will not lett them alone but terrifies them & incites them against their wills to this wrong, which now they attempted."[56] What else could be expected from a savage people who lived under the thumb of Satan? Nemattanew, with his feathers, diabolical ointment, and open defiance of the English, served well enough as the agent of the devil bent on the destruction of civil order. The English did not, however, detect any causal relationship between their own behavior and the Indians' desperate act of retaliation.

Yet they searched diligently for the cause of the massacre. It could have been, they thought, a punishment visited upon them by God for the laxness of their morals and their failure to fulfill the divine plan for the New World. God often used war, pestilence, and famine to punish the wicked. He permitted the devil to unleash the agents of savagism upon a people who had declined his grace. But most Virginians were not so addicted to pious self-doubt. They attributed the Indian attack largely to excessive leniency on the part of the English and a "wont of marshall discipline." If a firmer hand had been taken from the beginning or if the colonists had maintained a wary eye, kept arms and military knowledge from the Indians, and defended themselves properly, the massacre either would not have occurred or would have been a good deal less destructive. In the years after the establishment of peace in 1614, so the argument went, the colonists had scattered along the rivers in small groups, isolated from potential aid in case of an Indian attack. In effect they lived in the dispersed manner of the natives and abandoned the security afforded by numbers and formal defenses. In doing so they impinged upon native territory, but not in groups strong enough to check potential hostility. All these explanations assumed one underlying cause: the savagism that continued to form the native character.[57]

In the wake of the massacre, English propaganda turned to the conventional images of the savage. As John Smith described the scene, on "that fatall morning under the bloudy and barbarous hands of that perfidious and inhumane people" over 300 Englishmen were slain. Nor were the savages content merely to kill their victims. "They fell againe upon the dead bodies, making as well as they could a fresh murder, defacing, drugging, and mangling their dead carkases into many peeces, and carrying some parts away in derision, with base and brutish triumph." The Indians acted the familiar part of beasts. They slaughtered even their benefactors, which in Edward Waterhouse's view made them more "fell then Lyons and Dragons," who responded positively to kindness. "But these miscreants . . . put not off onely all humanity, but put on a worse and more than unnaturall bruitishnesse." It was essential that they be subdued with the severest means. "Though there be monsters both of men and beasts, fish and fowle, yet the greatest, the strongest, the wildest, cruellest, fiercest and cunningest, by reason, art and vigilancy, courage and industry hath beene slaine, subiected or made tame . . ." They were to be "tormented with a continuall pursuit." With "horses, and blood-Hounds to draw after them, the Mastives to seaze them, which take this naked, tanned, deformed Savage, for no other then wild beasts . . . ," the "ruine or subiection" of the Indians would soon be accomplished. Englishmen never stopped thinking of Indians as savages and beasts. The massacre merely intensified their primary perception.[58]

In truth the massacre changed nothing about the English conception of the native people. The contention that, from 1614 to 1622, the English lived peacefully among the Indians and sought an accommodation between the two societies was less than half accurate. They maintained peace as long as the Indians conformed to English designs. The two societies continued to live in a state of tension; their interests continued to diverge. The claim that the massacre interrupted a period of tranquility and that the Indians perfidiously betrayed the white man's trust was self-serving propaganda. The hostility between Europeans and Indians began before 1607 and continued throughout the period of formal peace. The massacre may have taken place when it did for specific reasons known only to the Indians, but it was not a startling event considering the character of the relations between the two societies. Moreover, the English response to the massacre—the extirpation of the Powhatan people—was fully consistent with their belief in the doctrine of savagism.

But the massacre did stun the English. They first concentrated the surviving population and dispatched ships to New England, Bermuda, and friendly Indian tribes for supplies. Then, in the fall of 1662, they put into effect a plan for the systematic destruction of the Indians. The colony sent armed bands into the native country with instructions to "pursue and follow them, surprisinge them in their habitations, intercepting them in theire hunting, burninge theire Townes, demolishing theire Temples, destroyinge theire Canoes, plucking upp theire weares, carrying away theire Corne, and depriving them of whatsoever may yeeld them succo[r] or relief. . ." The English fought a classic antiguerrilla campaign. They killed Indians when they could and with any means available—on one occasion with poison—

but they concentrated their efforts on wasting the natives' food base, thereby making life unbearably insecure for them.[59]

As befitted savage war, the English gave no quarter. Nor did they recognize any obligation to adhere to the common rules of conflict. The council in Virginia made the following reply to a word of caution from the company: "Wheras we are advised by you to observe rules of justice w[th] these barberous and p[er]fidious enemys, wee hold nothinge iniuste, that may tend to theire ruine, (except breach of faith). Strategems were ever allowed against all enemies, but w[th] these neither fayre Warr nor good quarter is ever to be held, nor is there other hope of theire subversione, who ever may informe you to the Contrarie." In the spring of 1623, Opechancanough asked for peace in order to save his people from starvation. He offered to return the twenty-two English prisoners held by the Indians. The English agreed because they wanted the prisoners back but also because a brief peace would solve the problem of elusive Indians who were "swift as Roebucks." If the Indians felt secure and planted crops again, the English would know exactly where they could be found. They waited patiently. When the native crops had ripened, the English renewed their attack. "[We] will trie," wrote George Sandys, "if wee can make them as secure as wee *were, that wee may followe their example in destroying them.*"[60]

Disagreement emerged over the desirability of exterminating the Indians. John Martin maintained that Scripture forbade it. Besides, he insisted, practicality dictated a role for the Indians in the Virginia colony. They controlled the wild animal population and kept down forest growth by periodic burnings. Also, the Indians could do valuable work that the English would not do for themselves. No doubt existed, however, about the need to subjugate and even enslave the natives. The argument for complete destruction was not without a practical side. With the disappearance of the Indians the colonists would reap "those benefits which the Plantations hath long promised." The best land would then be available for settlement, much of it already cleared by the Indians.[61] The discussion was largely academic. In the immediate situation, the English lacked the power to annihilate the Indians. For the time being they killed many, enslaved others, and drove the remnants out of the peninsula. Time and the acculturative process would largely accomplish their object before the end of the century.

Smith applauded the measures taken. The massacre, he thought, gave the English just cause to destroy or enslave the Indians. He counseled imitation of the Spaniards, who "forced the treacherous and rebellious Infidels to doe all manner of drudgery worke and slavery for them, themselves living like Souldiers upon the fruits of their labours." In fact the massacre marked no change in his thinking. He believed that the Indians had "given us an hundred times as iust occasion long agoe to subiect them. . ." The mistake, he believed, had been in not introducing repressive measures sixteen years earlier. As Purchas wrote in reference to conciliation of the Indians: "Civility is not the way to win Savages. . . Children are pleased with toyes and awed with rods. . ." He commended the severity of Smith's policy and disparaged the leniency of Newport's, though he was careful to distinguish the former from the Spanish approach. A "cruell mercy in awing Savages to feare us is better than that mercifull cruelty, which by too much kindenes hath made us feare them . . ."[62]

For the English the massacre fulfilled the prophecy of ignoble savagism. They had always expected treachery and violence from the Indians. When it burst upon them in 1622, they appealed immediately to the doctrine that linked the Indian with a brutal, virtually inhuman urge. Conflict between whites and Indians had never been merely a question of differing interests or of misunderstandings. The English interpreted it as a clash between cosmic forces. Defeat by the Indians meant the obliteration of civility and the triumph of savagism. The Indians were a constant threat because civility held only a tenuous grip upon existence and savagism seemed always on the verge of mastering it. While the Indians remained relatively tranquil and did the white man's bidding, savagism played only a minor role in the relations between the two societies. But when the Indians launched what was clearly a war of annihilation, the English saw it as an assault upon the civil condition. "o god!" cried Christopher Brooke, "Is *Uniformity*, and *Order* Turning to

Chaos?"[63] Thus, the colonists felt no uneasiness about implementing a plan to wipe out the natives or utterly subject them to English power.

But, of course, the English had never ceased their efforts to subjugate the Indians. From the beginning of the colonization movement, it had been the English intention to efface savagism or at least to fetter it with strong bonds. Proselytization, economic exploitation, and political manipulation all pointed to the destruction of the savage way of life. War with the Indians represented only the most decisive aspect of the English campaign to save America for civility. In the massacre of 1622, the English discovered overwhelming evidence that, thus far, they had failed. They also found in it a further warrant to proceed with their efforts. The decision to massacre the Indians was the immediate response to the native attack, but it was also a continuation of the English determination to rid the world of savagism.

AFTERWORD

The massacre of 1622 marked no decisive turning point in Anglo-Indian relations, unless it was that the English, after the massacre, felt free to do forcibly what they had long wished to accomplish peacefully. They sought the obliteration of savagism. By killing and subjugating Indians they would achieve that end. Hence the massacre and its aftermath fulfilled English policy, though not, of course, in the way most would have wished it. Few Englishmen who sailed to Virginia contemplated the physical destruction of native society, and certainly the official policy of crown and company intended no such outcome. But the Virginia colony was established, in large part, in order to expand the domain of civility and to diminish the sphere of savagism. Incorporating native society into the English political system, converting the Indians to Christianity, disseminating civil manners, and creating economic dependence through trade would shrink the power of savagism, but it would also lead inexorably to the collapse of social order among the native peoples. When they failed to implement their policy by peaceful means, the English were eager to adopt more forceful measures. The necessity for moderation and exhaustion at the magnitude of the task intervened. The English did not destroy the Powhatans as a result of the 1622 uprising. That was accomplished in the course of the seventeenth century as a result of English policy, but by slower, though no less lethal, methods.

The major result of the massacre was the English decision to separate themselves from the native people. From the beginning they had recognized the risk of settling among the more numerous and frequently hostile Indians, though they had never intended to displace the native tribes. The Spaniards had proved the feasibility of infiltrating a European population into the midst of a native society for the purpose of establishing European domination. In addition, the English required the presence of native farmers for survival. For good reason the Powhatans' threat to abandon their fields and move into the interior caused consternation among the colonial leadership. Nor could the English hope to further the process of conversion unless each side retained easy access to the other. Unfortunately, in 1622 this ready access had cost many English lives. Afterward the English were determined to keep the Indians at a distance.

In 1629, after seven years of killing Indians and burning their villages and fields, the English determined to clear some 300,000 acres of land on the lower peninsula of its native population. They agreed to fortify a line across the peninsula from Chiskiack on the York River, through Middle Plantation, to Jamestown. In 1633 a palisade was strung from the James to the York. In effect the Indians were confined to lands west of the line and north of the York. After the second Indian attack in 1644, the colony constructed four blockhouses, stretching from the forks of the York to the falls of the Appomattox River, to protect the frontier. According to the treaty made with the natives in 1646, they were forbidden to enter the territory east of the fall line without permission. This policy of exclusion had the indirect effect of recognizing Indian possession of at least some lands, and in 1653 the colony continued the practice by making a formal grant of fifty acres to each adult male Indian. Hence, by the middle of the century, the native peoples had been securely hemmed into lands assigned to them by the English and excluded from easy intercourse with the colonists.[1]

The English had planned wisely. When Opechancanough struck a second time in 1644 his warriors failed to penetrate beyond the frontier. The death toll was high. Some 500 Englishmen perished, but the Indians could no longer present a serious threat to the permanence of the colony. By 1646 Opechancanough had been murdered by a colonist and his people lay at the mercy of the English. They sued for peace. The resulting treaty recognized the overlordship of the English, required the Indians to pay tribute, and gave the governor a veto over the selection of native leaders. Apparently Necotowance, Opechancanough's successor, was the last chieftain to rule over a remnant of the Indians that Powhatan had brought together. After 1665 the various native leaders were chosen by the governor.[2] The English had first driven the Powhatans from their land and then established political hegemony over them. It remained only for native culture to experience the internal consequences of a generation of English influence.

Although the Indians seemed unaffected by liquor in the early years of contact, later in the seventeenth century drunkenness became a serious problem. The Indians never learned the art of moderate drinking. Instead they saw the white man's alcohol mainly as an efficient instrument for inducing inebriation. The natives' ordinary drink was water, commented John Clayton, an Anglican parson, "unless when they can get spirits, such as Rum, from the English, which they will allways drink to excess if they can possibly get them, but do not much care for them unless they can have enough to make them drunk . . ." Heavy drinking became an important symptom of the widespread breakdown of native society and a symbol to many Europeans of the paradoxical changes that civility had engendered among the native people. "To be drunk & swear," observed John Banister, "is the only peice of civility these bar[b] arous people have learnt of us Europeans[.]" In time the besotted Indian stood out as a major character in the white man's version of the Indians' decline.[3]

The maladies that infected the Virginia Indians in the early years of contact with the English continued to ravage the tribes in the decades after the massacre. Clayton described an array of distempers that afflicted both whites and Indians in Virginia. They suffered from a dropsy similar to scurvy, colic, scarlet fever, diphtheria, syphilis, yaws, psoriasis, lethargies, and general ill health. The toll from a variety of illnesses in addition to the seasoning process endured by all colonists remained high among whites throughout the seventeenth century. No doubt the Indians suffered even more severely. Smallpox, the most deadly of all the diseases brought to America by the Europeans, struck the Virginia Indians repeatedly during the century. The tribes of the Eastern Shore contracted it (probably for the second time) from an English sailor in 1667 and soon spread it to the mainland. Epidemics broke out again in 1679–80 and in 1696. For the Indians sickness of the body accompanied the more general decline of their societies.[4]

Under the pressure of defeat and subjugation the native people began to lose heart. They remembered that the shamans had told them "that bearded men . . . should come and take away their Country and that there should none of the original Indians be left within a certain number of years." In time even their gods turned against them. "Some of them say, that the God of the *English* is a good God, and gives them good things; but *their* God is an angry God, and oftentimes beats them." The traditional native spirits retained a certain potency in conflicts with traditional enemies but proved helpless against the hostility of the English. As Parson Clayton put it, despite long periods of peace between the two societies the Indians "seem insensibly to decay." A feeling of irresistible malaise overcame the tidewater Indians in the latter half of the seventeenth century as they suffered the effects of alcohol, disease, social breakdown, and a decline in population.[5]

The coming of the Europeans sparked a demographic catastrophe that touched all the native people of America. The effects of this catastrophe on the Powhatans were especially severe. War and disease reduced their numbers. Captured Indians were sold as slaves. Gradually villages and fields were abandoned, and were taken over by the English. The remnants of larger tribal entities consolidated into smaller but mixed groupings of natives. A decline in the birthrate ("they are undoubtedly no great breeders") contributed to the fall in absolute numbers. By the end of the century fewer than a thousand remained of the 12,000 Powhatans who had greeted the English in 1607.[6]

Although the attacks of 1622 and 1644 excited profound bitterness among the colonists, efforts to transform native society continued. In the hope of fostering the ownership of domestic animals, the English offered the Indians a cow for every wolf they could kill. Moreover, numbers of natives continued to live within the area marked off for the whites and to maintain working relations with their white neighbors. The treaty of 1646 provided for the placing of Indians under twelve years of age in English households, and the assembly appropriated money for their support. Later, native parents were permitted to select the English families with whom their children would live. At the same time the assembly found it necessary to forbid the enslavement of native children. Although Indian slavery was allowed by statute only between 1670 and 1691, throughout the colonial period Indians occupied positions of servitude that were often tantamount to enslavement. The education of young Indians became a possibility again in the 1690s when Sir Robert Boyle's legacy began paying for the Indian school at the College of William and Mary. In 1712 Governor Spotswood reported that twenty Indian boys were attending the college. But by English standards these efforts yielded little success. Despite limited progress in converting Indians to Christianity and infiltrating the artifacts and manners of civility, success always came at the expense of the integrity of native culture. Needless to say, no Indians gained admittance to colonial society. They tended to become disintegrated Indians rather than Englishmen.[7]

When the tribesmen were no longer a threat and their society showed signs of imminent collapse, a significant shift occurred in English thinking about Indians. While the fighting continued, as it did in the 1640s and 1670s, they were an "ignorant and unpolisht people," and their leader Opechancanough a "bloody Monster,"[8] but by the turn of the century the conception of the noble savage had once again come into vogue, this time with a new twist. The idea had always been associated with the failure of Europeans to retain the innocence of a past age. Now, with the decline of the natives, white men experienced a profound sense of remorse that the noble savage, the exemplar against which they measured their own world, had fallen into a state of decay. They had often felt guilty about their own failure to match the ideal of noble savagism, and they now bore the burden of having destroyed that ideal. The fate of the Indian once again became a symbol for the white man's internal afflictions–this time for a sense of guilt he could never quite assuage.

The appearance of Robert Beverley's *History and Present State of Virginia* in 1705 marked this new turn in the history of the idea of savagism. His work was the most important English treatment of native society since John Smith's *Generall Historie*.[9] He drew on the major written sources for the story of Anglo-Indian relations and recorded much new information obtained in his own investigations. For his time he wrote sound anthropology and informative history. But he could not forsake the doctrine of savagism. At the same time that he announced his own sense of discontentment by calling himself an Indian, he argued that real Indians resided in a "state of Nature." "For they live barely up to the present relief of their Necessities, and make all things easy and comfortable to themselves, by the indulgence of a kind Climate, without toiling and perplexing their mind for Riches, which other people often trouble themselves to provide for uncertain and ungrateful Heirs." The Indians, unfortunately, seemed to Beverley to be more like "soft Wax, ready to take any Impression" than self-contained savages ready to resist the cultural incursions of the white man. As a consequence they had "reason to lament the arrival of the Europeans." They "lost their Felicity, as well as their Innocence. The *English* have taken away great part of their Country, and consequently made every thing less plenty amongst them, which have multiply'd their Wants, and put them upon desiring a thousand things, they never dreamt of before."[10] Beverley perceived the impact of acculturation, but he was incapable of explaining it without invoking the idea of savagism. He knew that the English had to bear the responsibility for the fate of the native people, an acknowledgment of guilt he found all the more distressing because of the state of innocence from which the Indians had fallen. Beverley pitied them, which gave to the doctrine of savagism a distinctively eighteenth-century cast. To the English conviction that the natives were savages who had once threatened civil society (but could no longer), he added a sense of sentimental regret, an attitude quite foreign to the thinking and feeling of the early colonists.

NOTES

―――――――――

INTRODUCTION

1 Margaret T. Hodgen, *Early Anthropology in the Sixteenth and Seventeenth Centuries* (Philadelphia, 1964), 113. Scholars still argue over the significance of the New World for the Old. See J. H. Elliott, *The Old World and The New, 1492–1650* (Cambridge, 1970), ch. 1, and Arthur J. Slavin, "The American Principle from More to Locke," Fredi Chiappelli et al., eds., *First Images of America: The Impact of the New World on the Old* (Berkeley, 1976), I: 139–64.

2 Mircea Eliade, *The Myth of the Eternal Return*, trans. Willard R. Trask (New York, 1954), ch. 1; Michael Novak, *The Experience of Nothingness* (New York, 1970).

3 Roy Harvey Pearce, *The Savages of America: A Study of the Indian and the Idea of Civilization*, rev. ed. (Baltimore, 1965), ch. I; Andrew Sinclair, *The Savage: A History of Misunderstanding* (London, 1977), chs. 2 and 3. For a discussion of European nomenclature concerning the native people, see Robert F. Berkhofer, Jr., *The White Man's Indian: Images of the American Indian from Columbus to the Present* (New York, 1978), 4–25.

4 Theodore Spencer, *Shakespeare and the Nature of Man*, 2nd ed. (New York, 1961), ch. 2; Myrick H. Carre, *Phases of Thought in England* (Oxford, 1949), ch. 6; C. S. Lewis, *English Literature in the Sixteenth Century, Excluding Drama* (Oxford, 1954), 3; Arthur O. Lovejoy, *The Great Chain of Being: A Study of the History of an Idea* (Cambridge, Mass., 1936), ch. 4; Felix Raab, *The English Face of Machiavelli: A Changing Interpretation, 1500–1700* (London, 1964), chs. 1 and 2; Douglass Bush, *The Renaissance and English Humanism* (Toronto, 1939), 72–3; H. R. Trevor-Roper, *The Crisis of the Seventeenth Century: Religion, the Reformation and Social Change* (New York, 1968), ch. 1; Lawrence Stone, *The Crisis of the Aristocracy, 1558–1641* (Oxford, 1965), pt. 1; E. M. W. Tillyard, *The Elizabethan World Picture* (London, 1948), 16; Don Cameron Allen, "The Degeneration of

Man and Renaissance Pessimism," *Studies in Philology* 35 (1938): 202–27.

5 See Gary B. Nash, "The Image of the Indian in the Southern Colonial Mind," *William and Mary Quarterly*, 3d ser., XXIX (1972): 197–220.

1. PARADISE

1 Henri Baudet, *Paradise on Earth: Some Thoughts on European Images of Non-European Man*, trans. Elizabeth Wenthold, (New Haven, 1965), chs. 1 and 2; Howard Mumford Jones, *O Strange New World: American Culture, The Formative Years* (New York, 1964), ch. 1; Mircea Eliade, "The Yearning for Paradise in Primitive Tradition," *Daedalus* 88 (1959): 255–67.

2 C. Raymond Beazley, *The Dawn of Modern Geography* (New York, 1949), III: 319–21; John Parker, *Books to Build an Empire: A Bibliographical History of English Overseas Interests to 1620* (Amsterdam, 1965), 16–17.

3 John Mandeville, *The Voiage and Trayayle of Sir John Maundeville* . . . , ed. John Ashton (London, 1887; reprint of 1568 ed.), 128, 210–12.

4 Sebastian Munster, "Treatyse of the Newe India," ed. Richard Eden in Edward Arber, ed., *The First Three English Books on America* (Birmingham, Eng., 1885), 19; [Stephen Batman], *Batman vppon Bartholome* . . . (London, 1582), 237ᵛ; "A Voyage Made Out of England into Guinea in Affricke . . . 1553," Richard Hakluyt, *The Principall Navigations Voiages and Discoveries of the English Nation*, ed. David Beers Quinn and Raleigh Ashlin Skelton (Cambridge, 1965), 85; "A Relation of the Commodities of Noua Hispania . . . by Henry Hawkes . . . 1572," *ibid.*, 551.

5 Loren E. Pennington, "The Origins of English Promotional Literature for America, 1553–1625" (Ph.D. diss., University of Michigan, 1962); Roderick Nash, *Wilderness and the American Mind* (New Haven, 1967), 25.

6 Samuel Purchas, *Pvrchas His Pilgrimage* . . . (London, 1617), 18.

7 Edmundo O'Gorman, *The Invention of America* (Bloomington, Ind., 1961), 97–9, describes Columbus's flirtation with Paria as the terrestrial paradise. He associated America with the paradisaic myth, though he failed to realize that he had discovered a new continent. Paradise, for Columbus, was at the edge of the East.

8 Peter Martyr, "Decades of the Newe Worlde," ed. Eden in Arber, ed., *First Three English Books on America*, 90; "Arthur Barlowe's Discourse of the First Voyage," David B. Quinn, ed., *The Roanoke Voyages, 1584–1590* (London, 1955), I: 93–4; Pennington, "Origins of English Promotional Literature for America," 106; "To the

Virginian Voyage," *The Works of Michael Drayton*, ed. J. William Hebel (Oxford, 1931–41), II: 336–64.

9 Antonello Gerbi, *The Dispute of the New World: The History of a Polemic, 1750–1900*, rev. ed., trans. Jeremy Moyle (Pittsburgh, 1973), 3; William Symonds, "Virginea Brittania," Alexander Brown, ed., *The Genesis of the United States* (Boston, 1890), I: 289; [Robert Johnson], *Nova Britannia* . . . (Rochester, N.Y., 1897; orig. pub., 1609), 6; "The 1586 Voyages," Quinn, ed., *Roanoke Voyages*, I: 479.

10 "George Percy's Discourse," Philip L. Barbour, ed., *The James-town Voyages Under the First Charter, 1606–1609* (Cambridge, 1969), I: 133; *The Original Writings and Correspondence of the Two Richard Hakluyts*, ed. E. G. R. Taylor (London, 1935), II: 222–3; Purchas, *Pvrchas His Pilgrimage*, 945. Smith described Massachusetts as "the Paradise of all those parts" in "A Description of New England," *Travels and Works of Captain John Smith* . . . , ed. Edward Arber and A. G. Bradley (Edinburgh, 1910), I: 204.

11 Stephen J. Greenblatt, *Sir Walter Ralegh: The Renaissance Man and His Roles* (New Haven, 1973), 164–5.

12 Sir Walter Ralegh, *The History of the World* in *The Works of Sir Walter Ralegh* (Oxford, 1829), II: 69, 74, 88.

13 *Ibid.*, II: 89, 100, 126–7, 336, VI: 113–14; Greenblatt, *Sir Walter Ralegh*, 140.

14 J. A. Manso, "The Quest of El Dorado," *Pan American Union Bulletin* 34 (1912): 55–66, 165–76, 317–27, 447–57, 607–21, 732–43; Wayland D. Hand, "The Effect of the Discovery on Ethnological and Folklore Studies in Europe," Chiappelli et al., eds., *First Images of America*, I: 50–1.

15 Sir Walter Ralegh, *The Discoverie of the Large and Beautiful Empire of Guiana*, ed. V. T. Harlow (London, 1928), 31n, 73; Lawrence Kemys, *A Relation of the Second Voyage to Guiana* (London, 1596), A3^v.

16 Ralegh, *History of the World*, II: 336; "De Guiana, Carmen Epicum," *The Poems of George Chapman*, ed. Phyllis Brooks Bartlett (New York, 1941), 354; V. T. Harlow, ed., *Ralegh's Last Voyage* (London, 1932), 151–2; Greenblatt, *Sir Walter Ralegh*, 14, 30; Agnes M. C. Latham, "Sir Walter Ralegh's Gold Mine: New Light on the Last Guiana Voyage," *English Association Essays and Studies*, new ser., 4 (1951): 94–111; David B. Quinn, *Raleigh and the British Empire*, rev. ed. (New York 1962), ch. 9.

17 Raphael Holinshed, *Holinshed's Chronicles of England, Scotland, and Ireland* (London, 1808), IV: 905–6. See also Richard Hakluyt, *Principal Navigations Voyages Traffiques & Discoveries of the English Nation* (Glasgow, 1903–5), I: lxvi.

18 Francisco López de Gómara, *The Pleasant Historie of the Conquest of West India* . . . , trans. Thomas Nicholas (London, 1578), 48, 57; Joseph de Acosta, *The Natural and Moral History of the Indies* . . . , ed. Clements R. Markham (London, 1880; orig. pub., London, 1604), 202–3; [Giovanni Botero], *The Worlde, or an Historicall Description of the Most Famous Kingdomes and Commonweales Therein* . . . (London, 1601), 40; Augustín de Zárate, *The Strange and Delectable History of the Discoverie and Conquest of the Provinces of Peru* . . . , [trans. Thomas Nicholas] (London, 1581), Aaii-Aaiii.

19 Zárate, *Strange and Delectable History* . . . , [trans. Nicholas], Li–Li^v; "A Discourse of the West Indies and South Sea Written by Lopez Vaz . . . ," Hakluyt, *Principal Navigations*, XI: 283; "The Conquest of Peru . . . by Francisco de Xeres . . . ," Samuel Purchas, *Hakluytus Posthumus or Purchas His Pilgrimes* (Glasgow, 1905–7), XVII: 425–6; Wayland Hand, "The Effect of the Discovery on Ethnological and Folklore Studies in Europe," Chiappelli et al., eds., *First Images of America*, I: 54n, estimates the value of the gold and plate in Pizarro's room at $17,500,000. "Observations . . . by the Inca Garcilasso de la Vega . . . ," Purchas, *Hakluytus Posthumus*, VXII: 340; "Briefe Notes of Francis Pizarro . . . ," *ibid.*, XVII: 416–18; "Relations of Occurrents in the Conquest of Peru . . . by Pedro Sancho . . . ,"*ibid.*, XVII: 429.

20 Acosta, *Natural and Moral History of the Indies*, ed. Markham, 186–7.

21 Peter Martyr, "Decades of the Newe Worlde . . . ," ed. Eden in Arber, ed., *First Three English Books on America*, 67, 80–1; Purchas, *Pvrchas His Pilgrimage*, 898–900; [George Abbot], *A Briefe Description of the Whole Worlde* . . . (London, 1605), R3–R3^v; John Frampton, *A Briefe Description of the Portes, Creekes, Bayes, and Havens of the West India* . . . (London, 1578), 4; "The Observations of Sir Richard Hawkins . . . ," Purchas, *Hakluytus Posthumus*, XVII: 129; "The Historie of Lopez Vaz . . . ," *ibid.*, XVII: 278; "Observations . . . of the Inca Garcilasso de la Vega," *ibid.*, XVII: 374.

22 Gómara, *Pleasant Historie of the Conquest of West India*, Aii^v; "A Letter of Francis Vasquez de Coronado . . . ," Hakluyt, *Principal Navigations*, IX: 119; "The Relation of Nicholas Burgoingnon . . . ," *ibid.*, IX: 113–14; "A Notable Historie . . . by Monsieur Laudonnière . . . ," *ibid.*, VIII: 452, 466–7.

23 Samuel Eliot Morison, *The European Discovery of America: The Northern Voyages, A.D. 500–1600* (New York, 1971), 510, 530–1, 544.

24 "Ralph Lane's Discourse . . . ," Quinn, ed., *The Roanoke Voyages*, I: 272–3; "Letters Patent to Sir Thomas Gates . . . ," Barbour, ed., *Jamestown Voyages*, I: 28; [Gabriel Archer], "Description of

the River and Country," *ibid.*, I: 98; "Letter from William Brewster," *ibid.*, I: 107; Sir Walter Cope to Lord Salisbury, Aug. 12, 1607, *ibid.*, I: 108–9; Cope to Salisbury, Aug. 13, 1607, *ibid.*, I: III; Sir Thomas Smythe to Lord Salisbury, Aug. 17, 1607, *ibid.*, I: 112.

25 Franklin T. McCann, *English Discovery of America to 1585* (New York, 1952), 198–209.

26 *The Jew of Malta, The Complete Works of Christopher Marlowe*, ed. Fredson Bowers (Cambridge, 1973), I: 305; Ben Jonson, George Chapman, and John Marston, *Eastward Ho!*, ed. C. G. Petter (London, 1973), 61–2; *Orlando Furioso, The Dramatic Works of Robert Greene . . .*, ed. Alexander Dyce (London, 1831), I: 6; "Four Plays or Moral Representation in One," *The Works of Francis Beaumont and John Fletcher*, ed. A. R. Waller (Cambridge, 1905–12), X: 360; "Sir George Peckham's *True Reporte . . .*," David B. Quinn, ed., *The Voyages and Colonising Enterprises of Sir Humphrey Gilbert* (London, 1940), II: 442.

27 Millar MacLure, *George Chapman: A Critical Study* (Toronto, 1966), 231–3; "The Memorable Masque," ed. G. Blackmore Evans in *The Plays of George Chapman: The Comedies, A Critical Edition*, ed. Allan Holaday (Urbana, 1970), 583, 565–6; G. P. V. Akrigg, *Jacobean Pageant, or the Court of King James I* (London, 1962), 153–4.

28 Keith Thomas, *Religion and the Decline of Magic* (New York, 1971), ch. 8; A. L. Rowse, *Sex and Society in Shakespeare's Age: Simon Forman the Astrologer* (New York, 1974); C. S. Lewis, *English Literature in the Sixteenth Century; Excluding Drama* (Oxford, 1954), 8.

29 Thomas, *Religion and the Decline of Magic*, 222–3; Harry Levin, *The Myth of the Golden Age in the Renaissance* (Bloomington, Ind., 1969), ch. 3; A. Bartlett Giamatti, *The Earthly Paradise and the Renaissance Epic* (Princeton, 1966), 15–33.

30 Peter J. French, *John Dee: The World of an Elizabethan Magus* (London, 1972), 76–7.

31 Norman O. Brown, *Life Against Death: The Psychoanalytical Meaning of History* (New York, 1959), 247; Mircea Eliade, *The Forge and the Crucible*, trans. Stephen Corrin (New York, 1962), 147–8, 171; C. G. Jung, *Psychology and Alchemy*, 2nd ed. (Princeton, 1968), 343–4; Thomas, *Religion and the Decline of Magic*, 267–70; McCann, *English Discovery of America*, 13–14; Carl Ortwin Sauer, *The Early Spanish Main* (Berkeley, 1969), 23–9.

32 Munster, "Treatyse of the Newe India," ed. Eden in Arber, ed., *First Three English Books on America*, 7; Amerigo Vespucci and Andreas de Corsali, "Of the Pole Antarctic . . . ," *ibid.*, 278; Roger Barlow, *A Brief Summe of Geographie*, ed. E. G. R. Taylor (London, 1932), 180; McCann, *English Discovery of America*, 164–7.

33 Margaret T. Hodgen, *Early Anthropology in the Sixteenth and Seventeenth Centuries* (Philadelphia), chs. 1–3; Mircea Eliade, *The Myth of the Eternal Return*, trans. Willard R. Trask (New York, 1954), 121–2.

34 Baudet, *Paradise on Earth*, 11. Wilcomb E. Washburn, "The Clash of Morality in the American Forest," Chiappelli et al., eds., *First Images of America*, I: 335–50, argues for the anthropological accuracy of the noble savage conception or at least for its usefulness in understanding "primitive people." For a more subtle examination of the function of savagism in European thinking, see Hayden White, "The Noble Savage Theme as Fetish," *ibid.*, I: 121–35, and Hayden White, "The Forms of Wilderness: Archeology of an Idea," Edward Dudley and Maximillian E. Novak, eds., *The Wild Man Within: An Image in Western Thought from the Renaissance to Romanticism* (Pittsburgh, 1972), 3–38.

35 Margaret T. Hodgen, "Montaigne and Shakespeare Again," *Huntington Library Quarterly* XVI (1952): 30; Arthur O. Lovejoy and George Boas, *Primitivism and Related Ideas in Antiquity* (Baltimore, 1935), 14–15.

36 John Donne, "To the Countess of Huntington," 1597, quoted in Gerbi, *Dispute of the New World*, 3; Mandeville, *Voiage and Trayayle*, ed. Ashton, 134–6; Martyr, "Decades of the Newe World," ed. Eden in Arber, ed., *First Three English Books on America*, 78, 138; [Pierre d' Avity], *The Estates, Empires, & Principallities of the World* . . . , trans. Edw. Grimstone (London, 1615), 221, 252; "A Treatise of Brasil . . . ," Purchas, *Hakluytus Posthumus*, XVI: 422.

37 Marc Lescarbot, *Nova Francia: A Description of Acadia, 1606*, trans. P. Erondelle (London, 1928), 264; [Archer], "Description of the River and Country," Barbour, ed., *Jamestown Voyages*, I: 100–1, 103; John Smith, "The Generall Historie of Virginia, New England and the Summer Isles," *Travels and Works of Captain John Smith*, ed. Arber and Bradley, II: 577.

38 *Original Writings and Correspondence of the Two Richard Hakluyts*, ed. Taylor, II: 222–3; "The Second Voyage into Florida . . . by Captaine Laudonnière . . . ," Hakluyt, *Principal Navigations*, IX: 8; John Nicholl, *An Houre Glass of Indian Newes* . . . (London, 1607), C2–C2ᵛ.

39 Lescarbot, *Nova Francia*, 101–2; Martyr, "Decades of the Newe Worlde," ed. Eden in Arber, ed., *First Three English Books on America*, 83; John Smith, "A True Relation," Barbour, ed., *Jamestown Voyages*, I: 185–6.

40 Leo Marx, *The Machine in the Garden: Technology and the Pastoral Ideal in America* (New York, 1964), 37–40; Richard A. Lanham, *The Old Arcadia* (New Haven, 1965), 389; W. T. Jewkes,

"The Literature of Travel and the Mode of Romance in the Renaissance," Warner G. Rice, ed., *Literature as a Mode of Travel* . . . (New York, 1963), 14–15.

41 "Arthur Barlowe's Discourse," Quinn, ed., *Roanoke Voyages*, II: 93–7, 105–8.

42 "A Notable Historie . . . written . . . by Monsieur Laudonnière . . . ," Hakluyt, *Principal Navigations*, VIII: 459; "The Second Voyage into Florida . . . by Captaine Laudonnière . . . ," *ibid.*, IX: 13; "A Discourse of the West Indies . . . by Lopez Vaz . . . ," *ibid.*, XI: 235–6.

43 Bartolomé de Las Casas, *The Spanish Colonie* . . . (London, 1583), A1–A1ᵛ. Las Casas wrote of the natives of Hispaniola. Elsewhere he referred to the "policie and prudencie" of the people of Yucatan: *ibid.*, F3ᵛ. For Las Casas as cultural relativist, see Bartolomé de Las Casas, *A Selection of His Writings*, ed. George Sanderlin (New York, 1971), 144.

44 Michael de Montaigne, *The Essayes or Morall, Politike and Millitarie Discourses*, trans. John Florio (London, 1603).

45 Hodgen, "*Montaigne and Shakespeare Again*," 26–7; Richard Sayce, *The Essays of Montaigne: A Critical Exploration* (London, 1972), 192–4; Aldo Scaglione, "A Note on Montaigne's 'Des Cannibales' and the Humanist Tradition," Chiappelli et al., eds., *First Images of America*, I: 63–70; Louis I. Bredvold, "The Naturalism of Donne in Relation to Some Renaissance Traditions," *Journal of English and Germanic Philology* XXII (1923): 494–9. Levin, *Myth of the Golden Age*, 74–9, contends that "for Montaigne the savage is not absolutely noble, he is relatively nobler than the European in some respects."

46 "Of the Caniballes," *The Essays of Montaigne Done into English by John Florio Anno 1603*, ed. George Saintsbury (London, 1892–3), I: 220, 223–5; "Of Coaches," *ibid.*, III: 142–3; Sayce, *Essays of Montaigne*, 91–2.

47 "Of the Caniballes," *Essays of Montaigne*, ed. Saintsbury, I: 221.

48 *Ibid.*, I: 222–3; "Of Coaches," *ibid.*, III: 142.

49 "Of the Caniballes," *ibid.*, I: 225–7; "Of Coaches," *ibid.*, III: 142.

50 George Boas, *The Happy Beast in French Thought of the Seventeenth Century* (Baltimore, 1933), 9.

51 "Of the Caniballes," *Essays of Montaigne*, ed. Saintsbury, I: 231.

52 Sir Thomas Chaloner, *The Praise of Folie*, ed. Clarence H. Miller (New York, 1965; orig. pub., n.p., 1549), 46–8.

53 H. P. Biggar, "The French Hakluyt; Marc Lescarbot of Vervins," *American Historical Review* VI (1900–1): 676–7; Pennington, "Origins of English Promotional Literature," 104.

54 Lescarbot, *Nova Francia*, 145–6, 255–9, 260–4, 277.

55 *Ibid.*, 62, 243.

56 *Ibid.*, 25, 127, 151, 227–8, 242–3.

57 *Ibid.*, 33, 58, 133–4, 226, 255–6. For Lescarbot's criticism of native society, see *ibid.*, 103.

58 *Faerie Queene*, bk. V, st. 1 and 2, *The Works of Edmund Spenser: A Variorum Edition*, ed. Edwin Greenlaw et al. (Baltimore, 1932–58). "De Guiana, Carmen Epicum," *Poems of George Chapman*, ed. Bartlett, 357; "Description of New England," *Travels and Works of Captain John Smith*, ed. Arber and Bradley, I: 195–6, 212–13.

59 Ralegh, *History of the World*, VI: 29–30.

60 John H. Elliott, "Renaissance Europe and America: A Blunted Impact," Chiappelli et al., eds., *First Images of America*, I: 20; Theodore Spencer, *Shakespeare and the Nature of Man*, 2nd ed. (New York, 1961), 27–8; E. M. W. Tillyard, *The Elizabethan World Picture* (London, 1948), 16. For a discussion of the millennial forboding that contributed so powerfully to the Elizabethan age, see Ernest Lee Tuveson, *Millennium and Utopia: A Study of the Background of the Idea of Progress* (Berkeley, 1949), 22–25. On Elizabethan pessimism, see Don Cameron Allen, "The Degeneration of Man and Renaissance Pessimism," *Studies in Philology* 35 (1938): 202–27.

61 Henry S. Burrage, ed., *Rosier's Relation of Weymouth's Voyage to the Coast of Maine, 1605* (Portland, Me., 1887), 149–50; "To the Virginian Voyage," *The Works of Michael Drayton*, ed. Hebel, II: 363; "Description of New England," *Travels and Works of Captain John Smith*, ed. Arber and Bradley, I: 197. For the relationship of alchemy and progress, see Eliade, *The Forge and the Crucible*, 172–3.

62 Stephen Parmenius, "An Embarkation Poem," David B. Quinn and Neil M. Cheshére, eds., *The New Found Land of Stephen Parmenius* (Toronto, 1972) 85–93.

2. IGNOBLE SAVAGISM

1 J. H. Elliott, *The Old World and New, 1492–1650* (Cambridge, 1970), 46; Denis Sinor, "The Barbarians," *Diogenes* 18 (1957): 58–9; George Lyman Kittredge, *Witchcraft in Old and New England* (New York, 1956), 362–3; Ronald Meek, *Social Science and the Ignoble Savage* (Cambridge, 1976), 49; Richard Slotkin, *Regeneration through Violence: The Mythology of the American Frontier, 1660–1860* (Middletown, Conn., 1973), 66, 73, 88, 119, 131.

2 James I, *Daemonologie (1597). Newes from Scotland Declaring the Damnable Life and Death of Doctor Fian, a Notable Sorcerer Who Was Burned at Edenbrough in January Last (1591)* (Edinburgh, 1966), 69; Arthur Dent, *The Plaine Mans Path-way to Heauen* ...

(London, 1603), 10–11; Henry Parry, *The Svmme of Christian Religion* . . . (Oxford, 1595), 41–2.

3 Thomas Palmer, *An Essay on the Meanes How to Make Our Trauailes, into Forraine Countries, the More Profitable and Honourable* (London, 1606), 74; Alan Macfarlane, *Witchcraft in Tudor and Stuart England: A Regional and Comparative Study* (New York, 1970), 213, 214; Lewes Lavater, *Of Ghostes and Spirits Walking by Nyght, 1572*, ed. J. Dover Wilson and May Yardley (Oxford, 1929), 75; "George Percy's Discourse," Philip L. Barbour, ed., *The Jamestown Voyages Under the First Charter, 1606–1609* (Cambridge 1969), I: 130.

4 [George Abbot], *A Briefe Description of the Whole Worlde* . . . (London, 1605), Q4.

5 Marc Lescarbot, *Nova Francia: A Description of Arcadia, 1606*, trans. P. Erondelle (London, 1928), 157–61, 234.

6 James I, *Daemonologie*, 44; H. W. Janson, *Apes and Ape Lore in the Middle Ages and the Renaissance* (London, 1952), 16–22, 26n.43; Richard Bernheimer, *Wild Men in the Middle Ages: A Study in Art, Sentiment and Demonology* (Cambridge, Mass., 1952), 97, 100–1; *The Tempest*, act I, sc. ii, lines 263–5, 319, 373; act IV, sc. i, line 188; act V, sc. i, lines 261, 272–5, *The Riverside Shakespeare*, ed. G. Blakemore Evans (Boston, 1974), II: 1615, 1616, 1631, 1635; Antonio Pigafetta, "The First Circumnavigation of the Globe, by Fernan de Magalhaens's Expedition, in 1519–22," ed. Richard Eden in Edward Arber, ed., *The First Three English Books on America* (Birmingham, Eng., 1885), 252.

7 Palmer, *An Essay*, 98.

8 Peter Martyr, "The Decades of the Newe Worlde . . . ," ed. Eden in Arber, ed., *First Three English Books on America*, 78; Loys Le Roy, *Of the Interchangeable Covrse, or Variety of Things in the Whole World* . . . (London, 1594), 27^v.

9 Thomas Hariot, "A Briefe and True Report," David B. Quinn, ed., *The Roanoke Voyages, 1584–1590* (London, 1955), I: 372–5. See also Lescarbot, *Nova Francia*, 164–6; Samuel Purchas, *Pvrchas His Pilgrimage* . . . (London, 1617), 932.

10 "Of Atheism," *The Works of Francis Bacon* . . . , ed. James Spedding et al. (Boston, 1857–74), VI: 414; Richard Hakluyt, *Divers Voyages Toughing the Discovery of America* . . . , ed. John Winter Jones (London, 1850; orig. pub., London, 1582), 71.

11 [Abbot], *Briefe Description of the Whole World*, 1599 ed., D6; 1605 ed., R2–R2^v; Walter Ralegh, *History of the World* in *Works of Sir Walter Ralegh* (Oxford, 1829), IV: 693–4; John Smith et al., "A Map of Virginia," Barbour, ed., *Jamestown Voyages*, II: 364. See also Sebastian Munster, "Treatyse of the New India . . . ," ed. Eden in Arber, ed., *First Three English Books on America*, 17–18;

Florio, *A Shorte and Briefe Narration of the Two Nauigations and Discoueries to the Northwest Partes Called Neue Fravnce* . . . (London, 1580), 58; William Symonds, "Virginea Brittania," Alexander Brown, ed., *The Genesis of the United States* (Boston, 1890), I: 289; P[eter] H[eylyn], *Microcosmus, or a Little Description of the Great World* . . . (Oxford, 1621), 407. John Aubrey reported that Thomas Hariot had left among his papers "an Alphabet that he had contrived for the American Language, like Devills." Oliver Lawson Dick, ed., *Aubrey's Brief Lives* (Ann Arbor, 1957), 123.

12 Joseph de Acosta, *The Natural and Moral History of the Indies* . . . , ed. Clements R. Markham (London, 1880; orig. pub., London, 1604), 298–325, 330–2, 337, 368–9, 370–1.

13 Thomas Nicholas, *The Pleasant Historie of the Conquest of West India* . . . (London, 1578), 334; Gómara gave the number of Spaniards as forty; see Lesley Byrd Simpson, ed., *Cortés: The Life of the Conqueror by His Secretary, Francisco López de Gómara* (Berkeley, 1964), 281–2.

14 [Pierre d'Avity], *The Estates, Empires, & Principallities of the World* . . . (London, 1615), 256; [Thomas Nicholas], *The Strange and Delectable History of the Discouerie and Conquest of the Prouinces of Peru* . . . (London, 1581), Ci^v; Purchas, *Pvrchas His Pilgrimage*, 975, 1076–7.

15 Purchas, *Pvrchas His Pilgrimage*, 961; William Strachey, *The Historie of Travell into Virginia Britania*, ed. Louis B. Wright and Virginia Freund (London, 1953), 89.

16 Smith et al., "Map of Virginia," Barbour, ed., *Jamestown Voyages*, II: 367–8; William White, "Fragments published in 1614," *ibid.*, I: 148–9; Strachey, *Historie of Travell*, ed. Wright and Freund, 98–100; Purchas, *Pvrchas His Pilgrimage*, 952–3. It is possible that the English adopted the term "black boys" because of the satanic implications they saw in the huskanaw ceremony. See Patrick Copland, *Virginia's God Be Thanked* . . . , 29.

17 Alexander Whitaker, *Good Newes from Virginia 1613* (New York, n.d.), 24–6; Strachey, *Historie of Travell*, ed. Wright and Freund, 89–90; John Smith, "A True Relation," Barbour, ed., *Jamestown Voyages*, I: 188–9; "Instruccons Orders and Constitucons . . . ," Susan Myra Kingsbury, ed., *The Records of the Virginia Company of London* (Washington, 1906–35), III: 14–15; David B. Quinn, "The Lost Colony in Myth and Reality, 1586–1625," *England and the Discovery of America, 1481–1620* (New York, 1974), 456–8.

18 "The Famous Voyage of Sir Francis Drake . . . 1577," Richard Hakluyt, *The Principall Navigations Voiages and Discoueries of the English Nation*, ed. David B. Quinn and Raleigh Ashlin Skelton (Cambridge, 1965; orig. pub., London, 1589), 643C; "The Second Voyage . . . Martin Frobisher . . . ," Richard Hakluyt, *The Principal Navigations Voyages Traffiques & Discoueries of the*

English Nation . . . (Glasgow, 1903–5), VII: 220; "The Generall Historie of Virginia, New England and the Summer Isles," *Travels and Works of Captain John Smith* . . . , ed. Edward Arber and A. G. Bradley (Edinburgh, 1910), II: 398–9; Purchas, *Pvrchas His Pilgrimage*, 954.

19 George Percy, " 'A Trewe Relacon' Virginia from 1609 to 1612," *Tyler's Quarterly Historical and Genealogical Magazine* III (1922): 277–8. For an account of the activities of Satan in early Virginia, see Richard Beale Davis, "The Devil in Virginia in the Seventeenth Century," *Literature and Society in Early Virginia, 1608–1840* (Baton Rouge, 1973), 14–42.

20 John Brinsley, *The Consolation of Ovr Grammar Schooles* . . . (London, 1622), A2ᵛ–A3.

21 "A Description of New-England," *Travels and Works of Captain John Smith*, ed. Arber and Bradley, I: 191; George Best, "A True Discourse," Vilhjalmur Stefansson, ed., *The Three Voyages of Martin Frobisher* . . . (London, 1938; orig. pub., London, 1587), 34–5; "The First Voyage of Robert Baker to Guinie . . . ," Hakluyt, *Principall Navigations*, ed. Quinn and Skelton, 132; Winthrop D. Jordan, *White Over Black: American Attitudes Toward the Negro, 1550–1812*, (Chapel Hill, 1968), ch. 1; Eldred D. Jones, *The Elizabethan Image of Africa* (Charlottesville, 1971). Strachey, *Historie of Travell*, ed. Wright and Freund, 54, identifies the Indians as descendants of Ham, but without drawing any racialist conclusions. From Ham "Ignoraunce of the true worship of god took beginning, the Inventions of Hethenisme and adoration of falce gods, and the Deuill," but not the Indian's Physiognomy.

22 Hakluyt, *Divers Voyages*, ed. Jones, 65; John Brereton, *A Briefe and True Relation of the Discourerie of the North Part of Virginia* . . . (London, 1602), 10; Lescarbot, *Nova Francia*, 193; Jean Ribaut, *The Whole & True Discouerye of Terra Florida* . . . , ed. H. P. Biggar (Gainesville, Fla., 1964; orig. pub., London, 1563), 69; [Gabriel Archer], "Description of the People," Barbour, ed., *Jamestown Voyages*, I: 103; "Generall Historie," *Travels and Works of Captain John Smith*, ed. Arber and Bradley, I: 361.

23 Hakluyt, *Divers Voyages*, ed. Jones, 56–7; Sir Walter Ralegh, *The Discoverie of the Large and Bewtiful Empire of Guiana*, ed. V. T. Harlow (London, 1928, orig. pub., London, 1596), 46–7. Oviedo found the Indians physically unattractive, though not in color: J. H. Elliott, *The Old World and the New, 1492–1650* (Cambridge, 1970), 43. On the problem of the Virginia Indians as "Redmen," see Wesley Frank Craven, *White, Red, and Black: The Seventeenth-Century Virginian* (Charlottesville, 1971), 39–41.

24 William C. Sturtevant, "First Visual Images of Native America," Fredi Chiappelli et al., eds., *First Images of America: The Impact of the New World on the Old* (Berkeley, 1976), II: 418–19; Paul

Hulton and David B. Quinn, *The American Drawings of John White* . . . , 2 vols. (London and Chapel Hill, 1964); W. P. Cumming et al., *The Discovery of North America* (New York, 1972), ch. 4; Johan-Theodoro de Bry, *America* . . . (Franckfurt, 1617).

25 Thomas Tvke, *A Treastise against Painting and Tinctvring of Men and Women* . . . (London, 1616), 17, 24–5; Joseph H. Marshburn and Alan R. Velie, *Blood and Knavery: A Collection of English Renaissance Pamphlets and Ballads of Crime and Sin* (Madison, N.J., 1973), 186; Millar MacLure, *The Paul's Cross Sermons, 1534–1642* (Toronto, 1958), 136.

26 Hulton and Quinn, *American Drawings of John White*, vol. II, pls. 47, 60, 61; Andrew Thevet, *The New Founde Worlde* . . . (London, [1568]), 51–51^v, 123; H[eylyn], *Microcosmus*, 408, 413; Smith et al., "Map of Virginia," Barbour, ed., *Jamestown Voyages*, II: 355–6. Not all Europeans found native body decoration displeasing: See "George Percy's Discourse," *ibid.*, I: 136; Lescarbot, *Nova Francia*, 203–4.

27 Thevet, *New Founde Worlde*, 46–46^v; "The Foresayd Francis Lopez de Gomara . . . ," Hakluyt, *Principal Navigations*, IX: 167–8; Purchas, *Pvrchas His Pilgrimage*, 963; "Dionyse Settles Account of the Second Voyages," Stefansson, ed., *Three Voyages of Martin Frobisher*, II: 20.

28 Smith et al., "Map of Virginia," Barbour, ed., *Jamestown Voyages*, II: 354–5; "General Historie," *Travels and Works of Captain John Smith*, ed. Arber and Bradley, II: 464; Ralegh, *Discoverie of the Large and Bewtiful Empire of Guiana*, ed. Harlow, 33; Edward Waterhouse, "A Declaration of the State of the Colony . . . ," Kingsbury, ed., *Records of the Virginia Company*, III: 562.

29 "The Foresayd Francis Lopez de Gomara," Hakluyt, *Principal Navigations*, IX: 168; Strachey, *Historie of Travell*, ed. Wright and Freund, 116; Acosta, *Natural and Moral History of the Indies*, ed. Markham, 449–50.

30 Whitaker, *Good Newes from Virginia, 1613*, 26; Acosta, *Natural and Moral History of the Indies*, ed. Markham, 410; H[eylyn], *Microcosmus*, 414; [Abbot], *A Briefe Description of the Whole Worlde* (1599 ed.), D6; "Generall Historie," *Travels and Works of Captain John Smith*, ed. Arber and Bradley, 377–8.

31 Hakluyt, "Preface to the Second Edition, 1598," *Principal Navigations*, I: li–liii; "Relations touching the Tartars . . . ," Samuel Purchas, *Hakluytus Posthumus or Purchas His Pilgrimes* . . . (Glasgow, 1905–7), XI: 173; John Frampton, *A Discourse of the Nauigation which the Portugales Doe Make to the Realmes and Prouinces of the East* . . . (London, 1579), 15.

32 "The First Voyage Made by Master Anthony Ienkinson . . . ,"

Hakluyt, *Principall Navigations*, ed. Quinn and Skelton, 335; Hakluyt, *Divers Voyages*, ed. Jones, 83–4.

33 "The Second Voyage to Guinea . . . ," Hakluyt, *Principall Navigations*, ed. Quinn and Skelton, 94; Munster, "Treatyse of the Newe India . . . ,"ed. Eden in Arber, ed., *First Three English Books on America*, 35; Caius Julius Solinus, *The Excellent and Pleasant Worke of Iulius Solinus Polyhistor . . .* , trans. Arthur Golding, (London, 1587), Iuᵛ.

34 David B. Quinn, *The Elizabethans and the Irish* (Ithaca, 1966); Nicholas P. Canny, *The Elizabethan Conquest of Ireland: A Pattern Established, 1565–76* (New York, 1976).

35 Canny, *Elizabethan Conquest of Ireland*, 117–19, 133–4; J. Frederick Fausz, "The Powhatan Uprising of 1622: A Historical Study of Ethnocentrism and Cultural Conflict" (Ph.D. diss., College of William and Mary, 1977), 182, 189; Richard Eden, "Preface" to Peter Martyr, "Decades of the Newe Worlde," Arber, ed., *First Three English Books on America*, 57.

36 Edmund Spenser, *A View of the Present State of Ireland*, ed. W. L. Renwick (London, 1934), 70, 72; Canny, *Elizabethan Conquest of Ireland*, 126–30; Meek, *Social Science and the Ignoble Savage*, 37–49.

37 Margaret T. Hodgen, *Early Anthropology in the Sixteenth and Seventeenth Centuries* (Philadelphia, 1964), 146; "Certain Considerations Touching the Plantation in Ireland," *Works of Francis Bacon*, ed. Spedding et al., XI: 117–18; Spenser, *View of the Present State of Ireland*, ed. Renwick, 70.

38 Canny, *Elizabethan Conquest of Ireland*, ch. 6; Quinn, *Elizabethans and the Irish*, ch. 7. Montaigne noted that despite the cold the Irish wore few clothes: Richard Sayce, *The Essays of Montaigne: A Critical Exploration* (London, 1972), 83; Las Casas accused the ancient Irish of cannibalism: Elliott, *Old World and New*, 34.

39 "A Discourse of the Original and Fundamental Cause of Natural, Arbitrary, Necessary, and Unnatural War," *Works of Sir Walter Ralegh*, VIII: 279–80; Ralegh, *History of the World, ibid.*, IV: 420-1.

40 "A Discourse of the Original and Fundamental Cause of Natural, Arbitrary, Necessary, and Unnatural War," *Works of Sir Walter Ralegh*, VIII: 253; Ralegh, *History of the World, ibid.*, VII: 699.

41 Munster, "Treatyse on the Newe India," ed. Eden in Arber, ed., *First Three English Books on America*, 37; Lescarbot, *Nova Francia*, 308; Thevet, *New Founde Worlde*, 59; "Generall Historie," *Travels and Works of Captain John Smith*, ed. Arber and Bradley, I: 366.

42 [d'Avity], *Estates, Empires, & Principallities of the World*, 225; "Certaine Notes of the Voyage to Brasill," Hakluyt, *Principall Navigations*, ed. Quinn and Skelton, 643; Purchas, *Pvrchas His Pilgrimage*, 959; "George Percy's Discourse," Barbour, ed., *Jamestown Voyages*, I: 141–2.

43 Martyr, "Decades of the Newe Worlde," ed. Eden in Arber, ed., *First Three English Books on America*, 180; Acosta, *Natural and Moral History of the Indies*, ed. Markham, 69; "Extracts Out of the Historie of John Lerius . . . ," Purchas, *Hakluytus Posthumus*, XVI: 542.

44 "Arthur Barlowe's Discourse of the First Voyage," Quinn, ed., *Roanoke Voyages*, I: 112–13; Acosta, *Natural and Moral History of the Indies*, ed. Markham, 170; Lescarbot, *Nova Francia*, 182, 219; Purchas, *Pvrchas His Pilgrimage*, 949.

45 "A Discourse of the Original and Fundamental Cause of Natural, Arbitrary, Necessary, and Unnatural War," *Works of Sir Walter Ralegh*, VIII, 253; Smith et al., "Map of Virginia," Barbour, ed., *Jamestown Voyages*, II: 361; Hariot, "Briefe and True Report," Quinn, ed., *Roanoke Voyages*, I: 371; Thevet, *New Found Worlde*, 59.

46 *Faerie Queene*, bk. II, can. xi, st. 21, *The Works of Edmund Spenser: A Variorum Edition*, ed. Edwin Greenlaw et al. (Baltimore, 1932); Florio, *A Shorte and Briefe Narration*, 57; "Generall Historie," *Travels and Works of Captain John Smith*, ed. Arber and Bradley, I: 367–8.

47 "A Notable Historie . . . by Monsieur Laudonnière," Hakluyt, *Principal Navigations*, VIII: 453; "The Second Voyage unto Florida . . . ," *ibid.*, IX: 57; "Generall Historie," *Travels and Works of Captain John Smith*, ed. Arber and Bradley, I: 378; Florio, *A Shorte and Briefe Narration*, 57. The English practice in Ireland should be contrasted with Indian scalping: Canny, *Elizabethan Conquest of Ireland*, 122. Regina Flannery, *An Analysis of Coastal Algonquian Culture* (Washington, 1939), 124–5. On scalping, see James Axtell, "Who Invented Scalping?," *American Heritage* XXVIII (April 1977), 96–9.

48 Robert Stafforde, *A Geographical and Anthologicall Description of All the Empires and Kingdomes, Both of Continent and Iland in this Terrestriall Globe* (London, 1607), 62; "William White, Fragments . . . ," Barbour, ed., *Jamestown Voyages*, I: 150; Percy, "Trewe Relaycon," 263, 265–6; "Generall Historie," *Travels and Works of Captain John Smith*, ed. Arber and Bradley, I: 377.

49 Eli Sagan, *Cannibalism: Human Aggression and Cultural Form* (New York, 1974), chs. 1, 2, and 3.

50 "Generall Historie," *Travels and Works of Captain John Smith*, ed. Arber and Bradley, II: 498–9; "A Briefe Declaration of the

Plantation of Virginia . . . ," H. R. McIlwaine, ed., *Journals of the House of Burgesses of Virginia, 1619–1658* (Richmond, 1915), 29; "A Relation of Alvaro Munez . . . ," Purchas, *Hakluytus Posthumus*, XVII: 463; "A Notable Historie . . . by Monsieur Laudonnière," Hakluyt, *Principal Navigations*, VIII: 485–6.

51 Munster, "Treatyse of the Newe India," ed. Eden in Arber, ed., *First Three English Books on America*, 30; Sturtevant, "First Visual Images of Native America," Chiappelli et al., eds., *First Images of America*, II: 420; Hodgen, *Early Anthropology in the Sixteenth and Seventeenth Centuries*, 152; Bry, *America*, 44, 128, 152, 161, 385.

52 Martyr, "Decades of the Newe Worlde," ed. Eden in Arber, ed., *First Three English Books on America*, 69–70.

53 "The Admirable Adventures . . . of Master Antonie Knivet . . . ," Purchas, *Hakluytus Posthumus*, XVI: 222–3. John Smith believed that the Indians fed him so well while he was held captive because they intended to eat him: See "Generall Historie," *Travels and Works of Captain John Smith*, ed. Arber and Bradley, II: 397.

3. *BESTIALITY*

1 Lewis Hanke, "Pope Paul III and the American Indians," *Harvard Theological Review* XXX (1937): 65–102; Lewis Hanke, *Aristotle and the American Indians: A Study in Race Prejudice in the Modern World* (Bloomington, Ind., 1970), *passim;* Edmundo O'Gorman, "Sobre la naturaleza bestial del indio americano," *Filosofía y Letras* I (1941): 141–56; Lino Gómez Canedo, "Hombres o bestias?," *Estudios de Historia Novohispaña* I (1966): 29–51.

2 William Meredith Carroll, *Animal Conventions in English Renaissance Non-Religious Prose (1550–1600)* (New York, 1954); P. Ansell Robin, *Animal Lore in English Literature* (London, 1932); Anthony Petti, "Beasts and Politics in Elizabethan Literature," S. Gorley Putt, ed., *Essays and Studies* XVI (1963): 68–90; George Boas, *The Happy Beast in French Thought of the Seventeenth Century* (Baltimore, 1933); Richard Bernheimer, *Wild Man in the Middle Ages: A Study in Art, Sentiment, and Demonology* (Cambridge, Mass., 1952); Helen C. White, *Social Criticism in Popular Religious Literature of the Sixteenth Century* (New York, 1944).

3 Hugh Honour, *The New Golden Land: European Images of America from the Discoveries to the Present Time* (New York, 1975), 272; "Of the Newe Landes . . . ," Edward Arber, ed., *The First Three English Books on America . . .* (Birmingham, Eng., 1885), xxvii.

4 G[eorge] S[andys], *Ovids Metamorphosis Englished, Mythologiz'd, and Represented in Figures* . . . (Oxford, 1632), 477–8; [Pierre d' Avity], *The Estates, Empires, & Principallities of the World* . . . (London, 1615), 268; John Bonoeil, *His Majesties Graciovs Letter to the Earle of Sovth Hampton* . . . (London, 1622), 85–6. The pertinent Aristotelian text may be found in the *Nicomachean Ethics*, VII: 1149a9f: "And of the foolish, those who are irrational by nature and live only by their senses are like the beasts, as are some of the races of the distant barbarians." See Arthur O. Lovejoy and George Boas, *Primitivism and Related Ideas in Antiquity* (Baltimore, 1935), 177–80.

5 Andrewe Thevet, *The New Found Worlde* . . . (London, [1568]), 43–43^v; [d'Avity], *The Estates, Empires, & Principalities of the World*, 236–7; John Brinsley, *The Consolation or Ovr Grammar Schooles* . . . (London, 1622), 3; "The Voyage of Samuel Champlaine . . . ," Samuel Purchas, *Hakluytus Posthumus or Purchas His Pilgrimes* . . . (Glasgow, 1905–7), XVIII: 195, 198–9.

6 Robert Gray, *A Good Speed to Virginia (1609)*, ed. Wesley F. Craven (New York, 1937), C2^v, C3^v–C4; [Robert Johnson], *Nova Britannia* . . . (Rochester, 1897; orig. pub., London, 1609), 10; William Alexander, *An Encouragement to Colonies* (London, 1624), 37; Joseph de Acosta, *The Natural and Moral History of the Indies* . . . , ed. Clements R. Markham (London, 1880), 426–7; "A True Declaration of the Estate in Virginia," Peter Force, ed., *Tracts and Other Papers* . . . (Washington, 1844), III: 6.

7 [d'Avity], *The Estates, Empires, & Principalities of the World*, 266–7; "The Drawings of John White," David B. Quinn, ed., *The Roanoke Voyages, 1584–1590* (London, 1955), I: 414; "The Last Voyage of . . . Thomas Candish . . . ," Richard Hakluyt, *The Principal Navigations Voyages Traffiques & Discoveries of the English Nation* . . . (Glasgow, 1903–5), XI: 410; "A Treatise of Brazil by a Portugall," Purchas, *Hakluytus Posthumus*, XVI: 448; "Extracts Out of Certaine Letters of Father Martin Perez . . . ," *ibid.*, XVIII: 74; William Cuningham, *The Cosmographical Glasse* . . . (London, 1559), 201–2; Marc Lescarbot, *Nova Francia: A Description of Arcadia, 1606*, trans. P. Erondelle (London, 1928), 221; "The Generall Historie of Virginia, New England, and the Summer Isles," *Travels and Works of Captain John Smith* . . . , ed. Edward Arber and A. G. Bradley (Edinburgh, 1910), I: 363; William Strachey, *The Historie of Travell into Virginia Britania*, ed. Louis B. Wright and Virginia Freund (London, 1953), 80.

8 Loys Le Roy, *Of the Interchangeable Course or Variety of Things in the Whole World* . . . (London, 1594), 27^v–28; Ernest Lee Tuveson, *Millennium and Utopia: A Study in the Background of the Idea of Progress* (Berkeley, 1949), 59–66. Le Roy anticipated Montaigne in the negative description of noble savagism; see

Margaret T. Hodgen, *Early Anthropology in the Sixteenth and Seventeenth Centuries* (Philadelphia, 1964), 199.

9 "Observations . . . by the Inca Garcilasso de la Vega . . . ," Purchas, *Hakluytus Posthumus*, XVII: 314–15, 371–2.

10 [Caius Plinius Secundus], *The Secrets and Wonders of the World* . . . (London, 1585); *The Voiage and Trayayle of Sir John Maundeville* . . . , ed. John Ashton (London, 1887; orig. pub., London, 1568); Hodgen, *Early Anthropology in the Sixteenth and Seventeenth Centuries*, 128; Sebastian Munster, "Treatyse of the Newe India . . . ," ed. Richard Eden in Arber, ed., *First Three English Books on America*, 11; "The Second Voyage to Guinea . . . 1554," Richard Hakluyt, *The Principall Navigations Voiages and Discoveries of the English Nation*, ed. David B. Quinn and Raleigh Ashlin Skelton (Cambridge, 1965), 96.

11 Thevet, *New Found Worlde*, 42; "The Voyage Made by . . . John Hawkins . . ." (1564), Clements R. Markham, ed., *The Hawkins' Voyages* . . . (London, 1878), 60; "The Traviales of Job Hortop . . . ," Hakluyt, *Principal Navigations*, IX: 446–7, 449; "An Abridgement of the Medieval Legend of Prester John," Arber, ed., *First Three English Books on America*, xxxiii; "A Relation of . . . Frier Marco de Nica . . . ," Hakluyt, *Principal Navigations*, IX: 137; Edward Webbe, *The Rare and Most Wonderful Thinges which Edward Webbe . . . Hath Seene* . . . (London, 1590), in Edward Arber, ed., *English Reprints* (London, 1869), I: 25; Martyr, "Decades of the Newe World," ed. Eden in Arber, ed., *First Three English Books on America*, 131; [George Abbot], *A Briefe Description of the Whole Worlde* . . . (London, 1599), R1ᵛ.

12 Edward Topsell, *The Historie of Fovre-Footed Beastes* . . . (London, 1607), 15; Richard Whitbourne, *A Discovrse and Discovery of New-Found-Land* . . . (London, 1622), R4–R4ᵛ. Purchas altered Whitbourne's description of the creature so as to stress its human qualities. He changed "blue streakes, resembling haire, but certainly was not haire" to "blew strakes, resembling haire, downe to the Necke (but certainly it was haire)"; see "Captaine Richard Whitbournes Voyages . . . ," Purchas, *Hakluytus Posthumus*, XIX: 439–40. "The First Voyage Made to Divers Parts of America . . . ," *ibid.*, XVI: 111; Thomas Glover, "An Account of Virginia . . . ," *Royal Society Philosophical Transactions* XI (1676): 625–6.

13 Sir Walter Ralegh, *The Discoverie of the Large and Bewtiful Empire of Guiana*, ed. V. T. Harlow (London, 1928; orig. pub., London, 1596), 56–7; Lawrence Kemys, *A Relation of the Second Voyage to Guiana* . . . (London, 1596), C3–C3ᵛ; Abbot, *A Briefe Description of the Whole Worlde*, V1ᵛ–V2; Samuel Purchas, *Purchas His Pilgrimage* . . . (London, 1617), 1020–1; "A Relation of the Habitations . . . of the River Marwin . . . ," Purchas, *Hakluytus Posthumus*, XVI: 408; Lescarbot, *Nova Francia*, 21–2. Shakespeare

noted the existence of people with faces between their shoulders in *Othello*, act I, sc. iii, lines 140–5, and in *The Tempest*, act III, sc. iii, line 47.

14 Carl Ortwin Sauer, *The Early Spanish Main* (Berkeley, 1969), 23; Thevet, *New Found Worlde*, 101–3; Purchas, *Hakluytus Posthumus*, XVII: 261; *Faerie Queene*, bk. IV, can. xi, st. 21, *The Works of Edmund Spenser: A Variorum Edition*, ed. Edwin Greenlaw et al. (Baltimore, 1932).

15 Peter Martyr, "The Decades of the Newe Worlde," ed. Eden in Arber, ed., *The First Three English Books on America*, 97; Samuel Eliot Morison, *The European Discovery of America: The Southern Voyages, A.D. 1492–1616* (New York, 1974), 212; Antonio Pigafetta, "A Briefe Declaration of the Vyage . . . Made Abowte the Worlde . . . ," ed. Eden in Arber, ed., *First Three English Books on America*, 251–2; Antonello Gerbi, "The Earliest Accounts on the New World," Fredi Chiappelli et al., eds., *First Images of America: The Impact of the New World on the Old* (Berkeley, 1976), I: 41–2; Acosta, *Natural and Moral History of the Indies*, ed. Markham, 453–4; Augustin de Zarate, *The Strange and Delectable History of the Descoverie and Conquest of the Provinces of of Peru . . .* , [trans. Thomas Nicholas] (London, 1581), Cii–Cii^v; "The Admirable Adventures . . . of Master Antonie Knivet . . . ," Purchas, *Hakluytus Posthumus*, XVI: 265–6; Sir Walter Ralegh, *The History of the World* in *The Works of Sir Walter Ralegh* (Oxford, 1829), VI: 29; Smith met Indians he called giants; see his "General Historie," *Travels and Works of Captain John Smith*, ed. Arber and Bradley, 350; Hayden White, "The Forms of Wildness: Archaeology of an Idea," Edward Dudley and Maximillian E. Novak, eds., *The Wild Man Within: An Image in Western Thought from the Renaissance to Romanticism* (Pittsburgh, 1972), 15.

16 Bernheimer, *Wild Man in the Middle Ages*, 5–6; Theodore Spencer, *Shakespeare and the Nature of Man*, 2nd ed. (New York, 1961), 11.

17 Bernheimer, *Wild Man in the Middle Ages*, 8, 30; *Faerie Queene*, bk. I, can. vi, st. 23, *Works of Edmund Spenser*, ed. Greenlaw et al.

18 Bernheimer, *Wild Man in the Middle Ages*, 3–4, 9–13; Thevet (*New Found World*, 47–47^v), after seeing American natives, claimed that wild men may "live in the woods and fields almost like the brute beasts," but that they were not covered with hair.

19 Bernheimer, *Wild Man in the Middle Ages*, 4–5, 112, 144–5; White, "Forms of Wildness," Dudley and Novak, eds., *Wild Man Within*, 22; Penelope B. R. Doob, *Nebuchadnezzar's Children: Conventions of Madness in Middle English Literature* (New Haven, 1974), ch. 4; Robert Hillis Goldsmith, "The Wild Man on the English Stage," *Modern Language Review* LIII (1958): 485, 488.

20 Bernheimer, *Wild Man in the Middle Ages*, 11–15.

21 *Faerie Queene*, bk. VI, can. ii, st. 1, *Works of Edmund Spenser*, ed. Greenlaw et al.; A Bartlett Giamatti, "Primitivism and the Process of Civility in Spenser's *Faerie Queene*," Chiappelli et al., eds., *First Images of America*, I: 76; Donald Cheney, *Spenser's Image of Nature: Wild Man and Shepherd in "The Faerie Queene"* (New Haven, 1966), 182; Roy Harvey Pearce, "Primitivistic Ideas in the *Faerie Queene*," *Journal of English and Germanic Philology* XLIV (1945): 151.

22 *Faerie Queene*, bk. VI, can. i, st. 7 and 8, *Works of Edmund Spenser*, ed. Greenlaw et al.; John Erskine Hankins, *Source and Meaning in Spenser's Allegory: A Study of the Faerie Queene* (Oxford, 1971), 50, 72; Rosemary Freeman, *The Faerie Queene: A Companion for Readers* (London, 1970), 303–4; Cheney, *Spenser's Image of Nature*, 183–4.

23 *Faerie Queene*, bk. VI, can. v, st. 1–41, *Works of Edmund Spenser*, ed. Greenlaw et al.; Freeman, *The Faerie Queene*, 310–14; Cheney, *Spenser's Image of Nature*, 209–14.

24 *Faerie Queene*, bk. VI, can. ii, st. 6; bk. VI, can. ii, st. 11, 18; bk. VI, can. viii, st. 25, 26, *Works of Edmund Spenser*, ed. Greenlaw et al.

25 Topsell, *Historie of Fovre-Footed Beastes*, 3, 8, 12–14, 15. Topsell drew on the work of the German zoologist Conrad Gesner, who published his *Historia Anamalium* between 1551 and 1558. See Robin, *Animal Lore in English Literature*, 12–13.

26 "Of the Cannibals," *Montaigne's Essays*, trans. John Florio, Everyman edition (New York, 1965), I: 220.

27 "An Apologie of Raymond Sebond," *Montaigne's Essays*, II: 125–326; George Boas, *Happy Beast in French Thought of the Seventeenth Century*, chs. 1 and 2; R. A. Sayce, *The Essays of Montaigne; A Critical Exploration* (London, 1972), 189–92; Pierre Villey, *Les sources & l'evolution des Essais de Montaigne*, 2nd ed. (Paris, 1933), II: 175–6. For a discussion of the problem of theriophilism, see H. W. Janson, *Apes and Ape Lore in the Middle Ages and the Renaissance* (London, 1952).

28 "An Apologie of *Raymond Sebond*," *Montaigne's Essays*, II: 142–84.

29 *Ibid.*, II: 143, 151–52, 159, 172–4.

30 *Ibid.*, II: 146–9, 160–1, 190–1.

31 Joseph Jacobs, ed., *The Fables of Aesop as First Printed by William Caxton in 1484* . . . (New York, 1970); A. W. Pollard and G. R. Redgrave, comps., *The Short-Title Catalogue of Books Printed in England, Scotland, & Ireland and of English Books Printed Abroad, 1475–1640* (London, 1946), 5; Petti, "Beasts and Politics in Elizabethan Literature," Putt, ed., *Essays and Studies*, 68–9.

32 Sir Thomas Chaloner, *The Praise of Folie*, ed. Clarence H. Miller

(New York, 1965; orig. pub., 1549), 46–7; G. H. Mair, ed., *Wilson's Arte of Rhetorique 1560* (Oxford, 1909), 76–7, 191–4; Topsell, *Historie of Fovre-Footed Beastes*, A4.

33 Carroll, *Animal Conventions*, 46; Petti, "Beasts and Politics in Elizabethan Literature," Putt, ed., *Essays and Studies, passim*; Audrey Yoder, *Animal Analogy in Shakespeare's Character Portrayal* (New York, 1947), 34, 61; Robin, *Animal Lore in English Literature*, 18.

34 Alan Fager Herr, *The Elizabethan Sermon: A Survey and a Bibliography* (Philadelphia, 1940), 58; Abraham Fleming, *The Diamond of Devotion* . . . (London, 1602), 19; Christopher Sutton, *Disce Mori: Learne to Dye* . . . (London, 1634), 35.

35 Lewes Bayly, *The Practise of Pietie* . . . , 9th ed. (London, 1617), 62–3; Thomas Tymme, *A Silver Watch-Bell* . . . (London, 1634), 8–9.

36 Henry Parry, *The Svmme of Christian Religion* . . . (Oxford, 1595), 6; Thomas Tymme, *The Poore Mans Pater Noster* . . . (N.P., 1598), Q4–Q4^v; Arthvr Dent, *The Plaine Mans Path-way to Heauen* . . . (London, 1603), 128, 162, 168–72, 180, 188; [Robert Underwood], *A New Anatomie* . . . (London, 1605), 32; Thomas Dekker, *Foure Birds of Noahs Arke*, ed. F. P. Wilson (Oxford, 1924; orig. pub., London, 1609), 150, 182, 200; Richard Eburne, *A Plain Pathway to Plantations (1624)*, ed. Louis B. Wright (Ithaca, 1962), 38, 39; Christopher Sutton, *Disce Vivere: Learne to Live* . . . (London, 1634), 49, 108, 111–12; Louis B. Wright, *Middle-Class Culture in Elizabethan England* (Ithaca, 1958), 232–4.

37 Dent, *Plaine Mans Path-way to Heauen*, 251.

38 Thomas Hill, *A Pleasant History: Declaring the Whole Art of Phisiognomy* . . . (N.P., 1613), A3–A3^v, 1^v, 70^v, 84, 85^v, 110^v, 122^v. The vice of poverty and the "sturdy beggers" who practiced it were also described in the language of bestiality. "These idle beastes will devour al that we shal get by over sore labour . . . ." See Robert Crowley *The Way to Wealth* . . . (London, 1550), A4; Ro[bert] Wakeman, *The Poore-mans Preacher* . . . (London, 1607), 12; John Chamberlain to Sir Dudley Carleton, July 9, 1612, *The Letters of John Chamberlain*, ed. Norman Egbert McClure (Philadelphia, 1939), I: 367; White, *Social Criticism in Popular Religious Literature of the Sixteenth Century*, 248, 280; B. L. Joseph, *Shakespeare's Eden: The Commonwealth of England, 1558–1629* (London, 1971), 93; Joseph H. Marshburn and Alan R. Velie, eds., *Blood and Knavery: A Collection of English Renaissance Pamphlets and Ballads of Crime and Sin* (Madison, N.J., 1973), 24, 25, 71.

39 D. G. James, *The Dream of Prospero* (Oxford, 1967), 72–97; Robert Ralston Cawley, "Shakespeare's Use of the Voyagers in *The Tempest*," *PMLA* XLI (1926): 688–726.

40 W. Gordon Zeeveld, *The Temper of Shakespeare's Thought* (New Haven, 1974), 247–57; K. M. Abenheimer, "Shakespeare's 'Tempest': A Psychological Analysis," *The Psychoanalytic Review* XXXIII (1946): 399–415; for Gonzalo's speech see *The Tempest,* act II, sc. i, lines 148–57, *The Riverside Shakespeare,* ed. G. Blakemore Evans (Boston, 1974), II: 1620.

41 *The Tempest,* act II, sc. i, lines 24–36, 57–8, *Riverside Shakespeare,* ed. Evans, II: 1622, 1623.

42 *Ibid.,* act IV, sc. i, lines 188–92, II: 1631; Hallett Smith, *Shakespeare's Romances: A Study of Some Ways of the Imagination* (San Marino, Calif., 1972), 140–2.

43 Frank Kermode, ed., *The Tempest* (Cambridge, Mass., 1958), xxxviii, n. 2; Leslie A. Fiedler, *The Stranger in Shakespeare* (New York, 1972), 234; George Coffin Taylor, "Shakespeare's Use of the Idea of the Beast in Man," *Studies in Philology* XLII (1945): 530–43; John E. Hankins, "Caliban the Bestial Man," *PMLA* LXII (1947): 793–801; Thomas P. Harrison, Jr., "Aspects of Primitivism in Shakespeare and Spenser," *The University of Texas Studies in English,* no. 4026 (1940): 59.

4. DEPENDENCE

1 Bernardino de Escalante, *A Discourse of the Navigation Which the Portugales Doe Make to the Realmes and Provinces of the East . . .* , trans. John Frampton (London, 1579), 3ᵛ, 41–41ᵛ.

2 Joseph de Acosta, *The Natural and Moral History of the Indies . . .* , ed. Clements R. Markham (London, 1880; orig. pub., London, 1604), 390–1; [Giovanni Botero], *The Worlde, or an Historical Description of the Most Famous Kingdomes and Commonweales Therein . . .* , trans. Robert Johnson (London, 1601), 37; [George Abbot], *A Briefe Description of the Whole Worlde . . .* (London, 1605), S1ᵛ. Benjamin Keen, *The Aztec Image in Western Thought* (New Brunswick, N.J., 1971), 55–6.

3 Peter Martyr, "Decades of the Newe Worlde . . . ," ed. Richard Eden in Edward Arber, ed., *First Three English Books on America . . .* (Birmingham, Eng., 1885), 55, 186; Antonio de Espejo, *New Mexico . . .* (London, 1587), B1ᵛ – B4, B8⁴; Thomas Nicholas, *The Pleasant Historie of the Conquest of the West India . . .* (London, 1578), 67; "Examination of David Ingram," David B. Quinn, ed., *The Voyages and Colonising Enterprises of Sir Humphrey Gilbert* (London, 1940), II: 281.

4 "The Generall Historie of Virginia, New England and the Summer Isles," *Travels and Works of Captain John Smith . . .* , ed. Edward Arber and A. G. Bradley (Edinburgh, 1910), I: 347–8. Estimates of the Powhatan population have increased since Mooney and Mook examined the question. See Maurice A. Mook,

"The Aboriginal Population of Tidewater Virginia," *American Anthropologist*, n.s., 46 (1944): 194–8; James Mooney, "The Powhatan Confederacy, Past and Present," *American Anthropologist*, n.s., 9 (1907): 129–52. Christian F. Feest, "Seventeenth Century Virginia Algonquian Population Estimates," *Archaeological Society of Virginia Quarterly Bulletin* XXVIII (1973): 74, estimates the total Algonquin population of Tidewater Virginia in 1607 to have been between 14,300 and 22,300 people; J. Frederick Fausz, "The Powhatan Uprising of 1622: A Historical Study of Ethnocentrism and Cultural Conflict" (Ph.D. diss., College of William and Mary, 1977), 60, puts the Powhatan population at about 12,000. See also Lewis Roberts Binford, "Archaeological and Ethnohistorical Investigation of Cultural Diversity and Progressive Development among Aboriginal Cultures of Coastal Virginia and North Carolina" (Ph.D. diss., University of Michigan, 1964), 74–82.

5 John Smith et al., "A Map of Virginia," Philip L. Barbour, ed., *The Jamestown Voyages under the First Charter, 1606–1609* (Cambridge, 1969), II: 371; William Strachey, *The Historie of Travell into Virginia Britania*, ed. Louis B. Wright and Virginia Freund (London, 1953), 57–8, 60–1.

6 William Powell to Edwin Sandys, April 12, 1621, Susan Myra Kingsbury, ed., *The Records of the Virginia Company of London* (Washington, 1906–35), III: 436.

7 "Generall Historie," *Travels and Works of Captain John Smith*, ed. Arber and Bradley, I: 375; Alexander Whitaker, *Good Newes from Virginia, 1613* (New York, n.d.), 26–7; Stanley Pargellis, ed., "An Account of the Indians in Virginia," *William and Mary Quarterly*, 3rd ser., XVI (1959): 230–1, 233, 235. See also Regina Flannery, *An Analysis of Coastal Algonquian Culture* (Washington, 1939), 122–3; Binford, "Archaeological and Ethnohistorical Investigation," 87–101.

8 "General Historie," *Travels and Works of Captain John Smith*, ed. Arber and Bradley, I: 306, II: 413; "A Relatyon ... Written ... by a Gent. of yᵉ Colony [Captain Gabriel Archer?]," Barbour, ed., *Jamestown Voyages*, I: 92; "George Percy's Discourse," *ibid.*, I: 137; Strachey, *Historie of Travell*, ed. Wright and Freund, 65.

9 Thomas Hariot, "A Briefe and True Report," David B. Quinn, ed., *The Roanoke Voyages, 1584–1590* (London, 1955), I: 370; Strachey, *Historie of Travell*, ed. Wright and Freund, 69, 87; Binford, "Archaeological and Ethnohistorical Investigation," 90–1; Christian Feest, "Powhatan: A Study in Political Organization," *Wiener Volkerkundliche Mitteilungen* XII (1966): 71, 73. Marc Lescarbot, *Nova Francia: Description of Arcadia, 1606*, trans. P. Erondelle (London, 1928), 180–1, relates the diversity of lan-

guages among the Indians to the consequences of the Tower of Babel.

10 Smith et al., "Map of Virginia," Barbour, ed., *Jamestown Voyages,* II: 257; "Description of the People," *ibid.,* I: 104; Pargellis, ed., "Account of the Indians in Virginia," 232; Lescarbot, *Nova Francia,* 252–3, 271.

11 Lescarbot, *Nova Francia,* 215–20; Henry S. Burrage, ed., *Rosier's Relation of Waymouth's Voyage to the Coast of Maine, 1605* (Portland, Me., 1887), 112; "The Second Voyage . . . by Captain Laudonnière . . . ," Richard Hakluyt, *The Principal Navigations Voyages Traffiques & Discoveries of the English Nation . . .* (Glasgow, 1903–5), IX: 56; "The Relation of . . . Captaine Fernando Alarchon, . . . ," *ibid.,* IX: 286, 308–9.

12 "A Relation of a Voyage to Guiana . . . by Robert Harcourt . . . ," Samuel Purchas, *Hakluytus Posthumus or Purchas His Pilgrimes . . .* (Glasgow, 1905–7), XVI: 362; Strachey, *Historie of Travell,* ed. Wright and Freund, 71, 98, 100; "William White, Fragments . . . ," Barbour, ed., *Jamestown Voyages,* I: 150; John Smith, "A True Relation . . . ," *ibid.,* I: 191–2; Binford, "Archaeological and Ethnohistorical Investigation," 96.

13 "Generall Historie," *Travels and Works of Captain John Smith,* ed. Arber and Bradley, I: 346, 361, 377; Whitaker, *Good Newes from Virginia,* 26–7; Kaj Berkit-Smith, "Powhatan and Pamlico," *Primitive Man and His Ways . . .* (London, 1960), 184.

14 "The Relation of . . . Captaine Fernando Alarchon," Hakluyt, *Principal Navigations,* IX: 315.

15 Walter Ralegh, *The History of the World,* in *The Works of Sir Walter Ralegh . . .* (Oxford, 1829), II: 334; Quinn, ed., *Roanoke Voyages,* I: 368; II: 853; "A Relatyon . . . Written . . . by a Gent of yᵉ Colony [Captain Gabriel Archer?], Barbour, ed., *Jamestown Voyages,* I: 94; "Letter to Virginia Company of London," January 1622, Kingsbury, ed., *Records of the Virginia Company,* III: 584. "Discourse on Western Planting . . . ," *The Original Writings & Correspondence of the Two Richard Hakluyts,* ed. E. G. R. Taylor (London, 1935), II: 215; Strachey, *Historie of Travell,* ed. Wright and Freund, 21–22; "A Notable Historie . . . ," Hakluyt, *Principal Navigations,* VIII: 466; "The Third Voyage . . . by Captaine Jaques Cartier, 1540," *ibid.,* 269–70; Andrewe Thevet, *The New Found Worlde . . .* (London, [1568]), 45ᵛ; "The Relation of Master John Wilson . . . ," Purchas, *Hakluytus Posthumus,* XVI: 351; "Generall Historie," *Travels and Works of Captain John Smith,* ed. Arber and Bradley, I: 381–2; "The Second Voyage . . . by Master John Davis . . . ," Richard Hakluyt, *The Principall Navigations Voiages and Discoveries of the English Nation,* ed. David B. Quinn and Raleigh Ashlin Skelton (Cambridge, 1965),

783; John Florio, *A Shorte and Briefe Narration of the Two Navigations and Discoveries to the Northwest Partes Called Newe Fraunce* . . . (London, 1580), 27, 78–80.

16 John Frampton, *Joyfull Newes Out of the Newe Founde Worlde* . . . , ed. Stephen Gaselee, 2 vols. (London, 1925), Frampton put out editions of Monardes in 1577, 1580, and 1596; see Lawrence C. Wroth, "An Elizabethan Merchant and Man of Letters," *Huntington Library Quarterly* XVII (1954): 307–9.

17 James I, "A Counterblaste to Tobacco," Edward Arber, ed., *English Reprints* (London, 1869), VIII: 100; "The Masque of Flowers," E. A. J. Honigmann, ed., *A Book of Masques in Honour of Allardyce Nicoll* (Cambridge, 1967), 165; "Tobacco Memorandum," Alexander Brown, ed., *The Genesis of the United States* (Boston, 1890), II: 772; [Abbot], *A Briefe Description of the Whole Worlde*, T3^v; Lescarbot, *Nova Francia*, 298–9; Florio, *A Shorte and Briefe Narration*, 60; Carl Bridenbaugh, *Vexed and Troubled Englishmen, 1590–1642* (New York, 1968), 195–6.

18 Frampton, *Joyfull Newes Out of the Newe Founde Worlde*, ed. Gaselee, I: 28, 134, 144; Joseph Ewan, "The Columbian Discoveries and the Growth of Botanical Ideas with Special Reference to the Sixteenth Century," Fredi Chiappelli et al., eds., *First Images of America: The Impact of the New World on the Old* (Berkeley, 1976), II: 808. On venereal disease, see Francisco Guerra, "The Problem of Syphilis," *ibid.*, 845–51; Alfred W. Crosby, Jr., *The Columbian Exchange: Biological and Cultural Consequences of 1492* (Westport, Conn., 1972), ch. 4.

19 Lescarbot, *Nova Francia*, 240; Florio, *A Shorte and Briefe Narration*, 64–9; Bruce R. Trigger, *The Children of Aataentsic: A History of the Huron People to 1660* (Montreal, 1976), I: 194; Smith et al., "Map of Virginia," Barbour, ed., *Jamestown Voyages*, II: 363–4; "Description of the River and Country," *ibid.*, I: 102; Hariot, "Briefe and True Report," Quinn, ed., *Roanoke Voyages*, I: 329; Pargellis, ed., "Account of the Indians in Virginia," 233. In 1601 the French botanist F. B. de l'Ecuse obtained guaiac wood from James Garth, a London druggist; see Cornelius Jaenen, *Friend and Foe: Aspects of French-Amerindian Cultural Contract in the Sixteenth and Seventeenth centuries* (New York, 1973), 118n. For a survey of the white man's early acceptance of native medicine, see Virgil J. Vogel, *American Indian Medicine* (Norman, Okla., 1970), ch. 3.

20 Ronald L. Meek, *Social Science and the Ignoble Savage* (Cambridge, 1976), ch. 2, maintains that the four-stage theory of development was not clearly formulated until the eighteenth century, though something like it was implicit in the doctrine of savagism in the early years of discovery and settlement. Nicholas P. Canny, *The Elizabethan Conquest of Ireland: A Pattern Established,*

1565–76 (New York, 1976), 13–15, notes that the English claimed that the Irish were savage because they did not cultivate the land.

21 Ester Boserup, *The Conditions of Agricultural Growth: The Economics of Agrarian Change under Population Pressure* (Chicago, 1965), discusses primitive agriculture and argues for its relatively high productivity; Marshall Sahlins, *Stone Age Economics* (Chicago, 1972), ch. 2 and 3, sees it as relatively more productive given the underuse of resources as compared with more intensive methods of farming. Smith et al., "Map of Virginia," Barbour, ed., *Jamestown Voyages*, II: 351; Strachey, *Historie of Travell*, ed. Wright and Freund, 118–19. See also Binford, "Archaeological and Ethnohistorical Investigation," 35–6, 161–3; Feest, "Powhatan: A Study in Political Organization," 76.

22 "Instructions for the Virginia Colony of 1606," *Original Writings & Correspondence of the Two Richard Hakluyts*, ed. Taylor, II: 495; Strachey, *Historie of Travell*, ed. Wright and Freund, 67, 79; "Generall Historie," *Travels and Works of Captain John Smith*, ed. Arber and Bradley, I: 363; Birket-Smith, "Powhatan and Pamlico," 181–3; Philip Alexander Bruce, *Economic History of Virginia in the Seventeenth Century* . . . (New York, 1935), 154, 156–7; Hariot, "Briefe and True Report," Quinn, ed., *Roanoke Voyages*, I: 342; Feest, "Powhatan: A Study in Political Organization," 74–5.

23 Strachey, *Historie of Travell*, ed. Wright and Freund, 79–80; "Arthur Barlowe's Discourse of the First Voyage," Quinn, ed., *Roanoke Voyages*, I: 105; Charles C. Willoughby, "The Virginia Indians in the Seventeenth Century," *American Anthropologist*, n.s., 9 (1907): 84–5; Ben C. McCary, *Indians in Seventeenth Century Virginia* (Charlottesville, 1957), 17.

24 "A Notable Historie . . . by Monsieur Laudonnière . . . ," Hakluyt, *Principal Navigations*, VIII: 477–84; "The Second Voyage . . . by Captaine Laudonnière . . . ," *ibid.*, IX: 3–4.

25 "The Second Voyage . . . by Captaine Laudonnière . . . ," Hakluyt, *Principal Navigations*, IX: 59–66; "Notes of Voyages and Plantations of the French in the Northerne America . . . ," Purchas, *Hakluytus Posthumus*, XVIII: 183–4; John Sparke, "The Voyage Made by . . . John Hawkins . . . ," Clements R. Markham, ed., *The Hawkins' Voyages* . . . (London, 1878), 54, 55–7; Nicolas Le Challeux, *A True and Perfect Description of the Last Voyage . . . Attempted by Capitaine John Rybaut* . . . (London, 1566), Bvi.

26 "The Second Voyage . . . by Captaine Laudonnière . . . ," Hakluyt, *Principal Navigations*, IX: 65–6, 73–4.

27 "Ralph Lane's Discourse on the First Colony," Quinn, ed., *Roanoke Voyages*, I: 276–83; David B. Quinn, *England and the Discovery of America, 1481–1620* . . . (New York, 1974), 290, 303–4.

28 Edmund S. Morgan, *American Slavery, American Freedom: The*

Ordeal of Colonial Virginia (New York, 1975), ch. 4; Karen Ordahl Kupperman, "Apathy and Death in Early Jamestown," *Journal of American History* 66 (1979): 24–40.

29 "The London Council's Instructions . . . ," Barbour, ed., *Jamestown Voyages*, I: 51–2; "Instruccͦons . . . to Sʳ Thomas Gates," Kingsbury, ed., *Records of the Virginia Company*, III: 16; Samuel Purchas, *Pvrchas His Pilgrimage* . . . (London, 1617), 947; "Generall Historie," *Travels and Works of Captain John Smith*, ed. Arber and Bradley, II: 562.

30 Darrett B. Rutman and Anita H. Rutman," Of Agues and Fevers: Malaria in the Early Chesapeake," *William and Mary Quarterly*, 3d ser., XXXIII (1976): 31–60, stress the impact of malaria on the Jamestown colonists; "George Percy's Discourse," Barbour, ed., *Jamestown Voyages*, I: 145; "Generall Historie," *Travels and Works of Captain John Smith*, ed. Arber and Bradley, II: 402, 434; Samuel Argall to Nicholas Hawes, June 1613, Brown, ed., *Genesis of the United States*, II: 641–2; John Smith, "A True Relation," Barbour, ed., *Jamestown Voyages*, I: 199; Ralph Hamor, *A True Discourse of the Present State of Virginia*, ed. A. L. Rowse (Richmond, 1957; orig. pub., London, 1615), 2.

31 "Francis Perkin[s] in Jamestown to a Friend in England," March 28, 1608, Barbour, ed., *Jamestown Voyages*, I: 160; Smith et al., "Map of Virginia," *ibid.*, I: 443–4, 446; "Generall Historie," *Travels and Works of Captain John Smith*, ed. Arber and Bradley, II: 452, 463, 580.

32 "Proclamation," May 9, 1623, Kingsbury, ed., *Records of the Virginia Company*, IV: 172–3.

33 Bruce, *Economic History of Virginia*, I: 165; Wesley Frank Craven, *Dissolution of the Virginia Company: The Failure of a Colonial Experiment* (New York, 1932), 37, 167–8; "Commission to Captain Ralph Hamor," May 7, 1622, Kingsbury, ed., *Records of the Virginia Company* III: 622.

34 Purchas, *Pvrchas His Pilgrimage*, 963; "A Relation of Alvaro Nunez . . . ," Purchas, *Hakluytus Posthumus*, XVII: 465–7, 475; "A Treatise of Brasil . . . ," *ibid.*, XVI: 420–1; "The Voyage of Samuel Champlaine . . . ," *ibid.*, XVIII: 195; Lescarbot, *Nova Francia*, 225; Christopher Carleill, "A Briefe and Summary Discourse . . . ," Quinn, ed., *Voyages and Colonising Enterprises of Sir Humphrey Gilbert*, II: 362; Florio, *Short and Briefe Narration*, 60.

35 "Generall Historie," *Travels and Works of Captain John Smith*, ed. Arber and Bradley, II: 570; George Somers to Earl of Salisbury, June 15, 1610, Brown, ed., *Genesis of the United States*, I: 401; Smith, "True Relation," Barbour, ed., *Jamestown Voyages*, I: 177–8; Smith et al., "Map of Virginia," *ibid.*, II: 416–17, 477.

36 William Strachey, "True Reportory," Louis B. Wright, ed., *A Voyage to Virginia in 1609* . . . (Charlottesville, 1964), 64, 74–5; Strachey, *Historie of Travell*, ed. Wright and Freund, 80, 84; "Generall Historie," *Travels and Works of Captain John Smith*, ed. Arber and Bradley, I: 360, II: 464, 590.

37 Strachey, *Historie of Travell*, ed. Wright and Freund, 62, 80, 87; Smith et al., "Map of Virginia," Barbour, ed., *Jamestown Voyages*, II: 370, 437; Binford, "Archaeological and Ethnohistorical Investigation," 93–5. Fausz, "The Powhatan Uprising of 1622," 98–9, argues that the discrepancy between the plenty produced by the Indians and the scarcity perceived by the colonists can be explained by the maldistribution of wealth between the native classes. Morgan, *American Slavery, American Freedom*, 50–1, denies that Powhatan took eighty percent of native resources and kept a well-stocked hoard of goods on the grounds that such a practice would belie the Indians' lack of acquisitiveness. For an account of the Feast of the Dead, an institution of redistribution found among the Hurons, see Trigger, *Children of Aataentsic*, I: 425–9.

38 The issue of white Indians would soon become a celebrated cause in the history of America, producing a mountainous literature. See in particular J. Norman Heard, *White into Red: A Study of the Assimilation of White Persons Captured by Indians* (Metuchen, N.J., 1973), and James Axtell, "The White Indians of Colonial America," *William and Mary Quarterly*, 3rd ser., XXXII (1975): 55–88.

39 "A Description of the West Indies, by Antonio De Herrera . . . ," Purchas, *Hakluytus Posthumus*, XIV: 583; "The Admirable Adventures . . . of Master Antonie Knivet . . . ," *ibid.*, XVI: 223–4; Walter Ralegh, *The Discoverie of the Large and Bewtiful Empire of Guiana*, ed. V. T. Harlow (London, 1928; orig. pub., London, 1596), LXXVII–LXXVIII.

40 Nicholas, *Pleasant Historie of the Conquest of the West India*, 34; "Second Voyage . . . by Captain Laudonnière," Hakluyt, *Principal Navigations*, IX: 49–51; "The Relation of Peter Carder . . . ," Purchas, *Hakluytus Posthumus*, XVI: 141–2, 145–56.

41 Strachey. "True Reportory," Wright, ed., *Voyage to Virginia*, 41–4. According to Smith, one of the rebels, Edward Carter, made his way to Virginia and at the time of the massacre was held captive, together with his wife, by the Nansemonds. Both escaped. "Generall Historie," *Travels and Works of Captain John Smith*, ed. Arber and Bradley, II: 638, 640–1. Wesley Frank Craven, *An Introduction to the History of Bermuda* ([Williamsburg, Va.], 1937), 18n, believes that the colonists remained in Bermuda in order to retain possession for future settlement.

42 Smith, "True Relation," Barbour, ed., *Jamestown Voyages,* I: 194, 205–6; Smith et al., "Map of Virginia," *ibid.,* 391–2; Hamor, *True Discourse,* ed. Rouse, 37; Kingsbury, ed., *Records of the Virginia Company,* IV: 276, 514; Brown, ed., *Genesis of the United States,* II: 996; Philip L. Barbour, *The Three Worlds of Captain John Smith* (Boston, 1964), 195, 351; Henry Fleet, "A Brief Journal of a Voyage Made in the Bark Virginia, to Virginia and Other Parts of the Continent of America," Edward D. Neill, ed., *The Founders of Maryland . . .* (Albany, 1876), 25, 37; "Francis Magnel's Relation . . . ," Barbour, ed., *Jamestown Voyages,* I: 154.

43 "Spelman's Relation," Brown, ed., *Genesis of the United States,* I: 487–8; "Generall Historie," *Travels and Works of Captain John Smith,* ed. Arber and Bradley, II: 498, 503; Peter Arundel to Caninge, April 1623, Kingsbury, ed., *Records of the Virginia Company,* IV: 89; John Pory, "A Reporte of the Manner and Proceeding in the General Assembly Convented at James City, 1619," *ibid.,* III: 174–5; Richard L. Morton, *Colonial Virginia . . .* (Chapel Hill, 1960), I: 78–81.

44 *Faerie Queene,* bk. III, can. x, st. 36, *The Works of Edmund Spenser: A Variorum Edition,* ed. Edwin Greenlaw et al. (Baltimore, 1932); Hamor, *True Discourse,* ed. Rowse, 44; "Generall Historie," *Travels and Works of Captain John Smith,* ed. Arber and Bradley, II: 520–1; "Notes Taken from Letters Which Came from Virginia in the 'Abigail,'" June 19, 1623, Kingsbury, ed., *Records of the Virginia Company,* IV: 232, 238; William S. Powell, "Aftermath of the Massacre; The First Indian War, 1622–1632," *Virginia Magazine of History and Biography* 66 (1958): 59–60.

45 Flores (Zuñiga) to Philip III, August 1, 1612, Brown, ed., *Genesis of the United States,* II: 572; "Mr. Wroth. Notes from Lists Showing Total Number of Emigrants to Virginia, 1622," Kingsbury, ed., *Records of the Virginia Company,* III: 536; George Percy, "'A Trewe Relaycon' Virginia from 1609 to 1612," *Tyler's Quarterly Historical and Genealogical Magazine* III (1922): 267; "Edward Maria Wingfield, Discourse, 1608," Barbour, ed., *Jamestown Voyages,* I: 216; "Gabriel Archer, from Virginia . . . ," August 31, 1609, *ibid.,* II: 281; William Strachey, *For the Colony in Virginea Britannia Laws Divine, Moral and Martiall, etc.,* ed. David H. Flaherty (Charlottesville, 1969; orig. pub., London, 1612), 20, 47–8; "Generall Historie," *Travels and Works of Captain John Smith,* ed. Arber and Bradley, II: 474, 542, 568; Hamor, *True Discourse,* ed. Rowse, 27; Richard Beale Davis, *George Sandys . . . ,* (London, 1955), 133.

46 Smith et al., "Map of Virginia," Barbour, ed., *Jamestown Voyages,* II: 425, 430, 436–7, 441–2, 449–50; "Generall Historie," *Travels and Works of Captain John Smith,* ed. Arber and Bradley, II: 466–7, 477, 487.

5. *CONVERSION*

1 Louis B. Wright, *Religion and Empire: The Alliance between Piety and Commerce in English Expansion, 1558–1625* (Chapel Hill, 1943); Perry Miller, "Religion and Society in the Early Literature of Virginia," *Errand into the Wilderness* (New York, 1964), 100–40; H. C. Porter, *The Inconstant Savage: England and the North American Indian, 1500–1660* (London, 1979), chs. 5 and 6; Theodore K. Rabb, *Enterprise & Empire: Merchant and Gentry Investment in the Expansion of England, 1575–1630* (Cambridge, Mass., 1967), 40–1.

2 Richard Hakluyt, "Epistle Dedicatory to Sir Walter Ralegh," *The Original Writings & Correspondence of the Two Richard Hakluyts*, ed. E. G. R. Taylor (London, 1935), II: 368; Christopher Carleill, "A Briefe and Summary Discourse . . . ," David B. Quinn, ed., *The Voyages and Colonising Enterprises of Sir Humphrey Gilbert* (London, 1940), II: 360–1; William Kempe, "The Education of Children in Learning," Robert D. Pepper, ed., *Four Tudor Books on Education* (Gainesville, Fla., 1966; orig. pub., London, 1588), 212; Henry Parry, *The Svmme of Christian Religion* . . . (Oxford, 1595), 94; J. H. Elliott, *The Old World and New, 1492–1650* (Cambridge, 1970), 15.

3 Thomas Nicholas, *The Pleasant Historie of the Conquest of the West India* . . . (London, 1578), 299.

4 *Original Writings & Correspondence of Two Richard Hakluyts*, ed. Taylor, II: 215.

5 "Virginea Brittania," Alexander Brown, ed., *The Genesis of the United States* . . . (Boston, 1890), I: 290–1; "Crashaw's Sermon," *ibid.*, I: 360–75; Richard Crakanthorpe, "Sermon," March 24, 1608, *ibid.*, I: 255–6; Alexander Whitaker, *Good Newes from Virginia 1613* (New York, n.d.), 15, 23–4; John Donne, *A Sermon upon the Eighth Verse of the First Chapter of the Acts of the Apostles* . . . (London, 1624), 46; Daniel Price, *Savls Prohibition Staide* . . . (London, 1609), F2–F3^v.

6 "Instructions for Government," November 20, 1606, Philip Barbour, ed., *The Jamestown Voyages Under the First Charter, 1606–1609* (Cambridge, 1969), I: 37; "Virginia Council, Instructions Orders and Constitucons . . . ," Susan Myra Kingsbury, ed., *The Records of the Virginia Company of London* (Washington, D.C., 1906–35), III: 27; "Orders and Constitutions," *ibid.*, III: 348.

7 "A Description of New-England," *Travels and Works of Captain John Smith* . . . , ed. Edward Arber and A. G. Bradley (Edinburgh, 1910), I: 208. See also Edward Bland et al., "The Discovery of New Brittaine . . . ," Alexander S. Salley, ed., *Narratives of Early Carolina, 1650–1708* (New York, 1911), 6.

8 "Extract from [Sir William] Alexander's Doomsday, 1614," Brown, ed., *Genesis of the United States*, II: 758; Dionyse Settle, *A True Reporte of the Laste Voyage into West and Northwest Regions . . .* (London, 1577), Aiiii^v. Also see Miller, "Religion and Society," 120–2.

9 "Crashaw's Sermon," Brown, ed., *Genesis of the United States*, I: 361–2; George Peckham, "True Reporte . . . ," Quinn, ed., *Voyages and Colonising Enterprises of Sir Humphrey Gilbert*, II: 448; Robert Tynley, *Two Learned Sermons . . .* (London, 1609), 67; Thomas Churchyarde, *A Prayse and Reporte of Maister Martyne Froboishers Voyage to Meta Incognita . . .* (London, 1578), Avi^v–Avii.

10 John Florio, *A Shorte and Briefe Narration of the Two Navigations and Discoveries to the Northwest Partes Called Newe Fraunce . . .* (London, 1580), 60; Thomas Palmer, *An Essay of the Meanes How to Make Our Travailes, into Forraine Countries, the More Profitable and Honourable* (London, 1606), 61–2; Whitaker, *Good Newes from Virginia*, 24–5.

11 Pomponius Mela, *The Worke of Pomponius Mela . . .* , trans. Arthur Golding (London, 1585), 32–3, 72; Marc Lescarbot, *Nova Francia: A Description of Arcadia, 1606*, trans. P. Erondelle (London, 1928), 203–4, 249; [Robert Johnson], *Nova Britannia . . .* (Rochester, N.Y., 1897; orig. pub., London, 1609), 13; William Strachey, "A True Repertory of the Wracke, and Redemption of Sir Thomas Gates . . . ," Samuel Purchas, *Hakluytus Posthumus or Purchas His Pilgrimes . . .* (Glasgow, 1905–7), XIX: 62–3; William Strachey, *The Historie of Travell into Virginia Britania*, ed. Louis B. Wright and Virginia Freund (London, 1953), 6, 23–5, 70–1; Richard Whitbourne, *A Discovrse and Discovery of New-Found-Land . . .* (London, 1622), 14–15; Richard Eburne, *A Plain Pathway to Plantations* (1624), ed. Louis B. Wright (Ithaca, N.Y., 1962), 29–30, 60–1; Joseph and Nesta Ewan, eds., *John Banister and His Natural History of Virginia, 1678–1692* (Urbana, Ill., 1970), 373–4, 381, 383.

12 "A Notable Historie . . . by Monsieur Laudonnière . . . ," Richard Hakluyt, *The Principal Navigations Voyages Traffiques & Discoveries of the English Nation . . .* (Glasgow, 1903–5), VIII: 443.

13 "Dedication of Florio's Cartier, 1580," *Original Writings & Correspondence of the Two Richard Hakluyts*, ed. Taylor, I: 164–5; Peter Martyr, "The Decades of the New Worlde . . . ," ed. Richard Eden in Edward Arber, ed., *The First Three English Books on America* (Birmingham, Eng., 1885), 106; Lescarbot, *Nova Francia*, 156, 161, 164; Stephen J. Greenblatt, "Learning to Curse: Aspects of Linguistic Colonialism in the Sixteenth Century," Fredi Chiappelli et al., eds., *First Images of America: The Impact of the New World on the Old* (Berkeley, 1976), II: 562–3.

14 "Instruccons Orders and Constitucons . . . ," Kingsbury, ed., *Records of the Virginia Company*, III: 14; Henrie Smith, *Gods Arrowe against Atheists* (London, 1593), B4–B4^v.

15 "Instruccons Orders and Constitucons . . . ," Kingsbury, ed., *Records of the Virginia Company*, III: 14, 27. Bacon to Duke of Buckingham, 1616, *The Works of Francis Bacon . . .* , ed. James Spedding et al. (Boston, 1857–74), XIII: 21.

16 Martyr, "Decades of the New Worlde," ed. Eden in Arber, ed., *First Three English Books on America*, 192; Nicholas, *Pleasant Historie of the Conquest of the West India*, 145–6; Joseph de Acosta, *The Natural and Moral History of the Indies . . .* , ed. Clements R. Markham (London, 1880; orig. pub., London, 1606), 310. Acosta was less sanguine about the conversion of more primitive Indians (*ibid.*, 528).

17 The question of English reliance on Spanish precedents bears upon the issue of the Black Legend. Loren E. Pennington, "The Origins of English Promotional Literature for America, 1553–1625" (Ph.D. diss., University of Michigan, 1962), 9n, plays down the impact of the legend in the sixteenth century on the grounds that Las Casas's writings were not extensively published in England until the next century. He sees the legend as more significant for the Dutch war than for competition between England and Spain for colonies. For further information on the influence of Las Casas in sixteenth-century England, see Porter, *The Inconstant Savage*, ch. 8. Edmund S. Morgan, *American Slavery, American Freedom: The Ordeal of Colonial Virginia* (New York, 1975), ch. 1, stresses the animosity between Spaniards and Englishman as early as the 1550s and, as a result, the alliance between the English and the Indians. On the Black Legend, see also William S. Maltby, *The Black Legend in England: The Development of Anti-Spanish Sentiment, 1558–1660* (Durham, N.C., 1971), and Philip Wayne Powell, *Tree of Hate: Propaganda and Prejudices Affecting United States Relations with the Hispanic World* (New York, 1971). Aside from the problem of the accuracy of the legend or the date of its origin, the pertinent point in reference to English attitudes toward conversion of the Indians was that the Spanish accounts offered an ambiguous lesson.

18 Nicholas P. Canny, *The Elizabethan Conquest of Ireland: A Pattern Established, 1565–76* (New York, 1976), 123–6.

19 Robert Gray, *A Good Speed to Virginia (1609)*, ed. Wesley F. Craven (New York, 1937), C1^v–C2; "The Generall Historie of Virginia, New England and the Summer Isles," *Travels and Works of Captain John Smith . . .* , ed. Arber and Bradley, II: 564.

20 "Crashaw's Sermon," Brown, ed., *Genesis of the United States*, I: 363; John Frampton, *A Discourse of the Navigation which the Portugales Doe Make to the Realmes and Provinces of the East*

Partes of the Worlde . . . (London, 1579), 2ᵛ; Samuel Purchas, "Virginias Verger," *Hakluytus Posthumus*, XIX: 237–8; see also Peckham, "True Reporte," Quinn, ed., *Voyages and Colonising Enterprises of Sir Humphrey Gilbert*, II: 468.

21 Thomas Hariot, "A Briefe and True Report," David B. Quinn, ed., *The Roanoke Voyages, 1584–1590* (London, 1955), I: 376–7. Perhaps Lescarbot, *Nova Franica*, 160n, was more realistic when he wrote: "I do not think that the theology may be expounded to these people, though one could perfectly speak their language."

22 "Instructions to George Yeardley," November 18, 1618, Kingsbury, ed., *Records of the Virginia Company*, III: 102; "A Broadside," *ibid.*, III: 276; "A Declaration of the State of the Colony . . . ," 1620, *ibid.*, III: 310; "Crashaws Epistle Dedicatory," Brown, *Genesis of the United States*, II: 615; Philip Alexander Bruce, *Institutional History of Virginia in the Seventeenth Century* . . . (New York, 1910), I: 194–9. Francis Jennings, *The Invasion of America: Indians, Colonization, and the Cant of Conquest* (Chapel Hill, 1975), 54–5, gives short shrift to missionary efforts in Virginia. Jennings's position is countered by J. Frederick Fausz, "The Powhatan Uprising of 1622: A Historical Study of Ethnocentrism and Cultural Conflict" (Ph.D. diss., College of William and Mary, 1977), 298–303. Porter, *The Inconstant Savage*, 380, n. 4, lists twenty clergy in Virginia between 1607 and 1622.

23 George Thorpe and John Pory to Sir Edwin Sandys, May 15 and 16, 1621, Kingsbury, ed., *Records of the Virginia Company*, III: 446; Edward Waterhouse, "A Declaration of the State of the Colony . . . ," *ibid.*, III: 550, 552; "Newes from Virginia . . . ," Purchas, *Hakluytus Posthumus*, XIX: 153; "Generall Historie," *Travels and Works of Captain John Smith*, ed. Arber and Bradley, II: 574.

24 John Rolfe, *A True Relation of the State of Virginia* . . . (Charlottesville, 1971), 12; "Instructions to the Governor and Council of State in Virginia," July 24, 1621, Kingsbury, ed., *Records of the Virginia Company*, III: 468; R[oger] G[reen], "Virginia's Cure . . . ," Peter Force, ed., *Tracts and Other Papers* . . . (Washington, 1844), III: 7, and *passim*.

25 [Robert Johnson], *The New Life of Virginia* . . . (Rochester, N.Y., 1897; orig. pub., London, 1612), 14; "Instruccons . . . to Sʳ Thomas Gates," May 1609, Kingsbury, ed., *Records of the Virginia Company*, III: 14–15; Sir George Yeardley to Sir Edwin Sandys, 1619, *ibid.*, III: 128–9; Treasurer and Council for Virginia to Sir George Yeardley, June 21, 1619, *ibid.*, III: 147–8; John Pory, "A Reporte of the Manner and Proceeding in the General Assembly . . . ," 1619, *ibid.*, III: 165–6; "The Putting Out of the Tennants that Came Over in the B.N. wᵗʰ Other Orders of the Councell," November 11, 1619, *ibid.*, III: 228; "At a Quarter Court . . . of Ianuar[y]

1621," *ibid.*, I: 586; G[reen], "Virginia's Cure . . . ," Force, ed., *Tracts*, III: 6.

26 "Generall Historie," *Travels and Works of Captain John Smith,* ed. Arber and Bradley, II: 571; Pory, "Reporte of the Manner and Proceeding in the General Assembly," Kingsbury, ed., *Records of the Virginia Company*, III: 165; "Instructions to the Governor and Council of State in Virginia," July 24, 1621, *ibid.*, III: 470.

27 Robert Hunt Land, "Henrico and Its College," *William and Mary Quarterly*, 2nd ser., 18 (1938): 453-98.

28 "At a Quarter Court . . . of Januar[y] 1621," Kingsbury, ed., *Records of the Virginia Company*, I: 588; "The Putting Out of the Tennants that Came Over in the B.N. wth Other Orders of the Councell," November 11, 1619, *ibid.*, III: 228; George Thorpe and John Pory to Sir Edwin Sandys, May 15 and 16, 1621, *ibid.*, III: 146.

29 Strachey, *Historie of Travell into Virginia Britania*, ed. Wright and Freund, 62, 72; Argall to Hawes, June 1613, Brown, ed., *Genesis of the United States*, II: 642-4; Ralph Hamor, *A True Discourse of the Present State of Virginia*, ed. A. L. Rowse (Richmond, Va., 1957; orig. pub., London, 1615), 42-3; "Generall Historie," *Works and Travels of Captain John Smith*, ed. Arber and Bradley, II: 511-12.

30 "Letter of John Rolfe, 1614," Lyon Gardiner Tyler, ed., *Narratives of Early Virginia, 1606-1625* (New York, 1907), 239-44. For an explication of the problem of intermarriage in the Book of Ezra, see Porter, *The Inconstant Savage*, 111-12. See also Philip Barbour, *Pocahontas and Her World* . . . (Boston, 1970), chs. 8-10; Grace Steele Woodward, *Pocahontas* (Norman, Okla., 1969), chs. 12 and 13.

31 "Generall Historie," *Travels and Works of Captain John Smith,* ed. Arber and Bradley, II: 529.

32 Barbour, *Pocahontas and Her World*, chs. 12-15; Woodward, *Pocahontas*, chs. 15 and 16.

33 Sidney Lee, "The Call of the West: America and Elizabethan England," Frederick S. Boas, ed., *Elizabethan and Other Essays* (Oxford, 1929), 274-5; Henry S. Burrage, ed., *Rosier's Relation of Waymouth's Voyage to the Coast of Maine, 1605* (Portland, Me., 1887), 130-1. For a survey of Indian visitors to Europe before Pocahontas, see Carolyn Thomas Foreman, *Indians Abroad, 1493-1938* (Norman, Okla., 1943), ch. 1.

34 Samuel Eliot Morison, *The European Discovery of America: The Northern Voyages, A.D. 500-1600* (New York, 1971), 215-16, 219, 254, 296-8, 331, 332; Lescarbot, *Nova Francia*, 112-13, 134; Gilbert Chinard, *L'exotisme Américain dans la litterature Française au XVIe siècle d'après Rabelais, Ronsard, Montaigne, etc.* (Paris, 1911), 6; Richard Sayce, *The Essays of Montaigne: A Critical Exploration* (London, 1972), 91-2; Clifford M. Lewis and Albert

J. Loomie, *The Spanish Jesuit Mission in Virginia, 1570–1572* (Chapel Hill, 1953), 15–18, 45–6; Quinn, ed., *Roanoke Voyages,* I: 251–2, 254–5.

35 "A Briefe Relation of the Discoverie and Plantation of New England . . . ," Purchas, *Hakluytus Posthumus,* XIX: 272–80; "A Relation or Journal of a Plantation Settled at Plymouth in New-England . . . ," *ibid.,* XIX: 332; "A Description of New-England," *Travels and Works of Captain John Smith,* ed. Aber and Bradley, I: 219; Philip L. Barbour, *The Three Worlds of Captain John Smith* (Boston, 1964), 163; David B. Quinn, *England and the Discovery of America . . .* (New York, 1974), 427–8.

36 Carleill, "A Briefe and Summary Discourse," Quinn, ed., *Voyages and Colonising Enterprises of Sir Humphrey Gilbert,* II: 363.

37 Richard Hakluyt, *Divers Voyages Toughing the Discovery of America and the Islands Adjacent . . . ,* ed. John Winter Jones (London, 1850; orig. pub., London, 1582), 23–4.

38 Quinn, ed., *Roanoke Voyages,* I: 116 n6, 119; "John White's Narrative of his Voyage," *ibid.,* II: 530–1, 543 n2. For a discussion of the probable experience of Taignoagny and Domagaya, the two Canadian Indians brought to France by Cartier, see Bruce B. Trigger, *The Children of Aataentsic: A History of the Huron People to 1660* (Montreal, 1976), I: 186–7.

39 John Smith, "A True Relation . . . ," Barbour, ed., *Jamestown Voyages,* I: 198–9; "Francis Magnel's Relation . . . ," *ibid.,* I: 154; Don Pedro de Zuniga to His Majesty, June 26, 1608, *ibid.,* I: 163; Smith et al., "Map of Virginia," *ibid.,* II: 391–2; "General Historie of the Bermudas," *Travels and Works of Captain John Smith,* ed. Arber and Bradley, II: 638–9. Strachey, *Historie of Travell into Virginia Britania,* ed. Wright and Freund, 61–2, claims that Machumps became an ally of the English.

40 "Generall Historie," *Travels and Works of Captain John Smith,* ed. Arber and Bradley, II: 534; "General Historie of the Bermudas," *ibid.,* II: 680–3; "The Court Book," Kingsbury, ed., *Records of the Virginia Company,* I: 485, 496; Chamberlain to Carleton, June 22, 1616, Brown, ed., *Genesis of the United States,* II: 789. Chanco, the Christian Indian who warned the English in 1622 that massacre was imminent, had spent time in England: See Robert C. Johnson, ed., "The Indian Massacre of 1622: Some Correspondence of the Reverend Joseph Mead," *Virginia Magazine of History and Biography* 71 (1963): 408–9.

41 "The Third Voyage of Discovery Made by Captaine Jaques Cartier, 1540 . . . ," Hakluyt, *Principal Navigations,* VIII: 263, 265; "A Voyage to Brasill, Made by . . . M. William Hankins . . . ," Richard Hakluyt, *The Principall Navigations Voiages and Discoveries of the English Nation,* ed. David B. Quinn and Raleigh

Ashlin Skelton (Cambridge, 1965), 520–1; George Best, "A True Discourse," Vilhjalmur Stefansson, ed., *The Three Voyages of Martin Frobisher* . . . (London, 1938), I: 50; "A Relation of a Voyage to Guiana performed by Robert Harcourt . . . ," Purchas, *Hakluytus Posthumus*, XVI: 400; Quinn, *England and the Discovery of America*, 421.

42 Charles Race, "Ancient Aboriginal Trade in North America," *Smithsonian Institution Annual Report, 1872* (Washington, 1873), 348–94; Harold A. Innis, *The Fur Trade in Canada: An Introduction to Canadian Economic History*, rev. ed. (Toronto, 1956), ch. 2; Regina Flannery, *An Analysis of Coastal Algonquian Culture* (Washington, 1939), 119–20. Trigger, *Children of Aataentsic*, 175–6, 409–29, argues that "the introduction of European goods did not alter the pattern of Huron development so much as it intensified it." The Hurons were already a trading people with an extraordinary capacity for maintaining the integrity of their culture and absorbing a wide variety of new products. They did eventually become dependent on the French as a result of a complex process of acculturation of which trade was only a part.

43 Palmer, *Essay of the Meanes How to Make Our Travailes into Forraine Countries, the More Profitable and Honourable*, 94.

44 Hakluyt, *Divers Voyages*, ed. Jones, 119–20, 133–4.

45 Jennings, *Invasion of America*, 88–9, stresses this point.

46 "Generall Historie," *Travels and Works of Captain John Smith*, ed. Arber and Bradley, II: 393, 403, 441; William Strachey, "True Reportory," Louis B. Wright, ed., *A Voyage to Virginia in 1609* . . . (Charlottesville, Va., 1964), 71–3; Strachey, *Historie of Travell into Virginia Britania*, ed. Wright and Freund, 107, 115; William Strachey, *For the Colony in Virginea Britannia Lawes Divine, Morall and Martiall, etc.*, ed. David H. Flaherty (Charlottesville, 1969; orig. pub., London, 1612), 15, 58; Governor Argall, "Proclamations or Edicts," May 18, 1618, Kingsbury, ed., *Records of the Virginia Company*, III: 93.

47 "The First Voyage of Master John Davis . . . ," Hakluyt, *Principall Navigations*, ed. Quinn and Skelton, 778; Florio, *Shorte and Briefe Narration*, 18; Lescarbot, *Nova Francia*, 100–1. For a discussion of gift giving, see Marcel Mauss, *The Gift: Forms and Functions of Exchange in Archaic Societies*, trans. Ian Cunnison (Glencoe, Ill., 1954).

48 "Generall Historie," *Travels and Works of Captain John Smith*, ed. Arber and Bradley, II: 405–6; Smith, "True Relation," Barbour, ed., *Jamestown Voyages*, I: 194–5.

49 Lescarbot, *Nova Francia*, 24.

50 "The Relation of Captaine Gosnols Voyage to the North Part of Virginia," Purchas, *Hakluytus Posthumus*, XVIII: 304; Best, "True

Discourse," Stefansson, ed., *Three Voyages of Martin Frobisher*, I: 126; Dionyse Settle, "Account of the Second Voyage," *ibid.*, II: 18; John Brereton, *A Briefe and True Relation of the Discoverie of the North Part of Virginia* . . . (London, 1602), 4.

51 "A Voyage Set Out from the Citie of Bristoll . . . ," Purchas, *Hakluytus Posthumus*, XVIII: 322–3; Martyr, "Decades of the New Worlde," ed. Eden in Arber, ed., *First Three English Books on America*, 146–7; "The Third Voyage Northwestward, Made by John Davis . . . 1587," Hakluyt, *Principall Navigations*, ed. Quinn and Skelton, 790; Andrewe Thevet, *The Newe Found Worlde* . . . (London, [1568]), 69; P[eter] H[eylyn], *Microcosmus* . . . (Oxford, 1621), 404.

52 "A Relayton . . . Written . . . by a Gent. of yᵉ Colony [Captain Gabriel Archer?]," Barbour, ed., *Jamestown Voyages*, I: 91, 92; "George Percy's Discourse," *ibid.*, I: 140.

53 Smith et al., "Map of Virginia," Barbour, ed., *Jamestown Voyages*, II: 395–6; "Generall Historie," *Travels and Works of Captain John Smith*, ed. Arber and Bradley, II: 400–1, 409–10, 450, 459, 529, 535, 563; "Arthur Barlowe's Discourse of the First Voyage," Quinn, ed., *Roanoke Voyages*, I: 105; Strachey, "True Reportory," Wright, ed., *Voyage to Virginia*, 90; Hamor, *True Discourse of the Present State of Virginia*, ed. Rowse, 6.

54 "The Primrose Journal of Drakes Voyage . . . ," Quinn, ed., *Roanoke Voyages*, I: 306; Hariot, "A Briefe and True Report," *ibid.*, I: 378; Clifford and Loomie, *Spanish Jesuit Mission in Virginia*, 89–90; John Ogilby, *America: Being the Latest and Most Accurate Description of the New World* . . . (London, 1671), 195–6; Smith et al., "Map of Virginia," Barbour, ed., *Jamestown Voyages*, II: 426; Samuel Argall to the Virginia Company, March 10, 1618, Kingsbury, ed., *Records of the Virginia Company*, III: 92; John Pory to "the Right Honble . . . ," September 30, 1619, *ibid.*, III: 220; John Rolfe to Edwin Sandys, January 1620, *ibid.*, III: 244, 246; "A Broadside," *ibid.*, III: 275; "Att a Greate and General Quarter Courte . . . ," February 16, 1619, March 16, 1619, *ibid.*, I: 310, 320; Gordon Jones, "The First Epidemic in English America," *Virginia Magazine of History and Biography* 71 (1963): 3–10; P. M. Ashburn, *The Ranks of Death: A Medical History of the Conquest of America*, ed. Frank D. Ashburn (New York, 1947), 118–23. For an account of disease among Indians before European discovery, see Lucile E. St. Hoyme, "On the Origins of New World Paleopathology," *American Journal of Physical Anthropology* 31 (1969): 295–302. Calvin Martin, *Keepers of the Game: Indian–Animal Relationships and the Fur Trade* (Berkeley, 1978), 130–44, finds a connection between human and animal disease among the northern Algonquins.

6. MASSACRE

1 Karen Ordahl Kupperman, "English Perceptions of Treachery, 1583–1640: The Case of the American 'Savages'," *The Historical Journal* XX (1977): 263–87, argues that "the expectation of treachery was deeply rooted in the Englishman's view of human relations" (266) and was not especially attached to the conception of the savage. It may be that people of the Machiavellian age did not require the doctrine of savagism to detect duplicity in the actions of the American natives. Englishmen of the period saw treachery as a normal component of human nature. But the fact remains that the idea of savagism informed virtually every relationship with the Indians and gave Englishmen a special reason for expecting the worst from them. The doctrine of savagism cannot be rendered meaningless to Indian–white relations because the English might have behaved as badly without it. Because they believed the Spanish or French to be treacherous for one set of reasons does not mean that they would interpret the supposed treachery of the American "savages" in the same light.

2 "The Generall Historie of Virginia, New England and the Summer Isles," *Travels and Works of Captain John Smith . . .* , ed. Edward Arber and A. G. Bradley (Edinburgh, 1910), II: 611; William Strachey, "True Reportory," Louis B. Wright, ed., *A Voyage to Virginia in 1609 . . .* (Charlottesville, 1964), 88–9, and note.

3 Paul A. Jorgensen, *Shakespeare's Military World* (Berkeley, 1956), ch. 5; Maurice J. D. Cockle, *Bibliography of English Military Books up to 1642*, 2nd ed. (London, 1957); "A Discourse of the Original and Fundamental Cause of Natural, Arbitrary, Necessary, and Unnatural War," *Works of Sir Walter Raleigh* (Oxford, 1829), VIII: 253–97.

4 Sir John Smythe, *Instructions, Observation, and Orders Mylitarie . . .* (London, 1595), ¶; [Thomas Procter], *Of the Knowledge and Conducte of Warres . . .* (N.P., 1578), fols. 44–5; G. Geoffrey Langsam, *Martial Books and Tudor Verse* (New York, 1951), 6, 12–13.

5 Bacon to Duke of Buckingham, 1616, *The Works of Francis Bacon . . .* , ed. James Spedding et al. (Boston, 1857–74), XIII: 51; Andrewe Thevet, *The New Found Worlde . . .* (London, [1568]), 41; "The Second Voyage into Florida . . . by Captaine Laudonnière . . . ," Richard Hakluyt, *The Principal Navigations Voyages Traffiques & Discoveries of the English Nation . . .* (Glasgow, 1903–5), IX: 7–8, 14; "The Worthy and Famous Voyage of Master Thomas Candishe . . . 1586," Richard Hakluyt, *The Principall*

Navigations Voiages and Discoveries of the English Nation, ed. David B. Quinn and Raleigh Ashlin Skelton (Cambridge, 1965; orig. pub., London, 1589), 810; John Florio, *A Shorte and Briefe Narration of the Two Navigations and Discoveries to the North-east Partes Called Newe Fraunce* . . . (London, 1580), 70; "Ferdinando de Soto His Voyage to Florida . . . ," Samuel Purchas, *Hakluytus Posthumus or Purchas His Pilgrimes* . . . (Glasgow, 1905–7), XVIII: 47–9. In fact, at Jamestown the colonists did not fortify themselves adequately until after the first Indian attack: John Smith et al., "A Map of Virginia," Philip Barbour, ed., *The Jamestown Voyages Under the First Charter, 1607–1609* (Cambridge, 1969), II: 380.

6 David B. Quinn, ed., *The Roanoke Voyages, 1584–1590* . . . (London, 1955), II: 15–17, 78–81.

7 Paul Hulton and David B. Quinn, *The American Drawings of John White, 1577–1590* . . . (London and Chapel Hill, 1964), I: 13, 17; William Strachey, *The Historie of Travell into Virginia Britania,* ed. Louis B. Wright and Virginia Freund (London, 1953), 26, 91; Purchas, "Virginias Verger . . . ," *Hakluytus Posthumus,* XIX: 228. For the persistence of interest in Roanoke survivors, see Philip Barbour," Ocanahowan and Recently Discovered Linguistic Fragments from Southern Virginia, *c.* 1650," William Cowan, ed., *Papers of the Seventh Algonquian Conference, 1975* (Ottawa, 1976), 2–17.

8 "The London Council's 'Instructions . . . ,' " Barbour, ed., *Jamestown Voyages,* I: 50, 52–3; "Description of the People," *ibid.,* I: 103–4; "George Percy's Discourse," *ibid.,* I: 131.

9 Sir Walter Cope to Lord Salisbury, August 12, 1607, Barbour, ed., *Jamestown Voyages,* I: 110; "George Percy's Discourse," *ibid.,* I: 141; "A Relatyon . . . Written . . . by a Gent. of yᵉ Colony [Captain Gabriel Archer?]," *ibid.,* I: 88; Strachey, *Historie of Travell into Virginia Britainia,* ed. Wright and Freund 58; Strachey, "True Reportory," Wright, ed., *Voyage to Virginia,* 92.

10 J. Frederick Fausz, "The Powhatan Uprising of 1622: A Historical Study of Ethnocentrism and Cultural Conflict" (Ph.D. diss., College of William and Mary, 1977), 310–13. For analyses of the complex problem of land and empire, see John Thomas Juricek, "English Claims to North America to 1660: A Study in Legal and Constitutional History" (Ph.D. diss., University of Chicago, 1970), *passim,* and 50, 422–5, 742–4, 763–4; Robert F. Berkhofer, Jr., *The White Man's Indian: Images of the American Indian from Columbus to the Present* (New York, 1978), 126–34.

11 John Smith, "A True Relation," Barbour, ed., *Jamestown Voyages,* I: 174–7; David B. Quinn, *England and the Discovery of America, 1481–1620* . . . (New York, 1974), 82–3; George Percy, " 'A Trewe Relaycon' Virginia from 1609 to 1612," *Tyler's Quar-*

   terly Historical and Genealogical Magazine III (1922): 265. See
   also "Second Voyage into Florida . . . by Captaine Laudonnière,"
   Hakluyt, *Principal Navigations*, IX: 76.

12 "The *Tiger* Journal of the 1685 Voyage," Quinn, ed., *Roanoke
   Voyages*, I: 191; "George Percy's Discourse," Barbour, ed., *James-
   town Voyages*, I: 139; "Description of the People," *ibid.*, I: 103;
   "Relatyon . . . Written . . . by a Gent. of yᵉ Colony," *ibid.*, I: 87;
   "Generall Historie," *Travels and Works of Captain John Smith*,
   ed. Arber and Bradley, II: 610–11; Alden T. Vaughan, *American
   Genesis, Captain John Smith and the Founding of Virginia* (Bos-
   ton, 1975), 46–7; [Robert Johnson], *The New Life of Virginia . . .*
   (Rochester, N.Y., 1897; orig. pub., London, 1612), 4.

13 The Powhatans had already foiled one serious effort to settle
   in their midst; see Clifford Lewis and Albert J. Loomie, *The
   Spanish Jesuit Mission in Virginia, 1570–1572* (Chapel Hill, 1953).

14 "Generall Historie," *Travels and Works of Captain John Smith*,
   ed. Arber and Bradley, II: 427.

15 "Civilization and Its Discontents," *The Standard Edition of the
   Complete Psychological Works of Sigmund Freud*, ed. James
   Strachey et al. (London, 1961), XXI: 114. For a summary of theories
   explaining ethnicity and aggression, see Robert A. Le Vine and
   Donald T. Campbell, *Ethnocentrism: Theories of Conflict, Ethnic
   Attitudes, and Group Behavior* (New York, 1972), ch. 8.

16 Quinn, *England and the Discovery of America*, 454–5; "George
   Percy's Discourse," Barbour, ed., *Jamestown Voyages*, I: 133–4;
   John Smith et al., "Map of Virginia" *ibid.*, II: 379.

17 Strachey, *Historie of Travel in Virginia Britania*, ed. Wright and
   Freund, 104–5; Strachey, *ibid.*, 44–5, described Powhatan's deci-
   mation and subjugation of the Kecoughtan Indians in 1608. Powhatan displayed the trophies of this episode ("lockes of haire with
   their skyns") to Englishmen who came to trade at Werowocomoco,
   "thincking to have terrefyed them with this Spectacle . . ." Nancy
   Oestreich Lurie, "Indian Cultural Adjustment to European Civilization," James Morton Smith, ed., *Seventeenth-Century America:
   Essays in Colonial History* (Chapel Hill, 1959), 41, 46, contends
   that Powhatan killed only some of the Chesapeakes and replaced
   the leadership with his own people, which was his common mode
   of operation with recalcitrant tribes. She also believes that the
   Chesapeakes attacked the English, thereby providing Powhatan
   with an opportunity to ingratiate himself with the English. The
   important point observed also by Lurie was that the English fell
   into an exceedingly complex and violent situation and became
   themselves actors in it.

18 John Smith, "A True Relation," Barbour, ed., *Jamestown Voyages*, I: 172; "Relatyon . . . Written . . . by a Gent. of yᵉ Colony,"
   ibid., I: 95–8. For the most recent treatment of Anglo–Indian

relations in Virginia before the massacre, see Alden T. Vaughan, " 'Expulsion of the Salvages': English Policy and the Virginia Massacre of 1622," *William and Mary Quarterly*, 3d ser., XXXV (1978): 57–84.

19 Sir George Peckham, "True Reporte," David B. Quinn, ed., *The Voyages and Colonising Enterprises of Sir Humphrey Gilbert* (London, 1940), II: 452.

20 Sebastian Munster, "Treatyse of the Newe India . . . ," ed. Richard Eden in Edward Arber, ed., *The First Three English Books on America* . . . (Birmingham, Eng., 1885), 29, 37–8; Joseph de Acosta, *The Natural and Moral History of the Indies* . . . , ed. Clements R. Markham (London, 1880; orig. pub., London, 1604), 529–31.

21 Sir Walter Ralegh, *The Discoverie of the Large and Bewtiful Empire of Guiana*, ed. V. T. Harlow, (London, 1928; orig. pub., London, 1596), 14, 15, 44; "The Relation of Master John Wilson . . . ," Purchas, *Hakluytus Posthumus*, XVI: 341, 344–5; Robert Harcourt, *A Relation of a Voyage to Guiana*, ed. C. Alexander Harris (London, 1928; orig. pub., London, 1613), 80, 86–9.

22 "A Notable Historie . . . Written . . . by Monsieur Laudonnière . . . ," Hakluyt, *Principal Navigations*, VIII: 458–9; "Second Voyage into Florida . . . by Captaine Laudonnière," *ibid.*, IX: 7, 12–13, 23–9, 33–5, 56.

23 Samuel Eliot Morison, *The European Discovery of America: The Northern Voyages, A.D. 500–1600* (New York, 1971), 406–7; Marc Lescarbot, *Nova Francia: A Description of Arcadia, 1606*, trans. P. Erondelle (London, 1928), 118–19, 132, 237.

24 James Mooney, "The Powhatan Confederacy, Past and Present," *American Anthropologist*, n.s., 9 (1907): 131; Lurie, "Indian Adjustment to European Civilization," 43–4.

25 "Generall Historie," *Travels and Works of Captain John Smith*, ed. Arber and Bradley, II: 437–8; Smith, "True Relation," Barbour, ed., *Jamestown Voyages*, I: 186, 196–7; "Relatyon . . . Written . . . by a Gent. of ye Colony," *ibid.*, I: 82, 85–6, 88; "Instruccons . . . to Sr Thomas Gates," May 1609, Susan Myra Kingsbury, ed., *The Records of the Virginia Company of London* (Washington, 1906–35), III: 19–20; "The Putting Out of the Tennants that Came Over in the B.N. . . . ," November 11, 1619, *ibid.*, III: 228; Samuel Argall to Nicholas Hawes, June 1613, Purchas, *Hakluytus Posthumus*, XIX; 91–4; Strachey, *Historie of Travell into Virginia Britinia*, ed. Wright and Freund, 105–7.

26 "Generall Historie," *Travels and Works of Captain John Smith*, ed. Arber and Bradley, I: 380, II: 514–15; Ralph Hamor, *A True Discourse of the Present State of Virginia*, ed. A. L. Rowse (Richmond, Va., 1957; orig. pub., London, 1615), 8–16; Theodore Stern, "Chickahominy: The Changing Culture of a Virginia Indian Com-

munity," *American Philosophical Society Proceedings* 96 (1952): 165–7.

27 "Generall Historie," *Travels and Works of Capjtain John Smith,* ed. Arber and Bradley, II: 586–7; Smith et al., "Map of Virginia," Barbour, ed., *Jamestown Voyages,* II: 361, 408–9; "Governor of Virginia. A Commission to Captain Maddison," June 17, 1622, Kingsbury, ed., *Records of the Virginia Company,* III: 654–5; Peter Arundel to William Caninge, April 1623, *ibid.,* IV: 89.

28 "Relatyon . . . Written . . . by a Gent. of ye Colony," Barbour, ed., *Jamestown Voyages,* I: 84–5; "Description of the People," *ibid.,* I: 102; "Instruccons . . . to Sr Thomas Gates," May 1609, Kingsbury, ed., *Records of the Virginia Company,* III: 19.

29 Smith, "True Relation," Barbour, ed., *Jamestown Voyages,* I: 185; Smith et al., "Map of Virginia," *ibid.,* II: 410–11, 414; "Generall Historie," *Travels and Works of Captain John Smith,* ed. Arber and Bradley, II: 434.

30 Richard Hakluyt, "Pamphlet for the Virginia Enterprise," *The Original Writings and Correspondence of the Two Richard Hakluyts,* ed. E. G. R. Taylor (London, 1935), II: 334; "A Notable Historie . . . Written . . . by Monsieur Laudonnière . . . ," Hakluyt, *Principal Navigations,* VIII: 447; "Of Plantations," *Works of Francis Bacon,* ed. Spedding et al., VI: 459.

31 Sir George Peckham, "True Reporte," Quinn, ed., *Voyages and Colonising Enterprises of Sir Humphrey Gilbert,* II: 451–3.

32 Robert Gray, *A Good Speed to Virginia (1609),* ed. Wesley F. Craven (New York, 1937), C2^v; "Anonymous Notes for the Guidance of Raleigh and Cavendish," Quinn, ed., *Roanoke Voyages,* I: 138; William Strachey, *For the Colony in Virginea Britannia Lawes Divine, Morall and Martiall, etc.,* ed. David H. Flaherty (Charlottesville, 1969), 12, 37, 48–9; "Instructions for Government," Nov. 20, 1606, Barbour, ed., *Jamestown Voyages,* I: 43; John Pory, "A Reporte of the Manner and Proceeding in the General Assembly Convented at James City," 1619, Kingsbury, ed., *Records of the Virginia Company,* III: 164; "Virginia Company. Instructions to the Governor and Council . . . ," July 24, 1621, *ibid.,* III: 469.

33 "Relatyon . . . Written . . . by a Gent. of ye Colony . . . ," Barbour, ed., *Jamestown Voyages,* I: 90.

34 Edward Waterhouse, "A Declaration of the State of the Colony . . . ," Kingsbury, ed., *Records of the Virginia Company,* III: 552; "A Voyage Set Out from the Citie of Bristoll . . . ," Purchas, *Hakluytus Posthumus,* XVIII: 325.

35 "Generall Historie," *Travels and Works of Captain John Smith,* ed. Arber and Bradley, II: 611.

36 [George Abbot], *A Briefe Description of the Whole Worlde . . .*

(London, 1605), R3ᵛ; "The London Council's 'Instructions Given by Way of Advice,'" Barbour, ed., *Jamestown Voyages*, I: 52.

37 J. R. Hale, ed., "Introduction, "Sir John Smythe, *Certain Discourses Military* (Ithaca, N.Y., 1964), xli–lvi; C. G. Cruickshank, *Elizabeth's Army* (London, 1946), ch. 5; Humfrey Barwick, *A Breefe Discourse, concerning the Force and Effect of All Manuall Weapons of Fire* . . . (London, [1594]), A4, 2; [Abbot], *Briefe Description of the Whole Worlde*, B2ᵛ.

38 "The London Council's 'Instructions Given by Way of Advice,'" Barbour, ed., *Jamestown Voyages*, I: 52; "Relatyon . . . Written . . . by a Gen. of yᵉ Colony," *ibid.*, I: 91, 92; "George Percy's Discourse," 1608, *ibid.*, I: 140; "Second Voyage into Florida . . . by Captaine Laudonnière," Hakluyt, *Principal Navigations*, IX: 13–14; Lescarbot, *Nova Francia*, 107–8.

39 "Generall Historie," *Travels and Works of Captain John Smith*, ed. Arber and Bradley, II: 396; Smith et al., "Map of Virginia," Barbour, ed., *Jamestown Voyages*, II: 390; Thomas Hariot, "A Briefe and True Report," Quinn, ed., *Roanoke Voyages*, I: 375–6.

40 J. H. Elliott *The Old World and New, 1492–1650* (Cambridge, 1970), 51–2.

41 Purchas, *Hakluytus Posthumus*, II: 27; Acosta, *Natural and Moral History of the Indies*, ed. Markham, 61–2; [Abbot], *A Briefe Description of the Whole Worlde* . . . (London, 1599), D6ᵛ.

42 Hariot, "Briefe and True Report," Quinn, ed., *Roanoke Voyages*, I: 375–6; Ralph Lane, "Discourse on the First Colony," *ibid.*, I: 278; Henry S. Burrage, ed., *Rosier's Relation of Waymouth's Voyage to the Coast of Maine, 1605* (Portland, Me., 1887), 117–18; "Generall Historie," *Travels and Works of Captain John Smith*, ed. Arber and Bradley, II: 423; Hamor, *True Discourse of the Present State of Virginia*, ed. Rowse, 36–7.

43 Hariot, "Briefe and True Report," Quinn, ed., *Roanoke Voyages*, I: 377; "Generall Historie," *Travels and Works of Captain John Smith*, ed. Arber and Bradley, I: 374; Smith et al., "Map of Virginia," Barbour, ed., *Jamestown Voyages*, II: 369, 449; William White, "Fragments Published in 1614," *ibid.*, I: 150; Strachey, *Historie of Travell into Virginia Britania*, ed. Wright and Freund, 101; Stanley Pargellis, ed., "An Account of the Indians in Virginia," *William and Mary Quarterly*, 3rd ser., XVI (1959): 236; "Good Newes from New England . . . ," Purchas, *Hakluytus Posthumus*, XIX: 381–2.

44 "Letter to the Virginia Company . . . ," January 1622, Kingsbury, ed., *Records of the Virginia Company*, III: 584; Waterhouse, "Declaration of the State of the Colony," *ibid.*, III: 552–3.

45 "Epistle Dedicatory to the Council of Virginia," *Original Writings and Correspondence of the Two Richard Hakluyts*, ed. Taylor, II: 502–3; Barbour, ed., *Jamestown Voyages*, I: 15–16; "Descrip-

tion of New England," *Travels and Works of Captain John Smith,* ed. Arber and Bradley, I: 228.

46 Ralph Lane to Sir Philip Sidney, August 12, 1585, Quinn, ed., *Roanoke Voyages,* I: 204; "The 1586 Voyages," *ibid.,* I: 478; Hariot, "Briefe and True Relation," *ibid.,* I: 381; John Pory, "A Reporte of the Manner and Proceeding in the General Assembly Convented at James City," 1619, Kingsbury, ed., *Records of the Virginia Company,* III: 170–2; "Sir Thomas Smyth and Alderman Johnson," November 1621, *ibid.,* III: 522; "Description of New England," *Travels and Works of Captain John Smith,* ed. Arber and Bradley, I: 200.

47 "Instruccons . . . to Sʳ Thomas Gates," May 1609, Kingsbury, ed., *Records of the Virginia Company,* III: 19; Pory, "Reporte of the Manner and Proceeding in the General Assembly Convented at James City," 1619, *ibid.,* III: 157–8, 163; Percy, "Trewe Relaycon," 266; "Description of New England," *Travels and Works of Captain John Smith,* ed. Arber and Bradley, I: 198.

48 Smith, "True Relation," Barbour, ed., *Jamestown Voyages,* I: 200–8; Smith et al., "Map of Virginia," *ibid.,* II: 443–5; Strachey, "True Reportory," Wright, ed., *Voyage to Virginia,* 93; Percy, "Trewe Relaycon," 273, 280–1.

49 Percy, "Trewe Relaycon," 271–3; "Generall Historie," *Travels and Works of Captain John Smith,* ed. Arber and Bradley, II: 503.

50 The traditional figure of 347 has been revised downward to between 325 and 330 by Fausz ("The Powhatan Uprising," 399).

51 Waterhouse, "Declaration of the State of the Colony," Kingsbury, ed., *Records of the Virginia Company,* III: 550–6; "Letter to Virginia Company," January 20, 1622, *ibid.,* IV: 10–11; Darrett Bruce Rutman, "A Militant New World, 1607–1640 . . ." (Ph.D. diss., University of Virginia, 1959), I: 260–1, note, rejects the idea of a Powhatan conspiracy.

52 Percy, "Trewe Relaycon," 279–80; "Generall Historie," *Travels and Works of Captain John Smith,* ed. Arber and Bradley, I: 372–3, II: 587; "Virginia Affaires since the Yeare 1620," Purchas, *Hakluytus Posthumus,* XIX: 168–9; Robert Beverley, *The History and Present State of Virginia,* ed. Louis B. Wright (Chapel Hill, 1947; orig. pub., London, 1705), 52–4.

53 Christian Feest, "Powhatan: A Study in Political Organization," *Wiener Volkerkundliche Mitteilungen* XIII (1966): 71–2; Lewis and Lomie, *Spanish Jesuit Mission in Virginia, 1570–1572,* 161; Regina Flannery, *An Analysis of Coastal Algonquian Culture* (Washington, 1939), 44, 182; Smith et al., "Map of Virginia," Barbour, ed., *Jamestown Voyages,* II: 355.

54 Paul S. Martin et al., *Indians before Columbus: Twenty Thousand Years of North American History Revealed by Archeology* (Chicago, 1947) 361–8; James B. Griffin, "The De Luna Expedition and

the 'Buzzard Cult' in the Southeast," *Journal of the Washington Academy of Sciences* 34 (1944): 299–303; Alex D. Krieger, "An Inquiry into Supposed Mexican Influence on a Prehistoric 'Cult' in the Southern United States," *American Anthropologist*, new ser., 47 (1945): 483–515.

55 J. Frederick Fausz and Jon Kukla, eds., "A Letter of Advise to the Governor of Virginia, 1624," *William and Mary Quarterly*, 3rd ser., XXIV (1977): 117. For this account of the massacre, I have drawn on Fausz, "The Powhatan Uprising of 1622," chs. 4 and 5. Fausz suggests (345–52) that Nemattanew was a prophet and the leader of an early revitalization movement among the Powhatans. On revitalization movements, see Anthony F. C. Wallace, "Revitalization Movements," *American Anthropologist*, new ser., 58 (1956): 264–81.

56 Robert C. Johnson, ed., "The Indian Massacre of 1622: Some Correspondence of the Reverend Joseph Mead," *Virginia Magazine of History and Biography* 71 (1963): 408–9.

57 "Letter to Governor and Council in Virginia," August 1, 1622, Kingsbury, ed., *Records of the Virginia Company*, III: 666; George Sandys to Sir Miles Sandys, March 30, 1623, *ibid.*, IV: 70–1; Edward Waterhouse. "A Declaration of the State of the Colony," *ibid.*, III: 542, 556, 559; "Generall Historie," *Travels and Works of Captain John Smith*, ed. Arber and Bradley, II: 616.

58 Waterhouse, "Declaration of the State of the Colony," Kingsbury, ed., *Records of the Virginia Company*, III: 551, 557–8; "Generall Historie," *Travels and Works of Captain John Smith*, ed. Arber and Bradley, II: 574, 594; Langsam, *Martial Books and Tudor Verse*, 8; Jorgensen, *Shakespeare's Military World*, 191; Christopher Brooke, "A Poem of the Late Massacre in Virginia," *Virginia Magazine of History and Biography* 72 (1964): 259–92. By mutilating Thorpe's body so brutally, the Indians may have been registering their profound opposition to his efforts to undermine their culture; see Fausz, "The Powhatan Uprising," 379.

59 "Letter to Governor and Council in Virginia," August 1, 1622, Kingsbury, ed., *Records of the Virginia Company*, III: 672; "A Commission to Sir George Yeardley," September 10, 1622, *ibid.*, III: 678–9; "Letter to Virginia Company of London," January 20, 1622/3, *ibid.*, IV: 9–10; Robert Bennett to Edward Bennett, June 9, 1623, *ibid.*, IV: 221–2; "Lord Sackville's Paper's respecting Virginia, 1613–1631," *American Historical Review* XXVII (1921–2): 507.

60 George Sandys to Sir Miles Sandys, March 30, 1623, Kingsbury, ed., *Records of the Virginia Company*, IV: 71; Council in Virginia to Virginia Company of London, April 4, 1623, *ibid.*, IV: 98–9, 102; Council in Virginia to Virginia Company of London, January 30, 1623/4, *ibid.*, IV: 451.

61 John Martin, "The Manner Howe to Bringe the Indians into

Subiection," Kingsbury, ed., *Records of the Virginia Company*, III: 704–7; Richard Ffrethorne to his Father and Mother, March 20, April 2 and 3, 1623, *ibid.*, IV: 58; Waterhouse, "Declaration of the State of the Colony," *ibid.*, III: 556–9, 564.

62 "Generall Historie," *Travels and Works of Captain John Smith*, ed. Arber and Bradley, II: 578–9; Purchas, *Hakluytus Posthumus*, XVIII: 268, 494, 497–8; "Virginias Verger," *ibid.*, XIX: 246.

63 Brooke, "A Poem of the Late Massacre in Virginia," 276.

AFTERWORD

1 Wesley Frank Craven, "Indian Policy in Early Virginia," *William and Mary Quarterly*, 3d ser., I (1944): 74–81; Richard L. Morton, *Colonial Virginia* . . . (Chapel Hill, 1960), I: 123–4.

2 Wesley Frank Craven, *White, Red, and Black: The Seventeenth-Century Virginian* (Charlottesville, 1971), 55–8; William Berkeley, "A Perfect Description of Virginia . . . ," Peter Force,. ed., *Tracts and Other Papers* (Washington, 1844), II: 13.

3 Edmund Berkeley and Dorothy Berkeley, eds., *The Reverend John Clayton: A Parson with a Scientific Mind* . . . (Charlottesville, 1965), 37–8; Robert Beverley, *The History and Present State of Virginia*, ed. Louis B. Wright (Chapel Hill, 1947; orig. pub., London, 1705), 182, echos Clayton's view; Joseph and Nesta Ewan, eds., *John Banister and His Natural History of Virginia, 1678–1692* (Urbana, Ill., 1970), 377; Stanley Pargellis, ed., "An Account of the Indians in Virginia," *William and Mary Quarterly*, 3rd ser., XVI (1959): 231; W. Stitt Robinson, "Tributary Indiana in Colonial Virginia," *Virginia Magazine of History and Biography* 67 (1959): 57 and note.

4 Berkeley and Berkeley, eds. *The Reverend John Clayton*, 25–7; Thomas Glover, "An Account of Virginia . . . ," *Royal Society Philosophical Transactions* XI (1676): 634; Thos. B. Robertson, "An Indian King's Will," *Virginia Magazine of History and Biography* XXXVI (1928): 193; John Duffy, "Smallpox and the Indians in the American Colonies," *Bulletin of the History of Medicine* XXV (1951): 332; John Duffy, *Epidemics in Colonial America* (Baton Rouge, 1953), 71; Wyndham B. Blanton, *Medicine in Virginia in the Seventeenth Century* (Richmond, 1930), ch. 2.

5 Berkeley and Berkeley, eds., *The Reverend John Clayton*, 39; Glover, "An Account of Virginia," 633; Pargellis, ed., "An Account of the Indians in Virginia," 232. Helen C. Rountree, "Change Came Slowly: The Case of the Powhatan Indians of Virginia," *Journal of Ethnic Studies* 3 (1975): 1–19, argues for the persistence of Powhatan culture despite the consequences of the invasion of the English.

6 Berkeley and Berkeley, eds., *The Reverend John Clayton*, 39;

Glover, "An Account of Virginia," 631–2; William Berkeley, "A Perfect Description of Virginia," Force, ed., *Tracts*, II: 7; Pargellis, ed., "An Account of the Indians in Virginia," 231; Beverley, *History and Present State of Virginia*, ed. Wright, 232; Clifford Lewis, ed., "Some Recently Discovered Extracts from the Last Minutes of the Virginia Council and General Court, 1642–1645," *William and Mary Quarterly*, 2nd ser., 20 (1940): 69; Craven, *White, Red, and Black*, 59–60, 64, 74; Christian F. Feest, "Seventeenth Century Virginia Algonquian Population Estimates," *Archeological Society of Virginia Quarterly Bulletin* 28 (1973): 74–7.

7 Craven, "Indian Policy in Early Virginia," 79; Craven, *White, Red, and Black*, 74; W. Stitt Robinson, "The Legal Status of the Indian in Colonial Virginia," *Virginia Magazine of History and Biography* 61 (1953): 254–6; 257; W. Stitt Robinson, "Indian Education and Missions in Colonial Virginia," *Journal of Southern History* XVIII (1952): 159–63.

8 Beverley, *History and Present State of Virginia*, ed. Wright, 216; William Berkeley, "Perfect Description of Virginia," Force, ed., *Tracts*, II: 7.

9 Gary B. Nash, "The Image of the Indian in the Southern Colonial Mind," *William and Mary Quarterly*, 3d ser., XXIX (1972): 223.

10 Beverley, *History and Present State of Virginia*, ed. Wright, 9, 16, 211, 226, 233. Ignoble savagism persisted despite the shift to the noble image and the prevalence of pity. Witness the views of Ebenezer Cook, a contemporary of Beverley:

> Whether this Race was framed by God
> Or whether some Malignant pow'r,
> Contriv'd them in a evil hour
> And from his own Infernal Look,
> Their Dusky form and Image took . . .

(Eben[ezer] Cook, "The Sot-weed Factor: Or, a Voyage to Maryland. A Satyr," Bernard C. Steiner, ed., *Early Maryland Poetry* [Baltimore, 1900], 19).

NOTE ON PRIMARY SOURCES

Any study of Anglo-Indian relations in the early period must begin with the major bibliographical work: A. W. Pollard and G. R. Redgrave, comps., *The Short Title Catalogue of Books Printed in England, Scotland, & Ireland and of English Books Printed Abroad, 1475–1640* (London, 1946). Older listings of books may be found in Henry Harrisse, *Biblioteca Americana Vetustissima: A Description of Works Relating to America Published Between the Years 1492 and 1551* (New York, 1865), and Joseph Sabin, *A Dictionary of Books Relating to America from Its Discovery to the Present Time*, 29 vols. (London, 1868–1936). Perhaps the most convenient introduction to the subject is John Parker, *Books to Build an Empire: A Bibliographical History of English Overseas Interests to 1620* (Amsterdam, 1965), which analyzes and lists the major works dealing with English colonization. A useful bibliography on Virginia is E. G. Swem, John M. Jennings, and James A. Servies, eds., *A Selected Bibliography of Virginia, 1607–1699* (Williamsburg, 1957). On the American Indians, the indispensable work is Francis Paul Prucha, *A Bibliographical Guide to the History of Indian-White Relations in the United States* (Chicago, 1977), which lists materials published on the subject through 1974.

Serious English interest in colonization and America begins with the publications of Richard Eden in the 1550s. His works have been brought together by Edward Arber, ed., *The First Three English Books on America* . . . (Birmingham, Eng., 1885). The work of collecting and translating materials on European travel and colonization was carried on by Richard Hakluyt, who brought out his *Divers Voyages Toughing the Discovery of America and the Islands Adjacent* in 1582. This work has been edited by John Winter Jones as volume VII of the Hakluyt Society Publications (London, 1850). For the rest of his days Hakluyt assembled materials. Two later collections testify to the importance of his efforts: *The Principall Navigations Voiages and Discoveries of the English Nation*, ed. David Beers Quinn and

Raleigh Ashlin Skelton, Hakluyt Society Extra Series, XXXIX, 2 vols. (Cambridge, 1965), originally published in London in 1589, and *The Principal Navigations Voyages Traffiques & Discoveries of the English Nation* . . . , 12 vols. (Glasgow, 1903–5), which appeared in a three-volume edition in London between 1598 and 1600. Hakluyt's work was largely cumulative, each succeeding edition building on the previous one. Samuel Purchas, the next great anthologizer, followed a similar procedure. He made his first offering to the public in 1613 (other editions appeared in succeeding years) as *Pvrchas His Pilgrimage, or Relations of the World and the Religions Observed in Al Ages and Places Discouered, from the Creation vnto the Present* (London, 1613). After Hakluyt's death in 1616, Purchas obtained his unpublished materials and used them as the basis for his great collection, *Hakluytus Posthumus, or Purchas His Pilgrimes, Contayning a History of the World in Sea Voyages and Lande Travells by Englishmen and Others*, 20 vols. (Glasgow, 1905–7), which he published in London in 1625. Hakluyt is generally reputed to be the greatest of the collectors, most astute in selecting materials and most scholarly in their presentation. But Purchas has the advantage of being more voluble in the expression of his own opinions and hence more revelatory of the views of the age. The anthologies of Eden, Hakluyt, and Purchas form the basis for any study of the character of life in America in the period of discovery and colonization.

Fortunately much of the material on exploration and colonization has been published in modern editions, many in the various series of the Hakluyt Society. E. G. R. Taylor has brought together *The Original Writings & Correspondence of the Two Richard Hakluyts*, Hakluyt Society Publications, 2nd ser., LXXVI–LXXVII (London, 1955). Clements R. Markham, in the last century, edited the materials bearing on the adventures of John Hawkins (Hakluyt Society Publications, LVII [London, 1878]). The records pertaining to the activities of Sir Humphrey Gilbert, Ralegh's predecessor, have been gathered by David Beers Quinn in *The Voyages and Colonising Enterprises of Sir Humphrey Gilbert*, Hakluyt Society Publications, 2nd ser., LXXXIII–LXXXIV (London, 1940). Vilhjalmur Stefansson has published the materials dealing with the career of Martin Frobisher: *The Three Voyages of Martin Frobisher: In Search of a Passage to Cathay and India by the Northwest A.D. 1576–78. From the Original 1578 Text of George Best* (London, 1938). The English version of Marc Lescarbot's *Nova Francia: A Description of Arcadia*, which Hakluyt was instrumental in publishing in 1606, can be found in *The Broadway Travellers* series edited by Sir E. Denison Ross and Eileen Power (London,

1928). For Ralegh's adventures in Guiana, see his *The Discoverie of the Large and Bewtiful Empire of Guiana*, edited by V. T. Harlow (London, 1928). His *The History of the World* can be found as volumes II through VII of *The Works of Sir Walter Ralegh . . .*, 8 vols. (Oxford, 1829). On Ralegh's North American enterprises, David Beers Quinn has produced the definitive account in *The Roanoke Voyages, 1584–1590*, Hakluyt Society Publications, 2nd ser., CIV–CV (London, 1955), which includes Thomas Hariot, "A Briefe and True Report," I: 317–87. Two older collections of materials remain useful: Peter Force, ed., *Tracts and Other Papers . . .*, 4 vols. (Washington, D.C., 1844; facsimile ed., Gloucester, Mass., 1963), and Alexander Brown, ed., *The Genesis of the United States*, 2 vols. (Boston, 1890).

The towering figure in the early years of the Virginia colony continues to be John Smith. He played a critical role in saving the colony from extinction and later wrote extensively about it. His two early accounts of his adventures, "A True Relation" and "A Map of Virginia," can be found in Philip L. Barbour, ed., *The Jamestown Voyages Under the First Charter, 1606–1609*, Hakluyt Society Publications, 2nd ser., CXXXVII–CXXXVIII (Cambridge, 1969). For the most extensive of Smith's works, "The Generall Historie of Virginia, New England and the Summer Isles," which appeared in 1624, one must still rely on *Travels and Works of Captain John Smith . . .*, ed. Edward Arber and A. G. Bradley, 2 vols. (Edinburgh, 1910). A new edition of Smith's writings will soon appear under the editorship of Philip L. Barbour. Smith seldom wrote favorably about the Indians, but they were a major topic in each of his works.

William Strachey followed Smith in his treatment of the native people. His major work, *The Historie of Travell into Virginia Britania*, has been edited by Louis B. Wright and Virginia Freund, Hakluyt Society Publications, 2nd ser., CIII (London, 1953). Wright has also edited his "True Reportory" in *A Voyage to Virginia in 1609 . . .* (Charlottesville, 1964). Strachey's compilation of the colony's law has been published by David H. Flaherty as *For the Colony in Virginea Britannia Lawes Divine, Morall and Martiall, etc.* (Charlottesville, 1969). Important material can be found in Ralph Hamor, *A True Discourse of the Present State of Virginia*, ed. A. L. Rowse (Richmond, 1957), a reprint of the 1615 edition; in George Percy, " 'A Trewe Relaycon' Virginia from 1609 to 1612," *Tyler's Quarterly Historical and Genealogical Magazine*, III (1922): 259–82; and in "Letter of John Rolfe, 1614," Lyon Gardiner Tyler, ed., *Narratives of Early Virginia, 1606–1625* (New York, 1907), 239–44. Robert Beverley's brilliant account of Virginia in the sixteenth century, *The*

History and Present State of Virginia, has been edited by Louis B. Wright (Chapel Hill, 1947). Although the colony records are fragmentary, Susan Myra Kingsbury, ed., *The Records of the Virginia Company of London*, 4 vols. (Washington, D.C., 1906–35), supplies a wealth of revealing information about relations with the native peoples.

Montaigne's views on noble savagism can be gleaned by a reading of the Everyman edition (E. P. Dutton) of John Florio's translation of the *Essays*, ed. L. C. Harmer, 3 vols. (New York, 1965), or of *The Essays of Montaigne Done into English by John Florio Anno 1603*, ed. George Saintsbury, (London, 1892–3). For Shakespeare, consult *The Riverside Shakespeare*, ed. G. Blakemore Evans, 2 vols. (Boston, 1974), and for Spenser, *The Works of Edmund Spenser: A Variorum Edition*, ed. Edwin Greenlaw et al., 10 vols. (Baltimore, 1932).

For the pictorial evidence concerning European views of native life, Paul Hulton and David Beers Quinn, *The American Drawings of John White, 1577–1590* . . . , 2 vols. (London and Chapel Hill, 1964), makes an essential contribution. See also Johan-Theodoro de Bry, *America* . . . (Franckfurt, 1617). Much interesting pictorial material may also be seen in W. P. Cumming, R. A. Skelton, and D. B. Quinn, *The Discovery of North America* (New York, 1972), and in Hugh Honour, *The European Vision of America* (Cleveland, 1975).

TITLES: PRIMARY SOURCES

[Abbot, George], *A Briefe Description of the Whole World* . . . (London, 1599; 2nd ed., London, 1605).

Acosta, Joseph de, *The Natural and Moral History of the Indies* . . . , ed. Clements R. Markham, Hakluyt Society Publications, LX–LXI (London, 1880).

Alexander, William, *An Encouragement to Colonies* (London, 1624). *The Political Works of Sir William Alexander, Earl of Stirling*, 3 vols. (Glasgow, 1870–2).

Bacon, Francis, *The Works of Francis Bacon* . . . , ed. James Spedding et al., 15 vols. (Boston, 1857–74).

Banister, John, *John Banister and His Natural History of Virginia, 1678–1692*, ed. Joseph and Nesta Ewan (Urbana, 1970).

Barclay, Alexander, *The Ship of Fools*, 2 vols. (Edinburgh, 1874).

Barlow, Roger, *A Brief Summe of Geographie*, ed. E. G. R. Taylor, Hakluyt Society Publications, 2nd ser., LXIX (London, 1932).

Barwick, Humfrey, *A Breefe Discourse, Concerning the Force and Effect of Manvall Weapons of Fire and the Disability of the Long Bowe or Archery* . . . (London, 1594?).

Basse, William, *The Poetical Works of William Basse (1602–1653)*, ed. R. Warwick Bond (London, 1893).

[Batman Stephen], *Batman vppon Bartholome* . . . (London, 1582).

Bayly, Lewes, *The Practise of Pietie*, 9th ed. (London, 1617).

Beaumont, Francis, and John Fletcher, *The Works of Francis Beaumont and John Fletcher*, ed. A. R. Waller, 10 vols. (Cambridge, 1905–12).

Benson, George, *A Sermon Preached at Paules Crosse* . . . (London, 1609).

Berkeley, William, "A Perfect Description of Virginia . . . ," Peter Force, ed., *Tracts and Other Papers* . . . , vol. II, no. viii (Washington, 1844).

[Bigges, Walter], *A Svmmarie and Trve Discovse of Sir Frances Drakes West Indian Voyage* . . . (London, 1589).

Bland, Edward, et al., "The Discovery of New Brittaine . . . ," Alexander S. Salley, Jr., ed., *Narratives of Early Carolina, 1650–1708*, 3–19 (New York, 1911).

[Boemus, Johann], *The Fardle of Facions* . . . , trans. William Watreman (London, 1555).

Bonoeil, Iohn, *His Majestres Graciovs Letter to the Earle of South-Hampton* (London, 1622).

[Botero, Giovanni], *The World, or an Historicall Description of the Most Famous Kingdomes and Commonweales Therein* . . . , trans. Robert Johnson (London, 1601).

Bourne, William, *A Booke Called the Treasure for Traueilers* . . . (London, 1578).

Brereton, John, *A Briefe and True Relation of the Discourerie of the North Part of Virginia* (London, 1602).

"A Briefe Declaration of the Plantation of *Virginia* . . . ," H. R. McIlwaine, ed., *Journals of the House of Burgesses of Virginia, 1619–1658/9*, 28–37 (Richmond, 1915).

Brinsley, Iohn, *A Consolation for Ovr Grammar Schooles* . . . (London, 1622).

Brooke, Christopher, "A Poem of the Late Massacre in Virginia," Robert C. Johnson, ed., *Virginia Magazine of History and Biography* 72 (1964): 259–92.

Bullokar, William, *Aesops Fablz* . . . (London, 1585).

Carlson, Leland, ed., *The Writings of John Greenwood and Henry Barrow, 1591–1593* (London, 1970).

Castaneda, Hernan Lopes de, *The First Booke of the Historie of the Discouerie and Conquest of the East Indias* . . . (London, 1582).

Certaine Sermons Appoynted by the Queenes Maiestie . . . (N.P., 1574).

Chaloner, Sir Thomas, *The Praise of Folie* (1549), ed. Clarence H. Miller (New York, 1965).

Chamberlain, John, *The Letters of John Chamberlain*, ed. Norman Egbert McClure, 2 vols. (Philadelphia, 1939).

Chapman, George, "De Guiana, Carmen Epicum," *The Poems of George Chapman*, ed. Phyllis Brooks Bartlett, 353–7 (New York, 1941).

"The Memorable Masque," ed. G. Blakemore Evans, *The Plays of George Chapman: The Comedies, A Critical Edition*, ed. Allan Holaday, 557–86 (Urbana, 1970).

Churchyarde, Thomas, *A Prayer and Reporte of Maister Martyne Forboishers Voyage to Meta Incognita* . . . (London, 1578).

[Clayton, John], "An Account of the Indians in Virginia," Stanley Pargellis, ed., *William and Mary Quarterly*, 3rd ser., XVI (1959): 228–43.

Clayton, John, "John Clayton's 1687 Account of the Medicinal Practices of the Virginia Indians," Bernard G. Hoffman, ed., *Ethnohistory* 11 (1964): 1–40.

The Reverend John Clayton: A Parson with a Scientific Mind; His Scientific Writings and Other Related Papers, ed. Edmund Berkeley and Dorothy Smith Berkeley (Charlottesville, 1965).

Cockle, Maurice J. D., *Bibliography of English Military Books up to 1642* (London, 1900; 2nd ed., 1957).

[Collier, J.P.], ed., *A Select Collection of Old Plays*, 12 vols. (London, 1825–7).

Cook, Eben[ezer], "The Sot-weed Factor: Or, a Voyage to Maryland. A Satyr," Bernard C. Steiner, ed., *Early Maryland Poetry*, 7–32 (Baltimore, 1900).

Copland, Patrick, *Virginia's God be Thanked, or A Sermon of Thanksgiving for the Happie Successe of the Affayres in Virginia This Last Yeare* (London, 1622).

Crakanthorpe, Richard, "Sermon," March 24, 1608, Alexander Brown, ed., *Genesis of the United States*, I: 255–6 (Boston, 1890).

Crowley, Robert, *The Way to Wealth* . . . (London, 1550).

Cuningham, William, *The Cosmographical Glasse* . . . (London, 1559).

Davies, James, "The Relation of a Voyage unto New England . . . ," *Massachusetts Historical Society Proceedings* XVIII (1880–1): 82–117.

[d'Avity, Pierre], *The Estates, Empires, & Principallities of the World* . . . , trans. Edw[ard] Grimstone (London, 1615).

Dekker, Thomas, *Foure Birds of Noahs Arke* (London, 1609).

Dent, Arthvr, *The Plaine Mans Path-way to Heaven* . . . , 6th ed. (London, 1603).

Donne, Iohn, *A Sermon* . . . (London, 1624).

Drayton, Michael, *The Works of Michael Drayton*, ed. William Hebel, 5 vols. (Oxford, 1931–41).

Eburne, Richard, *A Plain Pathway to Plantations (1624)*, ed. Louis B. Wright (Ithaca, 1962).

Ellis, Thomas, "Thomas Ellis's Account of the Third Voyage," Vilhjalmur Stefansson, ed., *Three Voyages of Martin Frobisher*, II: 27–51 (London, 1938).

Escalante, Bernardino de, *A Discourse of the Navigation Which the Portugales Doe Make to the Realms and Provinces of the East* . . . , trans. John Frampton (London, 1579).

Espejo, Antonio de, *New Mexico* . . . (London, 1587).

Fausz, J. Frederick, and Jon Kukla, eds., "A Letter of Advice to the Governor of Virginia, 1624," *William and Mary Quarterly*, 3rd ser., XXXIV (1977): 104–29.

Field, Nathan, "A Woman Is a Weather-cocke," *The Plays of Nathan Field*, ed. William Perry, 55–139 (Austin, 1950).

Fleet, Henry, "A Brief Journal of a Voyage Made in the Bark Virginia, to Virginia and Other Parts of the Continent of America," Edward D. Neill, ed., *The Founders of Maryland* . . . , 19–37 (Albany, 1876).

Flemming, Abraham, *The Diamond of Devotion* . . . (London, 1602).

Florio, John, *A Shorte and Briefe Narration of the Two Navigations and Discoueries to the Northweast Partes Called Newe Fravnce* . . . (London, 1580).

Frampton, John, *A Briefe Description of the Portes, Creekes, Bayes, and Havens, of the Weast India* . . . (London, 1578).

trans., *Joyfull Newes Out of the Newe Founde Worlde* . . . , ed. Stephen Gaselee (London, 1925).

Frost, George L., and Ray Nash, "Good Order: A Morality Fragment," *Studies in Philology* XLI (1944): 483–91.

Galvano, Antonio, *The Discoveries of the World* . . . *(1601)*, ed. Vice Admiral Bethune, Hakluyt Society Publications, XXX (London, 1862).

Glover, Thomas, "A Account of Virginia . . . ," *Royal Society Philosophical Transactions* XI (1676): 623–36.

Gómara, Francisco López de, *The Pleasant Historie of the Conquest of West India* . . . , trans. Thomas Nicholas (London, 1578).

"Good Newes From Virginia, 1623," *William and Mary Quarterly,* 3rd. ser., V (1948): 351–8.

Gray, Robert, *A Good Speed to Virginia,* (1609), ed. Wesley F. Craven (New York, 1937).

G[reen], R[oger], "Virginia's Cure: Or an Advisive Narrative concerning Virginia . . . ," Peter Force, ed., *Tracts and Other Papers* . . . , vol. III, no. 15 (Washington, 1844).

Greene, Robert, *The Dramatic Works of Robert Greene* . . . , ed. Alexander Dyce, 2 vols. (London, 1831).

Greepe, Thomas, *The True and Perfecte Newes of the Woorthy and Valiaunt Exploytes, Performed and Doone by* . . . *Syr Frauncis Drake* . . . (London, 1587).

Greville, Fulke, *The Works in Verse and Prose Complete of The Right Honourable Fulke Greville, Lord Brooke,* ed. Alexander B. Grosart, 4 vols. (N.P., 1870).

Harcourt, Robert, *A Relation of a Voyage to Guiana* . . . , ed. C. Alexander Harris, Hakluyt Society Publications, 2nd ser., LX (London, 1928).

Harlow, V. T., ed., *Ralegh's Last Volage* . . . (London, 1932).

H[eylyn], P[eter], *Microcosmus, or a Little Description of the Great World* . . . (Oxford, 1621).

Hickscorner (N.P., 1512c.).

Hill, Thomas, *A Pleasant History: Declaring the Whole Art of Phisiognomy, Orderly Vttering All the Speciall Parts of Man, from the Head to the Foot* (N.P., 1613).

Holinshed, [Raphael], *Holinshed's Chronicles of England, Scotland, and Ireland,* 6 vols. (London, 1808).

Honigmann, E. A. J., ed., "The Masque of Flowers," *A Book of*

Masques in Honour of Allardyce Nicoll, 149–77 (Cambridge, 1967).

Hortop, Job, *The Trauailes of an English Man* . . . (London, 1591).

Jacobs, Joseph, ed., *The Fables of Aesop as First Printed by William Caxton in 1484* . . . (New York, 1970).

James I, "A Counterblaste to Tobacco," Edward Arber, ed., *English Reprints* (London, 1869), VIII: 95–120.

Daemonologie (1597) . . . (Edinburgh, 1966).

[Johnson, Robert], *The New Life of Virginia* . . . *1612* (Rochester, N.Y., 1897).

Nova Britannia . . . *1609* (Rochester, N.Y., 1897).

Jonson, Ben, *Works of Ben Jonson,* ed. C. H. Herford and Percy and Evelyn Simpson, 11 vols. (Oxford, 1925–52).

Jonson, Ben, George Chapman, and John Marston, *Eastward Ho!,* ed. C. G. Petter (London, 1973).

Kempe, William, "The Education of Children in Learning (1588)," Robert D. Pepper, ed., *Four Tudor Books on Education,* 181–240 (Gainesville, Fla., 1966).

Kemys, Lawrence, *A Relation of the Second Voyage to Guiana* . . . (London, 1596).

Las Casas, Bartolomé de, *The Spanish Colonie, or Briefe Chronicle of the Acts and Gestes of the Spaniardes in the West Indies* . . . (London, 1583).

Lavater, Lewes, *Of Ghostes and Spirite§ Walking by Nyght, 1572,* ed. J. Dover Wilson and May Yardley (Oxford, 1929).

Le Challeaux, Nicolas, *A True and Perfect Description, of the Last Voyage on Navigation, Attempted by Capitaine John Rybaut* . . . (London, 1566).

Lederer, John, *The Discoveries of John Lederer* . . . , trans. William Talbot (London, 1672).

Le Roy, Loys, *Of the Interchangeable Covrse, or Variety of Things in the Whole World* . . . (London, 1594).

Lewis, Clifford, "Some Recently Discovered Extracts from the Last Minutes of the Virginia Council and General Court, 1642–1645," *William and Mary Quarterly,* 2nd ser., 20 (1940): 62–78.

Lightfoote, William, *The Complaint of England* . . . (London, 1587).

McIlwaine, H. R., ed., *Journals of the House of Burgesses of Virginia, 1619–1658/59* (Richmond, 1915).

Mandeville, John, *The Voiage and Trayayle of Sir John Maundeville* . . . , ed. John Ashton (London, 1887).

Manly, John Matthews, "Gorboduc; or, Ferrex and Porrex," *Specimens of the Pre-Shaksperean Drama,* II: 211–72 (Boston, 1897).

Marlowe, Christopher, *The Complete Works of Christopher Marlowe,* ed. Fredson Bowers, 2 vols. (Cambridge, 1973).

Marshburn, Joseph H., and Alan R. Velie, *Blood and Knavery: A*

Collection of English Renaissance Pamphlets and Ballads of Crime and Sin (Madison, N.J., 1973).

Mead, Joseph, "The Indian Massacre of 1622: Some Correspondence of the Reverend Joseph Mead," Robert C. Johnson, ed., *Virginia Magazine of History and Biography* 71 (1963): 408–10.

Meier, Albertus, *Certaine Briefe, and Speciall Instructions Gentlemen, Merchants, Students, Souldier, Marriners* . . . , trans. Philip Jones (London, 1589).

Mela, Pomponius, *The Worke of Pomponius Mela* . . . , trans. Arthur Golding (London, 1585).

Mexio, Pedro, *The Treasvrie of Avncient and Modern Times* . . . , 2 vols. (London, 1613–19).

More, St. Thomas, *The Best State of a Commonwealth and the New Island of Utopia* . . . , *The Complete Works of St. Thomas More*, ed. Edward Surtz, S.J., and J. H. Hexter, vol. 4 (New Haven, 1965).

Nicholl, Iohn, *An Houre Glasse of Indian Newes* . . . (London, 1607).

Nichols, John, *The Progresses, and Public Processions, of Queen Elizabeth*, 3 vols. (London, 1788–1802).

Norwood, [Henry], "A Voyage to Virginia" (1649), Peter Force, ed., *Tracts and Other Papers* . . . , vol. III, no. x (Washington, D.C., 1844).

Ogilby, John, *America: Being the Latest, and Most Accurate Description of the New World* . . . (London, 1671).

Palmer, Thomas, *An Essay of the Meanes How to Make Our Trauailes into Forraine Countries, the More Profitable and Honourable* (London, 1606).

Parry, Henry, *The S'vmme of Christian Religion* . . . (Oxford, 1595).

[Plinius Secundus, Caius], *The Secrets and Wonders of the World* . . . (London, 1585).

[Ponet, John], *A Shorte Treatise of Politike Pouuer* . . . (N.P., 1556).

Powell, [David], *The History of Wales* . . . (Shrewsbury, Eng., 1832).

Price, Daniel, *Savls Prohibition Staide* . . . (London, 1609).

[Procter, Thomas], *Of the Knowledge and Conducte of Warres* . . . (N.P., 1578).

Quinn, David B., and Neil M. Cheshire, eds., *The New Found Land of Stephen Parmenius* . . . (Toronto, 1972).

[Rastell, John], "The Interlude of the Four Elements: An Early Moral Play," James Orchard Halliwell, ed., Percy Society, *Early English Poetry, Ballads, and Popular Literature of the Middle Ages*, vol. XXII (London, 1848).

Ribaut, Jean, *The Whole & True Discouerye of Terra Florida: A Facsimile Reprint of the London Edition of 1563* . . . (Gainesville, Fla., 1964).

Rich, R., *Newes from Virginia (1610)*, ed. Wesley F. Craven (New York, 1937).

Roberts, Henry, *A Most Friendly Farewell, Given by a Welwiller to the Right Worshipful Sir Frauncis Drake* . . . (London, 1585).

Robertson, Thos. B., "A Indian King's Will," *Virginia Magazine of History and Biography* XXXVI (1928): 192–3.

Rolfe, John, *A True Relation of the State of Virginia Lefte by Sir Thomas Dale Knight in May Last 1616* (Charlottesville, 1971).

Rosier, James, *Rosier's Relation of Waymouth's Voyage to the Coast of Maine, 1605*, ed. Henry S. Burrage (Portland, Me., 1887).

Sackville, Lord, "Lord Sackville's Papers Respecting Virginia, 1613–1631," *American Historical Review* XXVII (1921–2): 493–538, 738–65.

Salley, Alexander S., Jr., ed., *Narratives of Early Carolina, 1650–1708* (New York, 1911).

S[andys], G[eorge], *Ovid's Metamorphosis* . . . (Oxford, 1632).

Seall, Robert, *A Cōmendation of the Aduēterus Viage of the Wurthy Captain. M. Thomas, Stutely* . . . (London, [1563]).

Settle, Dionyse, *A True Reporte of the Laste Voyage into West and Northwest Regions* . . . (London, 1577).

Simpson, Lesley Byrd, trans., *Cortes: The Life of the Conqueror by His Secretary, Francisco López de Gómara* (Berkeley, 1964).

Smith, Henrie, *Gods Arrowe against Atheists* (London, 1593).

Smithe, Sir Iohn, *Instrvctions, Obseruations, and Orders Mylitarie* . . . (London, 1595).

Smythe, Sir John, *Certain Discourses Military*, ed. J. R. Hale (Ithaca, 1964).

Solinus, Caius Julius, *The Excellent and Pleasant Worke of Iulius Solinus Polyhistor* . . . , trans. Arthur Golding (London, 1587).

Spenser, Edmund, *A View of the Present State of Ireland*, ed. W. L. Renwick (London, 1934).

Stafforde, Robert, *A Geographical and Anthologicall Description of All the Emperes and Kingdomes, Both of Continent and Ilands in This Terrestriall Globe* . . . (London, 1607).

Starkey, Thomas, *England in the Reign of King Henry the Eighth: A Dialogue between Cardinal Pole and Thomas Lupset* . . . , ed. J. M. Cowper, Early English Text Society, Extra Series, XXXII (London, 1878).

Sutton, Christopher, *Disce Mori: Learne to Dye* . . . (London, 1634). *Disce Vivere: Learne to Live* . . . (London, 1634).

Thevet, Andrewe, *The New Found Worlde* . . . (London, [1568]).

Topsell, Edward, *The Historie of Fovre-Footed Beastes* . . . (London, 1607).

Townshend, Aurelian, *Aurelian Townshends Poems and Masks*, ed. E. K. Chambers (Oxford, 1912).

"A Trve Declaration of the Estate of the Colonie in Virginia . . . ,"

Peter Force, ed., *Tracts and Other Papers* . . . , vol. III, no. i (Washington, D.C., 1844).

Tvke, Thomas, *A Treatise against Painting and Tinctving of Men and Women* . . . (London, 1616).

Tymme, Thomas, *A Silver Watch-Bell* . . . (London, 1634).
The Poore Mans Pater Noster . . . (N.P., 1598).

Tynley, Robert, *Two Learned Sermons* . . . (London, 1609).

[Underwood, Robert], *A New Anatomie* . . . (London, 1605).

[Vaughan, William], *The Golden Fleece* . . . (London, 1626).

[Verstegen, Richard], *A Declaration of the Trve Cavses of The Great Troubles, Presvpposed to Be Intended against the Realme of England* (N.P., 1592).

"Virginia in 1623–4," *Virginia Magazine of History and Biography* VI (1899): 373–4.

Wakeman, Ro., *The Poore-mans Preacher* . . . (London, 1607).

Webbe, Edward, *The Rare and Most Wonderful Thinges which Edward Webbe an Englishman Borne, Hath Seene and Passed in His Troublesome Trauailes* . . . (London, 1590).

Whitaker, Alexander, *Good Newes from Virginia 1613* (New York, n.d.).

Whitbourne, Richard, *A Discovrse and Discovery of New-Fovnd-Land* . . . (London, 1622).

Wilson, Sir Thomas, *Wilson's Arte of Rhetorique 1560*, ed. G. H. Mair (Oxford, 1909).

Yeardley, Francis, "Francis Yeardley's Narrative of Excursions into Carolina, 1654," Alexander S. Salley, Jr., ed., *Narratives of Early Carolina, 1650–1708*, 23–9 (New York, 1911).

Zárate, Augustín de, *The Discouverie and Conquest of the Provinces of Peru* . . . , trans. Thomas Nicholas (London, 1581).

TITLES: SECONDARY SOURCES

Abenheimer, K. M., "Shakespeare's 'Tempest' ": A Psychological Analysis," *Psychoanalytic Review* XXXIII (1946): 399–415.

Adams, Joseph Quincy, "Michael Drayton's *To the Virginia Voyage,*" *Modern Language Notes* XXXIII (1918): 405–8.

Akrigg, G. P. V., *Jacobean Pageant, or the Court of King James I* (London, 1962).

Allen, Don Cameron, "The Degeneration of Man and Renaissance Pessimism," *Studies in Philology* 35 (1938): 202–27.

The Legend of Noah: Renaissance Rationalism in Art, Science, and Letters (Urbana, 1949).

Ashburn, P. M., *The Ranks of Death: A Medical History of the Conquest of America,* ed. Frank D. Ashburn (New York, 1947).

Aubrey, John, *Aubrey's Brief Lives,* ed. Oliver Lawson Dick (Ann Arbor, 1957).

Axtell, James, "The White Indians of Colonial America," *William and Mary Quarterly,* 3rd ser. (1975): 55–88.

"Who Invented Scalping?," *American Heritage* XXVIII (April 1977): 96–9.

Barbour, Philip L., "The Earliest Reconnaissance of the Chesapeake Bay Area: Captain John Smith's Map and Indian Vocabulary," *Virginia Magazine of History and Biography* 79 (1971): 280–302; 80 (1972): 21–51.

Pocahontas and Her World . . . (Boston, 1970).

The Three Worlds of Captain John Smith (Boston, 1964).

Beazley, C. Raymond, *The Dawn of Modern Geography,* 3 vols. (New York, 1949).

Bennett, Josephine Waters, *The Evolution of "The Fairie Queene"* (New York, 1960).

Berkhofer, Robert F., Jr., *The White Man's Indian: Images of the American Indian from Columbus to the Present* (New York, 1978).

Bernheimer, Richard, *Wild Man in the Middle Ages: A Study in Art, Sentiment, and Demonology* (Cambridge, Mass., 1952).

Bidney, David, "The Idea of the Savage in North American Ethnohistory," *Journal of the History of Ideas* (1954): 322–7.

241

Biggar, H. P., "The French Hakluyt; Marc Lescarbot of Vervins," *American Historical Review* VI (1900–1): 671–92.

Binford, Lewis Roberts, "Archaeological and Ethnohistorical Investigation of Cultural Diversity and Progressive Development among Aboriginal Cultures of Coastal Virginia and North Carolina" (Ph.D. diss., University of Michigan, 1964).

Birket-Smith, Kaj, *Primitive Man and His Ways: Patterns of Life in Some Native Societies* (London, 1960).

Boas, George, *The Happy Beast in French Thought of the Seventeenth Century* (Baltimore, 1933).

Boserup, Ester, *The Conditions of Agricultural Growth: The Economics of Agrarian Change under Population Pressure* (Chicago, 1965).

Brasser, T. J. C., "The Coastal Algonkians: People of the First Frontiers," *North American Indians in Historical Perspective*, ed. Eleanor Burke Leacock and Nancy Oestreich Lurie, 64–91 (New York, 1971).

Bredvold, Louis I., "The Naturalism of Donne in Relation to Some Renaissance Traditions," *Journal of English and Germanic Philology* XXII (1923): 471–502.

Bridenbaugh, Carl, *Vexed and Troubled Englishmen, 1590–1642* (New York, 1968).

Brown, Norman O., *Hermes the Thief: The Evolution of a Myth* (Madison, 1947).

   Life Against Death: The Psychoanalytical Meaning of History (New York, 1959).

Bruce, Philip Alexander, *Economic History of Virginia in the Seventeenth Century* . . . , 2 vols. (New York, 1935).

   Institutional History of Virginia in the Seventeenth Century . . . , 2 vols. (New York, 1910).

Bush, Douglas, *The Renaissance and English Humanism* (Toronto, 1939).

Canedo, Lino Gómez, "Hombres o bestias?," *Estudios de Historia Novohispaña* I (1966): 29–51.

Canny, Nicholas P., *The Elizabethan Conquest of Ireland: A Pattern Established, 1565–76* (New York, 1976).

Carré, Meyrick H., *Phases of Thought in England* (Oxford, 1949).

Carroll, William Meredith, *Animal Conventions in English Renaissance Non-Religious Prose (1550–1600)* (New York, 1954).

Cawley, Robert Ralston, "Shakespeare's Use of the Voyagers in *The Tempest*," *PMLA* XLI (1926): 688–726.

   The Voyagers and Elizabethan Drama (Boston, 1938).

Chambers, R. W., *Thomas More* (New York, [1935]).

Cheney, Donald, *Spenser's Image of Nature: Wild Man and Shepherd in "The Faerie Queene"* (New Haven, 1966).

Chiappelli, Fredi, Michael J. B. Allen, and Robert L. Benson, eds.,

First Images of America: The Impact of the New World on the Old, 2 vols. (Berkeley, 1976).

Chinard, Gilbert, *L'exotisme Américain dan la litterature Française au XVIᵉ siècle d'après Rabelais, Ronsard, Montaigne, etc.* (Paris, 1911).

Cole, Richard G., "Sixteenth-Century Travel Books as a Source of European Attitudes Toward Non-White and Non-Western Culture," *American Philosophical Society Proceedings* 116 (1972): 59–67.

Cowan, William, ed., *Papers of the Seventh Algonquian Conference, 1975* (Ottawa, 1976).

——— ed., *Papers of the Sixth Algonquian Conference, 1974* (Ottawa, 1975).

Craven, Wesley Frank, *Dissolution of the Virginia Company: The Failure of a Colonial Experiment* (New York, 1932).

——— "Indian Policy in Early Virginia," *William and Mary Quarterly*, 3d ser., I (1944): 65–82.

——— *An Introduction to the History of Bermuda* ([Williamsburg, Va.], 1938).

——— *White, Red, and Black: The Seventeenth Century Virginian* (Charlottesville, 1971).

Crosby, Alfred W., Jr., *The Columbian Exchange: Biological and Cultural Consequences of 1492* (Westport, Conn., 1972).

Cruickshank, C. G., *Elizabeth's Army* (London, 1946).

Davis, Richard Beale, "The Devil in Virginia in the Seventeenth Century," *Literature and Society in Early Virginia, 1608–1840*, 14–42 (Baton Rouge, 1973).

——— *George Sandys, Poet Adventurer: A Study of Anglo-American Culture in the Seventeenth Century* (London and New York, 1955).

——— *Intellectual Life in the Colonial South, 1585–1763*, 3 vols. (Knoxville, Tenn., 1978).

Davis, Walter R., and Richard A. Lanham, *Sidney's Arcadia* (New Haven, 1965).

Day, Gordon M., "The Indian as an Ecological Factor in the Northeastern Forest," *Ecology* 34 (1953): 329–46.

Diamond, Sigmund, "From Organization to Society: Virginia in the Seventeenth Century," *American Journal of Sociology* LXIII (1958): 457–75.

Driver, Harold E., *Indians of North America*, 2nd ed., rev. (Chicago, 1969).

Dudley, Edward, and Maximillian E. Novak, eds., *The Wild Man Within: An Image in Western Thought from the Renaissance to Romanticism* (Pittsburgh, 1972).

Duffy, John, *Epidemics and Colonial America* (Baton Rouge, 1953).

——— "Smallpox and the Indians in the American Colonies," *Bulletin of the History of Medicine* XXV (1951): 324–41.

Eliade, Mircea, *The Forge and the Crucible*, trans. Stephen Corrin (New York, 1962).

The Myth of the Eternal Return, trans. Willard R. Trask (New York, 1954).

"The Yearning for Paradise in Primitive Tradition," *Daedalus* 88 (1959): 255–67.

Elliott, J. H., "The Discovery of America and the Discovery of Man," *British Academy Proceedings* LVIII (1972): 1–27.

The Old World and New, 1492–1650 (Cambridge, 1970).

Esler, Anthony, *The Aspiring Mind of the Elizabethan Younger Generation* (Durham, N.C., 1966).

Fairchild, Hoxie Neale, *The Noble Savage: A Study in Romantic Naturalism* (New York, 1961).

Falls, Cyril, *Elizabeth's Irish Wars* (London, 1950).

Fausz, J. Frederick, "The Powhatan Uprising of 1622: A Historical Study of Ethnocentrism and Cultural Conflict" (Ph.D. diss., College of William and Mary, 1977).

Feest, Christian, "Powhatan: A Study in Political Organization," *Wiener Volkerkundliche Mitteilungen* XIII (1966): 69–83.

"Seventeenth Century Virginia Algonquian Population Estimates," *Archeological Society of Virginia Quarterly Bulletin* 28 (December 1973): 66–79.

Fiedler, Leslie A., *The Stranger in Shakespeare* (New York, 1972).

Flannery, Regina, *An Analysis of Coastal Algonquian Culture* (Washington, 1939).

Foreman, Carolyn Thomas, *Indians Abroad, 1493–1938* (Norman, Okla., 1943).

Freeman, Rosemary, *The Faerie Queene: A Companion for Readers* (London, 1970).

French, Peter J., *John Dee: The World of an Elizabethan Magus* (London, 1972).

Freud, Sigmund, "Civilization and Its Discontents," *The Standard Edition of the Complete Psychological Works of Sigmund Freud*, ed. James Strachey et al., XXI: 57–145 (London, 1961).

Friede, Juan, and Benjamin Keen, eds., *Bartolomé de Las Casas in History: Toward an Understanding of the Man and His Work* (De Kalb, Ill., 1971).

Gearing, Frederick O., *The Face of the Fox* (Chicago, 1970).

Gerbi, Antonello, *The Dispute of the New World: The History of a Polemic, 1750–1900*, rev. ed., trans. Jeremy Moyle (Pittsburgh, 1973).

Giamatti, A. Bartlett, *The Earthly Paradise and the Renaissance Epic* (Princeton, 1966).

Glacken, Clarence J., *Traces on the Rhodian Shore: Nature and Culture in Western Thought from Ancient Times to the End of the Eighteenth Century* (Berkeley, 1967).

Glenn, Keith, "Captain John Smith and the Indians," *Virginia Magazine of History and Biography* LII (1944): 228–48.

Goldsmith, Robert Hillis, "The Wild Man on the English Stage," *Modern Language Review* LIII (1958): 481–91.

Greenblatt, Stephen J., *Sir Walter Ralegh: The Renaissance Man and His Roles* (New Haven, 1973).

Griffen, James B., "The De Luna Expedition and the 'Buzzard Cult' in the Southeast," *Journal of the Washington Academy of Sciences* 34 (1944): 299–303.

Hallowell, A. Irving, "The Backwash of the Frontier: The Impact of the Indian on American Culture," *The Frontier in Perspective*, ed. Walker D. Wyman and Clifton B. Kroeber, 229–58 (Madison, Wis., 1957).

Hanke, Lewis, *Aristotle and the American Indians: A Study in Race Prejudice in the Modern World* (Bloomington, Ind., 1959).

Bartolomé de Las Casas: Bookman, Scholar, & Propagandist (Philadelphia, 1952).

"Pope Paul III and the American Indians," *Harvard Theological Review* XXX (1937): 65–102.

Hankins, John E., "Caliban the Bestial Man," *PMLA* LXII (1947): 793–801.

Source and Meaning in Spenser's Allegory: A Study of The Faerie Queene (Oxford, 1971).

Harris, Victor, *All Coherence Gone* (Chicago, 1949).

Harrison, G. B., *The Life and Death of Robert Devereux, Earl of Essex* (New York, 1937).

Harrison, Thomas P., Jr., "Aspects of Primitivism in Shakespeare and Spenser," *University of Texas Studies in English*, no. 4026 (1940): 39–71.

Heard, J. Norman, *White into Red: A Study of the Assimilation of White Persons Captured by Indians* (Metuchen, N.J., 1973).

Henry, Bruce Ward, "British Imperialism to 1607" (Ph.D. diss., University of Southern California, 1975).

Herr, Alan Fager, *The Elizabethan Sermon: A Survey and a Bibliography* (Philadelphia, 1940).

Hexter, J. H., *More's Utopia: The Biography of an Idea* (Princeton, 1952).

Hill, Christopher, *Intellectual Origins of the English Revolution* (Oxford, 1965).

Hodgen, Margaret T., *Early Anthropology in the Sixteenth and Seventeenth Centuries* (Philadelphia, 1964).

"Montaigne and Shakespeare Again," *Huntington Library Quarterly* XVI (1952): 23–42.

Honour, Hugh, *The New Golden Land: European Images of America from the Discoveries to the Present Time* (New York, 1975).

Huddleston, Lee Eldridge, *Origins of the American Indians: European Concepts, 1492–1729* (Austin, Tex., 1967).

Innis, Harold A., *The Fur Trade in Canada: An Introduction to Canadian Economic History*, rev. ed. (Toronto, 1956).

Jaenen, Cornelius J., "Amerindian Views of French Culture in the Seventeenth Century," *Canadian Historical Review* LV (1974): 261–91.

Friend and Foe: Aspects of French-Amerindian Cultural Contact in the Sixteenth and Seventeenth Centuries (New York, 1973).

James, D. G., *The Dream of Prospero* (Oxford, 1967).

Jennings, Francis, *The Invasion of America: Indians, Colonialism, and the Cant of Conquest* (Chapel Hill, 1975).

Jewkes, W. T., "The Literature of Travel and the Mode of Romance in the Renaissance," Warner G. Rice, ed., *Literature as a Mode of Travel: Five Essays and a Postscript*, 11–30 (New York, 1963).

Johnson, Robert C., "The Indian Massacre of 1622," *Virginia Magazine of History and Biography* 68 (1960): 107–8.

Jones, Eldred D., *The Elizabethan Image of Africa* (Charlottesville, 1971).

Jones, Gordon, "The First Epidemic in English America," *Virginia Magazine of History and Biography* 71 (1963): 3–10.

Jones, Howard Mumford, *O Strange New World, American Culture: The Formative Years* (New York, 1964).

Jones, W. R., "The Image of the Barbarian in Medieval Europe," *Comparative Studies in Society and History* 13 (1971): 376–407.

Jordan, Winthrop D., *White Over Black: American Attitudes Toward the Negro, 1550–1812* (Chapel Hill, 1968).

Jorgensen, Paul A., *Shakespeare's Military World* (Berkeley, 1956).

Joseph, B. L., *Shakespeare's Eden: The Commonwealth of England 1558–1629* (London, 1971).

Jung, C. G., *Psychology and Alchemy*, 2nd ed. (Princeton, 1968).

Juricek, John Thomas, "English Claims in North America to 1660: A Study in Legal and Constitutional History" (Ph.D. diss., University of Chicago, 1970).

Keen, Benjamin, *The Aztec Image in Western Thought* (New Brunswick, N.J., 1971).

Kittredge, George Lyman, *Witchcraft in Old and New England* (New York, 1956).

Kocher, Paul H., *Science and Religion in Elizabethan England* (San Marino, Ca., 1953).

Krieger, Alex D., "An Inquiry into Supposed Mexican Influence on a Prehistoric 'Cult' in the Southern United States," *American Anthropologist*, new ser., 47 (1945): 483–515.

Kupperman, Karen Ordahl, "Apathy and Death in Early Jamestown," *Journal of American History* 66 (1979): 24–40.

"English Perceptions of Treachery, 1583–1640: The Case of the American 'Savages,'" *Historical Journal* XX (1977): 263–87.

Land, Robert Hunt, "Henrico and Its College," *William and Mary Quarterly*, 2nd ser., 18 (1938): 453–98.

Langsam, G. Geoffrey, *Martial Books and Tudor Verse* (New York, 1951).

Latham, Agnes M. C., "Sir Walter Ralegh's Gold Mine: New Light on the Last Guiana Voyage," *English Association Essays and Studies*, new ser., 4 (1951): 94–111.

Lee, Sidney, *Elizabethan and Other Essays*, ed. Frederick S. Boas (Oxford, 1929).

Levin, Harry, *The Myth of the Golden Age in the Renaissance* (Bloomington, Ind., 1969).

Le Vine, Robert, and Donald T. Campbell, *Ethnocentrism: Theories of Conflict, Ethnic Attitudes, and Group Behavior* (New York, 1972).

Lewis, C. S., *English Literature in the Sixteenth Century: Excluding Drama* (Oxford, 1954).

Lovejoy, Arthur O., *The Great Chain of Being: A Study of the History of an Idea* (Cambridge, Mass., 1936).

Lovejoy, Arthur O., and George Boas, *Primitivism and Related Ideas in Antiquity* (Baltimore, 1935).

Lurie, Nancy Oestreich, "Indian Cultural Adjustment to European Civilization," James Morton Smith, ed., *Seventeenth-Century America: Essays in Colonial History*, 33–60 (Chapel Hill, 1959).

MacAndrew, Craig, and Robert B. Edgerton, *Drunken Comportment: A Social Explanation* (Chicago, 1969).

MacFarlane, Alan, *Witchcraft in Tudor and Stuart England: A Regional and Comparative Study* (New York, 1970).

MacLure, Millar, *George Chapman: A Critical Study* (Toronto, 1966).
The Paul's Cross Sermons, 1534–1642 (Toronto, 1958).

Maltby, William S., *The Black Legend in England: The Development of Anti-Spanish Sentiment, 1558–1660* (Durham, N.C., 1971).

Manso, J. A., "The Quest of El Dorado," *Pan American Union Bulletin* 34 (1912): 55–66, 165–76, 317–27, 447–57, 607–21, 735–43.

Martin, Calvin, *Keepers of the Game: Indian-Animal Relationships and the Fur Trade* (Berkeley, 1978).

Martin, Paul S., et al., *Indians before Columbus: Twenty Thousand Years of North American History Revealed by Archeology* (Chicago, 1947).

Marx, Leo, *The Machine in the Garden: Technology and the Pastoral Ideal in America* (New York, 1964).

Mauss, Marcel, *The Gift: Forms and Functions of Exchange in Archaic Societies*, trans. Ian Cunnison (Glencoe, Ill., 1954).

Maxwell, Hu, "The Use and Abuse of Forests by the Virginia Indians," *William and Mary Quarterly*, 1st ser., XIX (1910): 73–103.

McCann, Franklin T., *English Discovery of America to 1585* (New York, 1952).

McCary, Ben C., *Indians in Seventeenth Century Virginia* (Charlottesville, 1957).

Meek, Ronald L., *Social Science and the Ignoble Savage* (Cambridge, 1976).

Miller, Perry, "Religion and Society in the Early Literature of Virginia," *Errand into the Wilderness*, 100–40 (New York, 1964).

Mook, Maurice A., "The Aboriginal Population of Tidewater Virginia," *American Anthropologist*, new ser., 46 (1944): 193–208.

"The Anthropological Position of the Indian Tribes of Tidewater Virginia," *William and Mary Quarterly*, 2nd ser., 23 (1943): 27–40.

"The Ethnological Significance of Tindall's Map of Virginia, 1608," *William and Mary Quarterly*, 2nd ser., (1943): 371–408.

"Virginia Ethnology from an Early Relation," *William and Mary Quarterly*, 2nd ser., 23 (1943): 101–29.

Mooney, James, "The Powhatan Confederacy, Past and Present," *American Anthropologist*, new ser., 9 (1907): 129–52.

Morgan, Edmund S., *American Slavery, American Freedom: The Ordeal of Colonial Virginia* (New York, 1975).

Morison, Samuel Eliot, *The European Discovery of America: The Northern Voyages, A.D. 500–1600* (New York, 1971).

The European Discovery of America: The Southern Voyages, A.D. 1492–1616 (New York, 1974).

Morton, Richard L., *Colonial Virginia* . . . , 2 vols. (Chapel Hill, 1960).

Nash, Gary B., "The Image of the Indian in the Southern Colonial Mind," *William and Mary Quarterly*, 3rd ser., XXIX (1972): 197–230.

Nash, Roderick, *Wilderness and the American Mind* (New Haven, 1967).

Novak, Michael, *The Experience of Nothingness* (New York, 1970).

O'Gorman, Edmundo, *The Invention of America* . . . (Bloomington, Ind., 1961).

"Sobre la naturaleza bestial del indio americano," *Filosofía y Letras* I (1941): 141–56.

Parks, George Bruner, *Richard Hakluyt and the English Voyages*, ed. James A. Williamson (New York, 1928).

Parry, J. H., *The Age of Reconnaissance* (Cleveland, 1963).

Pearce, Roy Harvey, "From the History of Ideas to Ethnohistory," *Journal of Ethnic Studies* II (1974): 86–92.

"Primitivistic Ideas in the Faerie Queene," *Journal of English and Germanic Philology* XLIV (1945): 139–51.

The Savages of America: A Study of the Indian and the Idea of Civilization, rev. ed. (Baltimore, 1965).

Pennington, Loren E., "*Hakluytus Posthumus*: Samuel Purchas and the Promotion of English Overseas Expansion," *Emporia State Research Studies* XIV (1966): 5–39.

"John Frampton and Thomas Nicholas: Two Sixteenth-Century Propagandists for English Expansion," *Emporia State Research Studies* XX (1972): 5–23.

"The Origins of English Promotional Literature for America, 1553–1625" (Ph.D. diss., University of Michigan, 1962).

Petti, Anthony, "Beast's and Politics in Elizabethan Literature," S. Gorley Putt, ed., *Essays and Studies* XVI (1963): 68–90.

Porter, H. C., *The Inconstant Savage: England and the North American Indian, 1500–1600* (London, 1979).

"Alexander Whitaker: Cambridge Apostle to Virginia," *William and Mary Quarterly*, 3d ser., XIV (1957): 317–43.

Powell, Philip Wayne, *Tree of Hate: Propaganda and Prejudices Affecting United States Relations with the Hispanic World* (New York, 1971).

Powell, William S., "Aftermath of the Massacre: The First Indian War, 1622–1632," *Virginia Magazine of History and Biography* 66 (1958): 44–75.

Quinn, David Beers, *The Elizabethans and the Irish* (Ithaca, 1966).
England and the Discovery of America, 1481–1620 . . . (New York, 1974).
Raleigh and the British Empire, rev. ed. (New York, 1962).
ed., *The Hakluyt Handbook*, 2 vols., Hakluyt Society Publications, 2nd ser., 144–5 (London, 1974).

Raab, Felix, *The English Face of Machiavelli: A Changing Interpretation, 1500–1700* (London, 1964).

Rabb, Theodore K., *Enterprise & Empire: Merchant and Gentry Investment in the Expansion of England, 1575–1630* (Cambridge, Mass., 1967).

Randel, William, "Captain John Smith's Attitudes Toward the Indians," *Virginia Magazine of History and Biography* XLVII (1939): 218–29.

Rau, Charles, "Ancient Aboriginal Trade in North America," *Smithsonian Institution Annual Report, 1872*, 348–94 (Washington, 1873).

Ray, Arthur J., *Indians in the Fur Trade: Their Role as Trappers, Hunters, and Middlemen in the Lands Southwest of Hudson Bay, 1660–1870* (Toronto, 1974).

Robin, P. Ansell, *Animal Lore in English Literature* (London, 1932).

Robinson, W. Stitt, "Indian Education and Missions in Colonial Virginia," *Journal of Southern History* XVIII (1952): 152–68.

"The Legal Status of the Indian in Colonial Virginia," *Virginia Magazine of History and Biography* 61 (1953): 247–59.

"Tributary Indians in Colonial Virginia," *Virginia Magazine of History and Biography* 67 (1959): 49–64.

Rountree, Helen C., "Change Came Slowly: The Case of the Powhatan Indians of Virginia," *Journal of Ethnic Studies* 3 (Fall 1975): 1–19.

Rowe, John Howland, "The Renaissance Foundations of Anthropology," Regna Darnell, ed., *Readings in the History of Anthropology*, 61–77 (New York, 1974).

Rowse, A. L., *The Expansion of Elizabethan England* (New York, 1955).

Sex and Society in Shakespeare's Age: Simon Forman the Astrologer (New York, 1974).

Sir Richard Grenville of the Revenge: An Elizabethan Hero (London, 1937).

Rutman, Darrett Bruce, "A Militant New World, 1607–1640: America's First Generation – Its Martial Spirit, Its Tradition of Arms, Its Militia Organization, Its Wars," 2 vols. (Ph. D. diss., University of Virginia, 1959).

Rutman, Darrett B., and Anita H. Rutman, "Of Agues and Fevers: Malaria in the Early Chesapeake," *William and Mary Quarterly*, 3d ser., XXXIII (1976): 31–60.

Sagan, Eli, *Cannibalism: Human Aggression and Cultural Form* (New York, 1974).

Sauer, Carl Ortwin, *The Early Spanish Main* (Berkeley, 1969).

Sixteenth Century North America: The Land and the People as Seen by the Europeans (Berkeley, 1971).

Sayce, Richard, *The Essays of Montaigne: A Critical Exploration* (London, 1972).

Sinclair, Andrew, *The Savage: A History of Misunderstanding* (London, 1977).

Sinor, Denis, "The Barbarians," *Diogenes* 18 (1957): 47–60.

Slotkin, Richard, *Regeneration Through Violence: The Mythology of the American Frontier, 1660–1860* (Middletown, Conn., 1973).

Smith, Hallett, *Shakespeare's Romances: A Study of Some Ways of the Imagination* (San Marino, Ca. 1972).

ed., *Twentieth Century Interpretations of "The Tempest,"* (Englewood Cliffs, N.J., 1969).

Spencer, Theodore, *Shakespeare and the Nature of Man*, 2nd ed. (New York, 1961).

Stern, Theodore, "Chickahominy: The Changing Culture of a Virginia Indian Community," *American Philosophical Society Proceedings* 96 (1952): 157–225.

St. Hoyme, Lucile E., "On the Origins of New World Paleopathology," *American Journal of Physical Anthropology* 31 (1969): 295–302.

Stone, Lawrence, *The Crisis of the Aristocracy, 1558–1641*, abridged ed. (London, 1967).

Strathmann, Ernest A., *Sir Walter Ralegh: A Study in Elizabethan Skepticism* (New York, 1951).

Sturtevant, William C., "Ethnographic Details in the American Drawings of John White, 1577–1590," *Ethnohistory* 12 (1965): 54–63.

——— ed., *Handbook of North American Indians,* vol. 15: *Northeast,* ed. Bruce G. Trigger (Washington, 1978).

Taylor, E. G. R., *Tudor Geography, 1485–1583* (London, 1930).

——— *Late Tudor and Early Stuart Geography, 1583–1650: A Sequel to Tudor Geography, 1485–1583* (London, 1934).

Taylor, George Coffin, "Shakespeare's Use of the Idea of the Beast in Man," *Studies in Philology* XLII (1945): 530–43.

Thomas, Keith, *Religion and the Decline of Magic* (New York, 1971).

Tillyard, E. M. W., *The Elizabethan World Picture* (London, 1948).

Trevor-Roper, H. R., *The Crisis of the Seventeenth Century: Religion, the Reformation and Social Change* (New York, 1968).

Trigger, Bruce G., "Brecht and Ethnohistory," *Ethnohistory* 22 (1975): 51–6.

——— *The Children of Aataentsic: A History of the Huron People to 1660,* 2 vols. (Montreal, 1976).

Turner, Randolph, "A New Population Estimate for the Powhatan Chiefdom of the Coastal Plain of Virginia," *Archeological Society of Virginia Quarterly Bulletin* 28 (December 1973): 57–65.

Tuveson, Ernest Lee, *Millennium and Utopia: A Study in the Background of the Idea of Progress* (Berkeley, 1959).

Vaughan, Alden T., *American Genesis: Captain John Smith and the Founding of Virginia* (Boston, 1975).

——— "'Expulsion of the Salvages': English Policy and the Virginia Massacre of 1622," *William and Mary Quarterly,* 3d ser., XXXV (1978): 57–84.

Villey, Pierre, *Les sources & l'évolution des essais de Montaigne,* 2nd ed., 2 vols. (Paris, 1933).

Vogel, Virgil J., *American Indian Medicine* (Norman, Okla., 1970).

Wagner, Henry R., *Sir Francis Drake's Voyage Around the World: Its Aims and Achievements* (San Francisco, 1926).

Wallace, Anthony F. C., "Revitalization Movements," *American Anthropologist,* new ser., 58 (1956): 246–81.

——— "Some Psychological Determinants of Culture Change in an Iroquoian Community," William N. Fenton, ed., *Symposium on Local Diversity in Iroquois Culture* (Smithsonian Institution, Bureau of American Ethnology) *Bulletin 149,* 55–76 (Washington, 1951).

Walne, Peter, "The Collections for Henrico College," *Virginia Magazine of History and Biography* 80 (1972): 258–66.

Washburn, Wilcomb E., "The Meaning of 'Discovery' in the Fifteenth and Sixteenth Centuries," *American Historical Review* LXVIII (1962): 1–21.

Red Man's Land/White Man's Law: A Study of the Past and Present Status of the American Indian (New York, 1971).

White, Helen C., *Social Criticism in Popular Religious Literature of the Sixteenth Century* (New York, 1944).

Willoughby, Charles C., "The Virginia Indians in the Seventeenth Century," *American Anthropologist*, new ser., 9 (1907): 57–86.

Woodward, Grace Steele, *Pocahontas* (Norman, Okla., 1969).

Wright, Louis B., *Middle-Class Culture in Elizabethan England* (Ithaca, 1958).

Religion and Empire: The Alliance between Piety and Commerce in English Expansion, 1558–1625 (Chapel Hill, 1943).

Wroth, Lawrence C., "An Elizabethan Merchant and Man of Letters," *Huntington Library Quarterly* XVII (1954): 299–314.

Yoder, Audrey, *Animal Analogy in Shakespeare's Character Portrayal* (New York, 1947).

Zeeveld, W. Gordon, *The Temper of Shakespeare's Thought* (New Haven, 1974).

INDEX

253